The Road to Outsourcing 4.0

Mohammadreza Akbari

The Road
to Outsourcing 4.0

Next-Generation Supply Chain

Mohammadreza Akbari
College of Business, Law
and Governance
James Cook University
Townsville, Australia

ISBN 978-981-97-2707-0   ISBN 978-981-97-2708-7   (eBook)
https://doi.org/10.1007/978-981-97-2708-7

Cover credit: @AerialPerspective Images

This Palgrave Macmillan imprint is published by the registered company Springer Nature
Singapore Pte Ltd.
The registered company address is: 152 Beach Road, #21-01/04 Gateway East, Singapore
189721, Singapore

Paper in this product is recyclable.

Dedicated to the three extraordinary lights in my life—my beloved wife and daughter, caring mother, and also to my father who passed away due to COVID-19. This is also dedicated to our eagerly anticipated newest member of the family, soon to arrive.

This book is a tribute to the warmth of your support and the boundless sea of love that has driven me to this moment. Without you, I would be a ship without a compass, lost in the vastness of uncertainty.

Preface and Acknowledgment

"The Road to Outsourcing 4.0: Next-Generation Supply Chain" offers readers a comprehensive voyage through the historical foundations, present dynamics, and future possibilities of outsourcing. Commencing with a historical lens, the narrative unveils the origins of outsourcing, weaving a tale that extends from the seventeenth century to the present, showcasing its transformation into a pivotal force within the globalized economy. The journey continues with an exploration of supply chain optimization, delving into the intricacies of cost reduction, expertise access, and the preservation of core competencies. Introducing the transformative concept of Outsourcing 2.0 and Vested Outsourcing, the narrative highlights the evolution toward enduring partnerships and collaborative problem-solving, transcending the traditional transactional nature of outsourcing.

As the narrative unfolds, readers are immersed in the realms of crowdsourcing for innovation, where diverse collective intelligence becomes a catalyst for creativity and effective problem-solving. Recent trends such as reshoring, nearshoring, and rightshoring are scrutinized against the dynamic backdrop of a rapidly changing global landscape, emphasizing their managerial implications. The exploration extends into the critical theme of sustainable outsourcing, shedding light on how organizations can positively contribute to the global ecosystem while navigating challenges such as environmental impact and ethical labor practices. The book's trajectory further extends into the captivating world of logistics outsourcing, from traditional models to the technology-driven 6PL, with real-world examples underscoring the significance of technological integration, collaboration, and adaptability. Climaxing in the era of Outsourcing 4.0, the narrative underscores the interconnected and technologically sophisticated landscape, emphasizing the pivotal role of Industry 4.0 technologies and digitalization in shaping the future of outsourcing. Throughout this transformative odyssey, *"The Road to Outsourcing 4.0: Next-Generation Supply Chain"* invites readers to contemplate the evolving landscape of outsourcing and its profound implications for businesses and supply chains navigating the challenges and opportunities of the contemporary global business ecosystem.

This exploration into the dynamics of outsourcing has been a collaborative effort, and my heartfelt gratitude extends to those who have played a pivotal role in bringing this work to fruition. My sincere thanks are owed to the diligent researchers, insightful practitioners, and visionary thought leaders in the field of outsourcing whose invaluable contributions have both inspired and shaped the content of this book.

To my cherished family, friends, and colleagues, your support has been my anchor throughout the writing process. The patience, encouragement, and understanding you have provided have served as catalysts, propelling my determination to delve into the intricacies of outsourcing and present a narrative characterized by both depth and clarity.

Lastly, to the discerning readership, an expression of sincere appreciation is extended. Your engagement with this exploration constitutes an integral facet of its trajectory, and it is earnestly hoped that the nuanced insights and perspectives encapsulated within these pages contribute substantively to a profound comprehension of the evolving landscape of outsourcing. The intellectual curiosity and scrutiny exercised by discerning readers such as yourself epitomize the essence of this collaborative scholarly undertaking, and the opportunity to disseminate this transformative discourse is met with deep gratitude.

Queensland, Australia   Dr. Mohammadreza Akbari

CONTENTS

LIST OF FIGURES

LIST OF TABLES

CHAPTER 1

Embarking on Outsourcing: An Introductory Overview

1.1 Outsourcing Background

The pursuit of continuous improvement is encapsulated by a crucial question in today's business environment: "Is there a better way?". This question motivated innovators such as Thomas Edison and Albert Einstein to challenge conventional thinking and create improved solutions (Vitasek et al., 2013). It also drives businesses to tackle the intricacies of globalization and satisfy the actual requirements of their end customers (Ha et al., 2023). The music industry, for instance, has undergone a remarkable transformation from cassette tapes to CDs to MP3s in the pursuit of improved methods of storage and mobility. However, simply identifying a better solution is not enough for inventors and engineers (Akbari, 2022).

"If you want something new, you have to stop doing something old"— Peter Drucker (1909–2005)

Outsourcing boasts a rich historical legacy (Akbari, 2013). For instance, the concept of outsourcing was prevalent in ancient Rome, when the government would outsource the construction of public buildings and roads to private contractors. However, the modern outsourcing industry as we know it today has its roots in the early 20th century (Akbari & Hopkins, 2016).

In 1900, when the Eastman Kodak Company contracted a company called Scovill Manufacturing to produce its cameras, it set a precedent for outsourcing that would influence business practices for decades to come (Claver et al., 2002). By outsourcing camera production to Scovill, Kodak was able to focus on its core competencies and save money on manufacturing costs. This allowed Kodak to remain competitive and become one of the most successful companies in the photography industry.

During the 1960s and 1970s, many manufacturing companies in the United States (US) began to outsource production to countries with lower labor costs (Kotabe & Murray, 2004), such as Japan, Taiwan, and South Korea. This was the beginning of the trend of outsourcing manufacturing to foreign countries, also known as offshoring.

In the 1980s, outsourcing became popular in the information technology (IT) industry when companies began to outsource their software development to specialist firms (Beaumont & Sohal, 2004). This was primarily driven by the shortage of IT professionals in the US and the lower labor costs in countries such as India, China, and the Philippines (David, 2007; Lee, 2003; Singh & Delios, 2005).

During the 1990s, outsourcing gained even more popularity, particularly after Eastman Kodak's successful information systems outsourcing to industry leaders like IBM, DEC, Businessland, and Xerox (Claver et al., 2002; Lacity & Hirschheim, 1993). During the 1990s, Business Process Outsourcing (BPO) also gained prominence, which involved outsourcing non-essential business functions like accounting, payroll, and human resources (Lacity et al., 2011). Outsourcing these functions to specialist service providers allowed businesses to concentrate on their core competencies and reduce costs.

In the 21st century, outsourcing has continued to evolve, and new outsourcing models have emerged (Krosh & Ghosh, 2010). For instance, Knowledge Process Outsourcing (KPO) involves outsourcing high-level business processes such as research and development, engineering, and design (Sen & Michael, 2006).

The COVID-19 pandemic in 2020 has had a significant impact on outsourcing and global supply chains (Tsai et al., 2021). The reliance on China as a major outsourcing hub was exposed by the pandemic, leading to disruptions in the global supply chain and increased costs. As a result, there has been a growing trend toward reshoring, nearshoring, and backshoring, which involves bringing outsourced operations back to the home country or relocating them to a nearby country (Barbieri et al.,

2020). This trend aims to reduce reliance on distant suppliers, enhance supply chain resilience, and ensure greater control over the supply chain. COVID-19 has accelerated this trend, with many companies re-evaluating their outsourcing strategies and seeking more secure and reliable supply chain alternatives (van Hoek & Dobrzykowski, 2021).

The historical evolution of outsourcing since 1900 is depicted in Fig. 1.1.

A company must engage personnel and utilize resources to attain its objectives, such as customer satisfaction, cost reduction, and reasonable returns for shareholders (Kantarelis, 2007). To operate effectively and achieve these objectives, a company must continuously strive for competitive and strategic advantage (Akbari et al., 2023). This benefits not only the company and its shareholders but also assists in the development of the economy and job creation.

The behavior, structure, and market association of firms are described by various economic theories, including the Neoclassical theory, which is based on profit maximization when marginal revenue equals marginal cost. However, this theory assumes the availability of complete information, which is not always the case. The Transaction Cost theory, introduced by Coase (1937) and elaborated on by Williamson (1975, 2008), describes the costs associated with a firm's involvement in the market or any economic activity. When external transaction costs are less than internal costs, firms may choose to scale down, for instance, through outsourcing. Conversely, if external transaction costs exceed internal costs, the firm may opt for insourcing.

The Agency theory deals with the possible conflicts between share holders and managers in companies, defining a contract for individuals to perform services on behalf of others (Shapiro, 2005). The Evolutionary Theory of the Firm highlights production capability and product inno vation, portraying the firm as a creator of competitive advantage and a catalyst for change (Gould, 2002; Sober, 2014).

When venturing into a new industry, companies must deploy competitive strategies to prepare for the intense competition posed by existing businesses. According to Porter (1980), a company's success or failure hinges on its strategic choices. To achieve a competitive advantage, a company must apply cost leadership, focus, and differentiation strategies (see Fig. 1.2).

Overall, the history of outsourcing shows that it has been a prevalent practice in various forms for centuries. Today, outsourcing is an integral

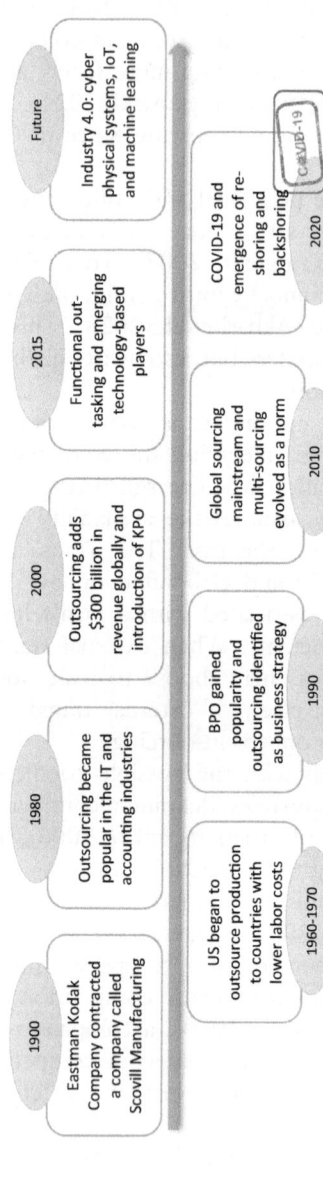

Fig. 1.1 History of outsourcing (*Source* Author's own work)

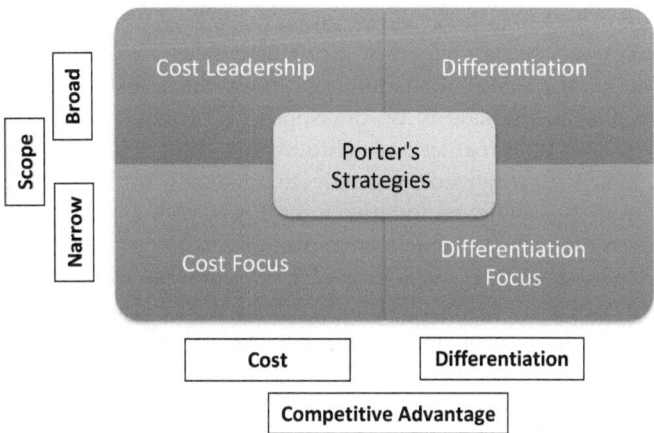

Fig. 1.2 Porter's competitive strategies (*Source* Author's own work—Adapted from Miller and Friesen [1986] and Porter [1980])

part of the global economy, and companies continue to outsource various business functions to enhance efficiency and reduce costs.

There are four key competitive strategies that companies can apply to achieve a competitive advantage (Miller & Friesen, 1986; Porter, 1980):

- Cost leadership: This strategy involves minimizing the costs of production or services within the organization.
- Differentiation: This strategy involves producing a product or service that differs from competitors or has better quality. The specific features, functionality, brand image, and support offered may vary depending on the nature of the company or firm.
- Cost focus: This strategy involves reducing costs within a specific and focused market niche.
- Differentiation focus: This strategy approach entails pursuing diversity within a specialized and narrowed market segment.

1.1.1 Definition of Outsourcing

In the late 1980s, the term "outsourcing" originally referred to delegating information systems work processes (Aubert et al., 2004; Lacity &

Hirschheim, 1993; Loh & Venkatraman, 1992). Over time, its scope expanded to encompass all outsourced activities across various sectors (Bhagwati et al., 2004). Outsourcing entails the transfer of previously in-house business functions or development processes to an external service provider on a regular basis (Blumberg, 1998; Fill & Visser, 2000; Sharpe, 1997). Recognized as an effective process, outsourcing enables organizations to sustain competitiveness (Rajabzadeh et al., 2008).

Based on the overall business operation of customers, they may receive various business services, including data processing, which were traditionally handled by vertically integrated ventures (Brown & Wilson, 2005). The definition of outsourcing has evolved to encompass services beyond the subdivisions of vertically integrated enterprises. This includes areas such as logistics, transportation, telecommunications, and website hosting, as outlined by Brown and Wilson (2005).

To better understand the concept, Table 1.1 presents a comprehensive overview of the significant definitions of outsourcing from the existing literature.

After examining the various definitions of outsourcing, it can be concluded that it typically involves engaging a third-party organization with expertise in a particular area to take on a process, such as manufacturing or development (Caldwell, 1996; Claver et al., 2002).

1.1.2   Differences Between Outsourcing, Offshoring, and Strategic Alliances

a. Outsourcing vs Offshoring

Outsourcing and offshoring are two business strategies that involve moving some of a company's operations or tasks outside of its own organization (Oshri et al., 2023). While both approaches involve the use of external resources, they have different meanings and implications.

Outsourcing involves contracting a third-party provider to perform a specific service or function on behalf of the company (Akbari, 2013). This provider may be located domestically or abroad. For example, a company might outsource its payroll processing to a specialized provider, or its customer service operations to a call center.

Offshoring, on the other hand, involves moving a company's operations or production to a foreign country, typically to take advantage

Table 1.1 Outsourcing definitions

Definition	Author
Make or buy decisions are a combination of conclusions made to ensure the necessary planning of resources and services required to produce goods and services within organizations	Harrigan (1985)
External vendors provide substantial human resources related to information technology processes for organizations	Loh and Venkatraman (1992)
External activities, including those that are typically seen as a fundamental aspect of a company, as long as they are not part of the company's essential competencies	Quinn and Hilmer (1994)
A strategic partnership is an agreement between different types of organizations where one company brings specialized knowledge and makes a significant contribution to another company by providing physical or human resources for a specific period with the goal of achieving a particular objective	Navarro (1999)
The act of transferring certain business operations and related services to a third-party organization for a required outcome, either temporarily or permanently	Bailey et al. (2002)
The process of transferring a business function or service that was previously managed internally to an external provider through a long-term agreement, which involves the complete transfer of responsibility to the vendor	Quélin and Duhamel (2003)
Goes beyond the mere procurement of goods/ services from external suppliers; it also involves the transfer of responsibility for business functions, and often the associated information, to the external corporation	McCarthy and Anagnostou (2004)
The act of obtaining goods or services from a government or governing authority	Mol et al. (2005)
To acquire necessary services and materials for production and delivery by compensating external distributors and/or suppliers	Krajewski et al. (2006)

of lower costs, such as labor or taxes (Manning et al., 2008; Metters, 2008). This can involve moving entire departments or business functions, including manufacturing, research and development, or customer service, to a location overseas (Brown & Wilson, 2005). For instance, companies like Hewlett Packard (HP) and IBM engage in offshoring by relocating various production processes to cities in India like Bangalore and Chennai, aiming to leverage cost-effective labor (Kripalani & Engardio, 2003). This offshoring strategy allowed HP and IBM to remain competitive in the market by reducing their overall costs while maintaining quality and meeting customer demand. In addition, offshoring can involve not only the relocation of production processes but also the outsourcing of services, such as call center operations, software development, and accounting. According to Bhagwati et al. (2004), India is the foremost provider of offshore services, encompassing roles like call center operators and software developers catering to customers beyond their national borders.

To further illustrate the difference between outsourcing and offshoring, let's consider an example. Suppose a software company needs to develop a new mobile application. They could either hire additional developers to work in-house, or they could outsource the development to a specialized provider located in their country or abroad. In this case, the company would be outsourcing the development of the mobile application.

On the other hand, suppose the same software company decides to move its entire development team to a country with lower labor costs, such as India. The company would be offshoring its development operations to a foreign location to reduce costs. While their motivations for offshoring may be similar to those for outsourcing, this approach is specifically aimed at accessing cheaper labor.

Companies offshore for a variety of reasons (Krajewski et al., 2006), including:

- Cost savings: One of the main drivers of offshoring is to take advantage of reduced labor costs in other countries. This can result in significant cost savings for companies, particularly in industries where labor is a significant expense.
- Access to talent: Offshoring can also provide access to a wider pool of skilled workers and specialized expertise that may not be available in the company's home country.
- Reduced regulatory and compliance costs: In some cases, companies may choose to offshore certain functions to countries with less stringent regulatory and compliance requirements, which can reduce costs and streamline operations.

- Expanded market access: Offshoring can also enable companies to establish a presence in new markets and gain a better understanding of local customers and preferences.
- Improved supply chain management (SCM): By offshoring certain manufacturing or logistics functions, companies can often streamline their supply chains and reduce costs associated with shipping, warehousing, and other logistics.

It's worth noting that offshoring can also have drawbacks, such as increased risks associated with cultural differences, language barriers, and political instability in some countries (Rost, 2006). Companies must carefully weigh the potential benefits and risks before deciding to offshore any of their operations.

b. *Outsourcing vs Strategic Alliances*

Outsourcing and strategic alliances are two distinct business strategies that involve working with external partners. While both approaches involve collaboration with external parties, they have different meanings and implications. Song et al. (2000) highlighted the significant distinctions between outsourcing and strategic alliances, underscoring that these are two separate strategic decisions made at the executive level.

Outsourcing is defined as the practice of contracting out services or functions to external providers with the aim of diminishing the internal resources needed for performing business functions. This often involves a contractual agreement between a company and a third-party provider, where the provider assumes responsibility for delivering the contracted services. The primary aim of outsourcing is to lower costs and enhance operational efficiency.

In contrast, a strategic alliance is a collaborative relationship between two or more companies, where they work together toward shared profits and goals by sharing resources and capital (Bryce & Useem, 1998). Thorelli (1986) defined strategic alliances as governance structures that exist between markets and hierarchies and are established between organizations. Unlike outsourcing, strategic alliances do not necessarily involve a contractual agreement or a financial commitment from one firm to another (Murray et al., 2005). The spectrum of strategic alliances is broad, encompassing informal and unofficial arrangements as well as more formal joint ventures with legal procedures and restrictions. The primary aim of strategic alliances is to create value through cooperation, share expertise, and gain access to new markets (Todeva et al., 2005). A good example of this is the strategic alliance between Starbucks and PepsiCo which began in 1994 when the two companies signed a licensing agreement, North American Coffee Partnership (NACP), to sell Starbucks-bottled Frappuccino drinks in North America. The partnership later expanded to include other ready-to-drink coffee products and has continued to this day, with the companies collaborating on new product launches and marketing initiatives. This demonstrates the benefits of collaboration between two companies to achieve shared business goals.

To further illustrate the difference between outsourcing and strategic alliances, let's consider another example. Suppose a car manufacturer wants to improve its supply chain efficiency. It has two options: outsource or form a strategic alliance. If the manufacturer chooses to outsource, it could hire a logistics company to manage its supply chain operations. The logistics company would be responsible for the transportation, warehousing, and distribution of the car manufacturer's products. In this case, the focus is on cost reduction and efficiency gains. If it chooses to form a strategic alliance, it could partner with a technology company to develop a new software platform to manage its supply chain operations. The car manufacturer and technology company would work together to design and develop the software platform, and both would benefit from the resulting efficiency gains. In this case, the focus is on creating value through cooperation and shared expertise.

According to Song et al. (2000), the utilization of outsourcing and strategic alliances is common for achieving diverse outcomes and commitments among participating entities. While outsourcing is primarily focused on cost reduction and efficiency gains, strategic alliances are aimed at creating new opportunities and value through cooperation and partnership.

Outsourcing and strategic alliances are important strategic decisions for executives. Outsourcing involves contracting out services or functions to external providers to reduce internal resources, while strategic alliances involve collaborative relationships between companies to create value through cooperation and shared goals (Akbari & Hopkins, 2016). The differences between these two strategies help define their distinct purposes and outcomes.

1.2   OUTSOURCING DECISIONS MODEL

There are several models of outsourcing decision-making that organizations can use to decide whether to outsource or not (Beaumont & Sohal, 2004). These models include:

- *Cost-based model*: This model focuses on the cost savings that can be achieved by outsourcing. It involves comparing the costs of in-house production with the costs of outsourcing to determine which option is more cost-effective. For example, a company may decide to outsource its customer service function to a vendor in another country to take advantage of lower labor costs. However, the company must also consider the potential impact of language barriers and cultural differences on customer satisfaction.
- *Strategic-based model*: This model considers outsourcing as a strategic decision that can help organizations achieve their long-term goals. It involves analyzing the organization's strategic objectives and determining whether outsourcing can help the organization achieve those objectives. For example, a manufacturing company may decide to outsource its logistics function to a vendor specializing in transportation and warehousing, freeing up resources to focus on product development and innovation.
- *Risk-based model*: This model considers the risks associated with outsourcing and determines whether outsourcing is worth the potential risks. It involves analyzing the risks associated with outsourcing, such as loss of control over production, quality issues, and supply chain disruptions. For example, a healthcare company may decide to outsource its data management function to a vendor with a proven track record of managing sensitive patient information.
- *Capability-based model*: This model focuses on the organization's capabilities and determines whether outsourcing can help the organization improve its capabilities. It involves analyzing the organization's strengths and weaknesses and determining whether outsourcing can help the organization leverage its strengths and improve its weaknesses.
- *Core-competency model*: This model focuses on outsourcing functions that are not core competencies of the organization. The idea is that outsourcing non-core functions can allow the company to concentrate on its core competencies, leading to enhanced overall

performance. For example, a technology company may decide to outsource its accounting function to a vendor specializing in accounting services, freeing up resources to focus on developing new products.

- *Combination model*: This model involves combining two or more of the above models to make a more comprehensive outsourcing decision. For example, an organization may use a cost-based model and a risk-based model to make a more informed outsourcing decision.

Outsourcing decision-making involves weighing a range of factors and considerations, and the best model for a given organization will depend on its specific needs and objectives.

1.3   ACTIVITY SELECTION MODEL FOR THE OUTSOURCING PROCESS

There is a fundamental rule of outsourcing that should be followed. This rule states that a company should not outsource its core activities, resources, or competencies to any other company, even if it could result in significant cost savings (Singh & Delios, 2005). The rationale behind this lies in the fact that outsourcing these essential components elevates the risk of the company jeopardizing its strategic resources or core competencies.

In other words, outsourcing activities that are essential to a company's competitive advantage or key operations can lead to a loss of control over those activities (Akbari et al., 2017). By outsourcing core activities, a company may lose its ability to innovate, maintain quality standards, or respond quickly to market changes. This can ultimately damage the company's long-term competitiveness and viability.

Singh and Delios (2005) extended their argument by contending that in the evaluation of outsourcing options, firms should exercise caution in outsourcing activities that constitute the core and generate substantial value for the organization. Nevertheless, this does not imply a blanket endorsement for outsourcing all routine activities. Leaders and managers shoulder the responsibility of a judicious evaluation process, considering two criteria (See Fig. 1.3).

- The first criterion involves the level of integration and management required for the activity. Firms are advised against contemplating outsourcing activities demanding high levels of integration or management. The rationale behind this caution is rooted in the critical nature of such activities to the firm's operations. Entrusting these crucial tasks to a third party can pose challenges in maintaining the requisite levels of management oversight, potentially jeopardizing the seamless execution and control essential for the smooth functioning of these activities within the organization. For instance, if a firm outsources its core activities or competencies, it may become challenging to manage the quality of the outsourced services, leading to a loss of control over its core functions.
- The second criterion involves the level of competition in the industry. If a firm operates in a highly competitive industry, outsourcing core activities or competencies may result in a loss of competitiveness because the firm may lose control over critical aspects of its business. Thus, in such cases, firms should avoid outsourcing activities that could have a significant impact on their competitive advantage.

Therefore, it is important for companies to carefully evaluate their business processes and identify which activities are truly core to their operations. Retaining essential core activities in-house, while contemplating outsourcing for non-core functions, enables companies to harness the advantages of outsourcing while safeguarding their strategic resources and competencies. As suggested by Singh and Delios (2005), the decision to outsource business activities rests on the shoulders of leaders or managers who bear the responsibility of this determination. They suggest using two criteria to make this evaluation, as depicted in Fig. 1.3.

The Activity Selection Model for outsourcing decision-making involves analyzing a company's business processes and selecting specific activities or functions that could potentially be outsourced to external vendors. The model involves identifying the specific activities or functions that are non-core or non-critical, and then evaluating the potential benefits and risks of outsourcing those activities.

For example, a software development company may use the Activity Selection Model to determine which specific software development activities can be outsourced to external vendors. The company may identify

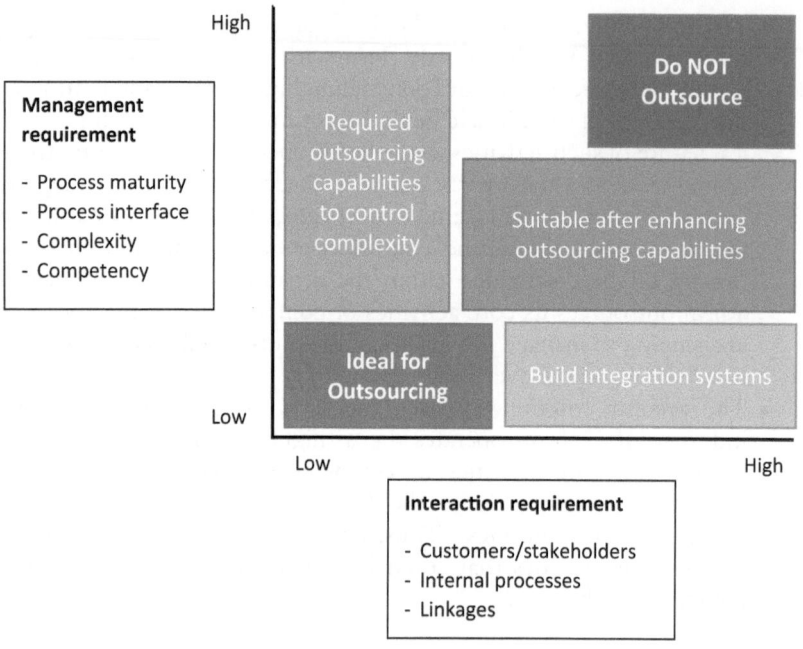

Fig. 1.3 Outsourcing selection criteria process (*Source* Author's own work—Adapted from Singh and Delios [2005])

activities such as software testing, documentation, or quality assurance as potential candidates for outsourcing.

The company would then evaluate the potential benefits and risks of outsourcing each of these activities. The benefits of outsourcing may include cost savings, access to specialized expertise or technology, or improved scalability. The risks may include loss of control over the outsourced activity, language or cultural barriers, or data security concerns.

Based on this evaluation, the company may decide to outsource certain activities to external vendors while keeping others in-house (Akbari et al., 2017). For example, the company may decide to outsource software testing and quality assurance to an external vendor, while keeping software development and project management in-house.

By using the Activity Selection Model, the company can make informed outsourcing decisions that align with its strategic objectives and core competencies, while also taking into account potential risks and benefits.

1.4   Aim and Structure of the Book

With the increasing complexity and competition in global business, firms have realized that they cannot do everything on their own and need to collaborate with third-party providers to gain a competitive advantage (Oshri et al., 2023). Outsourcing has become a strategic tool for companies that allow them to concentrate on their core competencies while leveraging the expertise and resources of specialized third-party providers.

The aim of this book is to provide a comprehensive insight into outsourcing in the context of global supply chains and the emerging trends and technologies that are shaping the future of outsourcing. The book is structured in a way that provides a holistic view of outsourcing and its impact on global supply chains. The book is organized into three parts:

Part I provides an introduction and overview of outsourcing (Chapter 1). This chapter covers common reasons for outsourcing, the benefits and risks involved, and the levels, types and success factors of outsourcing.

Part II of the book will delve into existing outsourcing models. Chapter 3 will look into outsourcing 2.0 which is mainly an advanced way to manage relationships. Chapter 4 will cover crowdsourcing, as one of the significant outsourcing practices in the modern supply chain era. This is followed by Chapter 5, which focuses on several varieties of outsourcing which currently, especially in the post-COVID-19 recovery period, are of more interest to supply chain firms.

Part III of the book will provide comprehensive insight regarding the emerging technologies in outsourcing. It will look into different Industry 4.0 technologies, including artificial intelligence (AI), cloud computing, the Internet of Things (IoT), and machine learning (ML). Additionally, it will examine the evolution toward Sixth-Party Logistics and sustainable outsourcing. Chapter 6 will examine sustainability in outsourcing, focusing on the integration of environmental, social, and governance (ESG) considerations with outsourcing initiatives and relationships. Chapter 7 will look into the development from 1PL (first-party logistics) to 3PL/TPL (third-party logistics) and its advancement all the way to 6PL (sixth-party logistics). After covering all parts of outsourcing, the concluding chapter (Chapter 8) delves into the progression of outsourcing, specifically highlighting the shift toward outsourcing 4.0. In this phase, businesses are harnessing cutting-edge technologies like AI, IoT, and blockchain to elevate the effectiveness of their outsourcing strategies.

Overall, this book provides valuable insights and information on outsourcing for companies and individuals who are interested in this field. The book's practical insights and real-world examples make it a valuable resource for professionals, managers, executives, students, and researchers interested in SCM and outsourcing. By enhancing our understanding of new trends in outsourcing, the book contributes to advancing the field and its impact on business, technology, and society.

References

Akbari, M. (2013). *Factors affecting outsourcing decisions in Iranian industries* (Doctoral thesis). Victoria University, Melbourne, Australia. https://vuir.vu.edu.au/22299/1/Mohammadreza%20Akbari.pdf

Akbari, M. (2022). Chapter 47—Outsourcing in supply chain management. In J. Sarkis (Ed.), *Handbook of supply chain management—A major reference work.* Palgrave. https://doi.org/10.1007/978-3-030-89822-9_47-1

Akbari, M., Clarke, S. J., & Maleki Far, S. (2017, July 31–August 5). Outsourcing best practice—The case of large construction firms in Iran. *Proceedings of the Informing Science and Information Technology Education Conference* (pp. 39–50). From: InSITE 2017: Informing Science and Information Technology Education Conference. Ho Chi Minh City, Vietnam. https://doi.org/10.28945/3737

Akbari, M., & Hopkins, J. (2016). The changing business landscape in Iran: Establishing outsourcing best practices. *Operations and Supply Chain Management: An International Journal, 9*(3), 184–197. https://doi.org/10.31387/oscm0250172

Akbari, M., Kok, S. K., Hopkins, J., Frederico, G. F., Nguyen, H., & Alonso, A. D. (2023). The changing landscape of digital transformation in supply chains: Impacts of industry 4.0 in Vietnam. *The International Journal of Logistics Management* (In-Press). https://doi.org/10.1108/IJLM-11-2022-0442

Aubert, B. A., Rivard, S., & Patry, M. (2004). A transaction cost model of IT outsourcing. *Information & Management, 41*(7), 921–932. https://doi.org/10.1016/j.im.2003.09.001

Bailey, W., Masson, R., & Raeside, R. (2002). Outsourcing in Edinburgh and the Lothians. *European Journal of Purchasing & Supply Management*, *8*(2), 83–95.

Barbieri, P., Boffelli, A., Elia, S., Frtocchi, L., Kalchschmidt, M., & Samson, D. (2020). What can we learn about reshoring after Covid-19? *Operations Management Research*, *13*, 131–136. https://doi.org/10.1007/s12063-020-00160-1

Beaumont, N., & Sohal, A. (2004). Outsourcing in Australia. *International Journal of Operations and Production Management*, *24*(7), 688–700. https://doi.org/10.1108/01443570410541993

Bhagwati, J., Panagariya, A., & Srinivasan, T. N. (2004). The muddles over outsourcing. *The Journal of Economic Perspectives*, *18*(4), 93–114. https://doi.org/10.1257/0895330042632753

Blumberg, D. F. (1998). Strategic assessment of outsourcing and downsizing in the service market. *Managing Service Quality*, *8*(1), 5–18. https://doi.org/10.1108/09604529810199340

Brown, D., & Wilson, S. (2005). *The black book of outsourcing*. Wiley.

Bryce, D., & Useem, M. (1998). The impact of corporate outsourcing on company value. *European Management Journal*, *16*(6), 635–643. https://doi.org/10.1016/S0263-2373(98)00040-1

Caldwell, B. (1996). The new outsourcing partnership. *Information Week*, *585*, 50–64.

Claver, E., Gonzalez, R., Gasco, J., & Llopis, J. (2002). Information systems outsourcing: Reasons, reservations and success factors. *Logistics Information Management*, *15*(4), 294–308.

Coase, R. H. (1937). The nature of the firm. *Economica*, *16*(4), 386–405.

David, F. R. (2007). *Strategic management: Concepts and cases* (11th ed.). Pearson International Edition.

Fill, C., & Visser, E. (2000). The outsourcing dilemma: A composite approach to the make or buy decision. *Management Decision*, *38*(1), 43–50. https://doi.org/10.1108/EUM0000000005315

Gould, S. J. (2002). *The structure of evolutionary theory*. Harvard University Press.

Ha, N. T., Akbari, M., & Au, B. (2023). Last mile delivery in logistics and supply chain management: A bibliometric analysis and future directions. *Benchmarking: An International Journal*, *30*(4), 1137–1170. https://doi.org/10.1108/BIJ-07-2021-0409

Harrigan, K. (1985). Strategies for intra-firm transfers and outside sourcing. *Academy of Management Journal*, *28*(4), 914–925. https://doi.org/10.5465/256244

Kantarelis, D. (2007). *Theories of the firm* (2nd ed.). Inderscience.

Kotabe, M., & Murray, J. Y. (2004). Global sourcing strategy and sustainable competitive advantage. *Industrial Marketing Management, 33*(1), 7–14. https://doi.org/10.1016%2Fj.indmarman.2003.08.004

Krajewski, L., Ritzman, L., & Malhotra, M. (2006). *Operations management: Process and value chains* (8th ed.). Prentice Hall.

Kripalani, M., & Engardio, P. (2003). The rise of India. *Business Week*, 38–46.

Krosh, J. R., & Ghosh, S. (2010). Outsourcing congruence with competitive priorities: Impact on supply chain and firm performance. *Journal of Operations Management, 28*(2), 124–143. https://doi.org/10.1016/j.jom.2009.09.004

Lacity, M. C., & Hirschheim, R. (1993). The information systems outsourcing bandwagon. *MIT Sloan Management Review, 35*(1), 73.

Lacity, M. C., Solomon, S., Yan, A., & Willcocks, L. P. (2011). Business process outsourcing studies: A critical review and research directions. *Journal of Information Technology, 26*, 221–258. https://doi.org/10.1057/jit.2011.25

Lee, L. (2003). Outsourcing: A necessary evil? *IDC Malaysia, 13*(8).

Loh, L., & Venkatraman, N. (1992). Determinants of information technology outsourcing: A cross sectional analysis. *Journal of Management Information Systems, 9*(1), 7–24. https://doi.org/10.1080/07421222.1992.11517945

Manning, S., Massini, S., & Lewin, A. Y. (2008). A dynamic perspective on next-generation off-shoring: The global sourcing of science and engineering talent. *Academy of Management Perspectives, 22*(3), 35–54. https://www.jstor.org/stable/27747462

McCarthy, I. P., & Anagnostou, A. (2004). The impact of outsourcing on the transaction costs and boundaries of manufacturing. *International Journal of Production Economics, 88*(1), 61–71. https://doi.org/10.1016/S0925-5273(03)00183-X

Metters, R. (2008). A typology of offshoring and outsourcing in electronically transmitted services. *Journal of Operations Management, 26*(2), 198–211. https://doi.org/10.1016/j.jom.2007.02.004

Miller, D., & Friesen, P. H. (1986). Porter's (1980) Generic strategies and performance: An empirical examination with American data—Part 1: Testing porter. *Organization Studies, 7*(1), 37–55. https://doi.org/10.1177/017084068600700103

Mol, M. J., Van Tulder, R. J. M., & Beije, P. R. (2005). Antecedents and performance consequences of international outsourcing. *International Business Review, 14*, 599–617. https://doi.org/10.1016/j.ibusrev.2005.05.004

Murray, J., Kotabe, M., Zhou, J. (2005). Strategic alliance-based sourcing and market performance: Evidence from foreign firms operating in China. *Journal of International Business Studies, 36*, 187–208. https://doi.org/10.1057/palgrave.jibs.8400120

Navarro, M.A.S. (1999). Consideraciones teóricas acerca del outsourcing. Boletín económico de ICE, Información Comercial Española, (2606), 27–41.

Oshri, I., Kotlarsky, J., & Willcocks, L. P. (2023). Overview of the global sourcing marketplace. In *The handbook of global outsourcing and offshoring*. Palgrave Macmillan. https://doi.org/10.1007/978-3-031-12034-3_1

Porter, M. E. (1980). *Competitive strategy*. Free Press.

Quélin, B., & Duhamel, F. (2003). Bringing together strategic outsourcing and corporate strategy: Outsourcing motives and risks. *European Management Journal, 21*(5), 647–661. https://doi.org/10.1016/S0263-2373(03)001 13-0

Quinn, J. B., & Hilmer, F. G. (1994). Strategic outsourcing. *Sloan Management Review, 8*, 43–55. https://sloanreview.mit.edu/article/strategic-outsou rcing/

Rajabzadeh, A., Rostamy, A., & Hosseini, A. (2008). Designing a generic model for outsourcing process in public sector: Evidence of Iran. *Management Decision, 46*(4), 521–538. https://doi.org/10.1108/00251740810865030

Rost, R. (2006). *The insider's guide to outsourcing risks and rewards* (1st ed.). Auerbach Publications. https://doi.org/10.1201/9781420013368

Sen, F., & Michael, S. (2006). From Business Process Outsourcing (BPO) to Knowledge Process Outsourcing (KPO): Some issues. *Human Systems Management, 25*(2), 145–155. https://doi.org/10.3233/HSM-2006-25207

Shapiro, S. P. (2005). Agency theory. *Annual Review of Sociology, 31*, 263–284. https://doi.org/10.1146/annurev.soc.31.041304.122159

Sharpe, M. (1997). Outsourcing organisational competitiveness, and work. *Journal of Labour Research, 18*(4), 535–549. https://doi.org/10.1007/s12 122-997-1021-8

Singh, K., & Delios, A. (2005). *Strategy for success in Asia in the mastering business in Asia*. Wiley.

Sober, E. (2014). *The nature of selection: Evolutionary theory in philosophical focus*. University of Chicago Press.

Song, Y., Maher, T. E., Nicholson, J. D., & Gurney, N. P. (2000). Strategic alliances in logistics outsourcing. *Asia Pacific Journal of Marketing and Logistics, 12*(4), 3–21. https://doi.org/10.1108/13555850010764640

Thorelli, H. B. (1986). Networks: Between markets and hierarchies. *Strategic Management Journal, 7*, 37–51. https://doi.org/10.1002/smj.4250070105

Todeva, E., & Knoke, D. (2005). Strategic alliances and models of collaboration. *Management Decision, 43*(1), 123–148. https://doi.org/10.1108/002 51740510572533

Tsai, C. A., Ho, T. H., Lin, J. S., Tu, C. C., & Chang, C.-W. (2021). Model for evaluating outsourcing logistics companies in the COVID-19 pandemic. *Logistics, 5*(3), 64. https://doi.org/10.3390/logistics5030064

van Hoek, R., & Dobrzykowski, D. (2021). Towards more balanced sourcing strategies—Are supply chain risks caused by the COVID-19 pandemic driving reshoring considerations? *Supply Chain Management, 26*(6), 689–701. https://doi.org/10.1108/SCM-09-2020-0498

Vitasek, K., Ledyard, M., & Manrodt, K. (2013). *Vested outsourcing: Five rules that will transform outsourcing* (2nd ed.). Palgrave Macmillan.

Williamson, O. E. (1975). *Markets and hierarchies, analysis and antitrust implications.* Free Press.

Williamson, O. E. (2008). Outsourcing: Transaction cost economics and supply chain management. *Journal of Supply Chain Management, 44*, 5–16. https://doi.org/10.1111/j.1745-493X.2008.00051.x

CHAPTER 2

Outsourcing: Optimizing Supply Chain Management for Efficiency and Growth

2.1 INTRODUCTION

Outsourcing has become prevalent in SCM because of its potential benefits, including cost reduction, access to specialized expertise, and flexibility (Tsay et al., 2018; Williamson, 2008). In SCM, outsourcing involves various forms, such as logistics (Akbari, 2018), manufacturing (Dong et al., 2016), and procurement (Skipworth et al., 2020), just to name some.

The decision to outsource is complex, and it requires careful analysis and evaluation of the potential risks and benefits (Brown & Wilson, 2005). Companies must consider factors such as the nature of the activity to be outsourced, the capabilities and expertise of the external provider, the cost and quality of the services, and the potential impact on the company's core competencies and competitive advantage (Akbari, 2018).

One of the main benefits of outsourcing in SCM is cost reduction. By outsourcing non-core activities, companies have the opportunity to reduce their overhead costs, such as labor, equipment, and facilities, and focus on their core competencies (Williamson, 2008). Outsourcing could also facilitate access to specialized expertise that may not be available internally, such as advanced logistics technology or specialized manufacturing processes (Akbari, 2022). Additionally, outsourcing can provide flexibility in terms of capacity and resources, allowing companies to swiftly adapt to evolving market conditions and demand (Choi et al., 2018; Lacity & Willcocks, 1995; Quinn & Hilmer, 1994).

However, outsourcing also involves potential risks and challenges (Kremic et al., 2006). For example, outsourcing may result in relinquishing control over the outsourced activity, which can affect the quality and reliability of services (Barthélemy, 2003). Moreover, outsourcing creates a dependency on external providers, which could be a significant risk if the provider fails to deliver or if there is a disruption in the supply chain (Lee et al., 2008). Outsourcing may also affect the company's reputation if the external provider does not adhere to the company's ethical and environmental standards.

Given these potential risks and benefits, companies must carefully evaluate their outsourcing decisions and develop effective outsourcing strategies (Akbari, 2022). This requires a thorough analysis of the company's internal capabilities and external opportunities and an understanding of the market dynamics and competitive landscape (Akbari et al., 2017).

This chapter will present an overview of outsourcing in SCM, including its benefits, risks, and challenges. I will review the different characteristics of outsourcing in SCM, such as the reasons for outsourcing and the levels and types of outsourcing. I will also present the key success factors for effective outsourcing in SCM, such as effective communication, strategic alignment, and risk management.

Overall, outsourcing in SCM can provide significant benefits for companies, but it also involves potential risks and challenges. To effectively leverage outsourcing, companies must carefully evaluate their outsourcing decisions and develop effective strategies that align with their business objectives and competitive positioning. This chapter offers a comprehensive summary of outsourcing in SCM which could help companies and practitioners develop effective outsourcing strategies that enhance their competitiveness and value proposition in the marketplace.

2.2   THE BACKGROUND

SCM has evolved into a crucial function in business operations since the mid-1990s, as highlighted by experts and practitioners (Akbari & Hopkins, 2016; König & Spinler, 2016). It is a relatively new field that emerged in the mid-1990s as a result of globalization and increased competition. The term "supply chain" encompasses the network of businesses, people, activities, information, and resources involved in creating

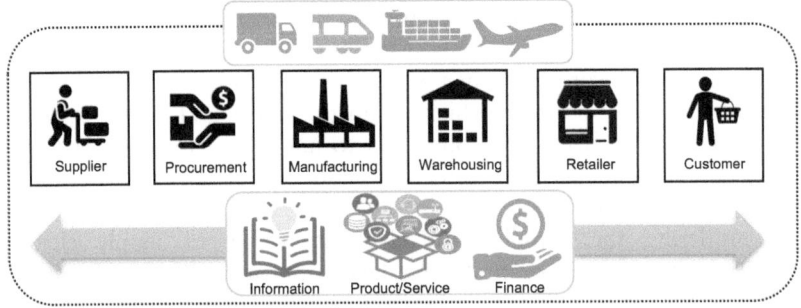

Fig. 2.1 Supply chain management (*Source* Author's own work—Adapted from Akbari [2018, 2022] and Wisner et al. [2012])

and delivering a product or service—from the raw material stage to the end customer (Wagner et al., 2003) (see Fig. 2.1).

The origins of SCM can be traced back to the early days of industrialization when businesses began to focus on optimizing their manufacturing processes to improve efficiency and reduce costs (Akbari, 2022). However, it was not until the advent of technology and the rise of global trade that SCM evolved into a distinct field of study and practice (Chopra & Meindl, 2015).

In the contemporary business landscape, competition takes place not just between companies, but also among supply chains themselves (Akbari et al., 2017; Christopher, 2016). This has placed immense importance on effective operations, transportation, and logistics within the supply chain (Chopra & Meindl, 2015; König & Spinler, 2016).

Today, SCM is considered a critical function in the success of businesses across diverse industries, including manufacturing, retail, healthcare, and hospitality. Supply chains are no longer just essential for the movement of goods in end-to-end production, but they are also rapidly changing how organizations connect, collaborate, and share information, leading to a transformation of the decision-making process (Ha et al., 2023; Wichmann et al., 2020). Therefore, effective SCM is essential for ensuring the timely and cost-effective delivery of products and services to customers, while simultaneously minimizing risks and maximizing profits (Akbari, 2023).

As supply chains continue to grow at an unprecedented pace, the need for robust SCM strategies has become even more pronounced. Organizations must ensure that their supply chain processes are optimized to meet customer demands while minimizing costs and risks (Aqlan & Lam, 2016). Effective SCM could lead to improved efficiency, reduced lead times, and enhanced customer satisfaction, ultimately translating into higher profits for businesses.

Considering the complex and dynamic nature of supply chains, managing them requires a multidisciplinary approach (Burgess & Singh, 2006). Supply chain managers must have a deep understanding of various functions, including procurement, manufacturing, transportation, warehousing, and distribution, among others. They must also be proficient in data analysis, risk management, and stakeholder engagement to effectively navigate the complexities of the global marketplace.

With the increasing complexity and competition in global business, firms have realized that they cannot do everything on their own and need to collaborate with third-party providers to secure a competitive advantage (Brown & Wilson, 2005). Outsourcing has become a strategic tool for firms to concentrate on their core competencies while leveraging the expertise and resources of specialized third-party providers. Outsourcing in SCM refers to the practice of contracting parts of the supply chain operations to third-party companies (Tsay et al., 2018). Companies may opt to outsource tasks like manufacturing, logistics, procurement, and inventory management to lower expenses, enhance productivity, and concentrate on their fundamental strengths.

One of the key benefits of outsourcing in SCM is cost savings (Williamson, 2008). By contracting certain tasks to companies that specialize in those areas, companies could potentially reduce labor and operational costs (Dong et al., 2016). In addition to accessing specialized expertise and technology that may not be available in-house, outsourcing enables companies to leverage lower labor costs and expertise and resources from providers in specific areas, including countries with specialized skills (Akbari, 2023).

However, outsourcing in the supply chain also poses risks, including a potential loss of control over the quality and delivery of goods, as well as the likelihood of disruptions if the third-party supplier encounters issues (Kremic et al., 2006). To mitigate these risks, companies must carefully select outsourcing partners and put in place proper contracts, monitoring systems, and contingency plans (Brown & Wilson, 2005).

Understanding the background and dynamics of outsourcing is crucial to distinguishing it from other strategic decisions such as offshoring and strategic alliances, which involve different approaches and considerations. As such, executives must carefully evaluate their business needs and goals to determine which approach is best suited to their organization, taking into account factors such as cost, control, and flexibility.

2.3 Benefits and Current Practices

When examining the benefits of outsourcing, it is crucial to note that companies can gain a multitude of advantages from various factors and situations (Kremic et al., 2006). While it is impossible to list every benefit of outsourcing, many benefits are general enough to apply to various organizations. Key advantages of outsourcing include cost reduction, the opportunity to concentrate on core competencies, and access to cutting-edge technology and global talent (Iqbal & Dad, 2013; Smadi & Al-Jawazneh, 2016; Somjai, 2017).

Cost reduction stands out as a paramount advantage of outsourcing, particularly advantageous for both small- to medium-sized enterprises (SMEs) and large corporations (Lankford & Parsa, 1999). For example, USS and Alcoa Inc. strategically opted to outsource their production activities to foreign countries—a move driven by the discernment of substantial operational cost reductions (Smith & Krivacek, 2019). Similarly, Somjai's (2017) investigation into the outsourcing practices of 20 SMEs underscored cost reduction as one of the most prominent and impactful benefits derived from such strategic business decisions.

In addition to cost reduction, outsourcing affords the invaluable advantage of enabling organizations to concentrate on their core competencies. Delegating non-core business processes empowers firms to judiciously allocate resources and direct their attention toward enhancing their fundamental strengths (Akbari et al., 2017). Despite the intricacies involved in selecting which functions to outsource, exemplar companies like Dell, which places a premium on research and development, and Tesco, focusing on online shopping as a core competency, have adeptly outsourced non-core activities to external entities (Windrum et al., 2008).

The acquisition of new technology stands as another compelling advantage of outsourcing, particularly for businesses seeking to tap into capabilities beyond their in-house expertise. A case in point is the experience of Augustana Care Corporation, which, faced with the challenges of a labor-intensive and potentially error-prone manual payroll process, opted to outsource to Minneapolis' Payroll Control Systems in 2017. This strategic move not only streamlined their payroll operations but also granted them access to cutting-edge technology, illustrating how outsourcing can be instrumental in harnessing advanced tools and systems that may be otherwise unavailable within the organization (Infinit-O Global, 2017).

2.3.1   Reasons for Outsourcing

Organizations frequently turn to outsourcing for their business functions with the dual objectives of boosting profits and concentrating on core activities. Scholars such as McCarthy (1996) and Beaumont and Sohal (2004) have elucidated numerous reasons and benefits that underscore the rationale behind outsourcing decisions in SCM. Embracing an outsourcing strategy empowers SCM firms to channel their focus on core business functions, concurrently mitigating challenges related to staffing levels and management complexities, thus freeing up resources for other critical tasks. The advantages extend to enhanced flexibility, improved risk management, facilitation of business process reengineering, reduction of both short- and long-term costs, broader access to domain experts, and, crucially, the facilitation of seamless integration of new technologies into SCM operations.

Furthermore, companies that opt to outsource their business functions are primarily driven by the overarching goal of profit enhancement. The motivations for outsourcing can be systematically categorized into six key factors: strategic, management, technology, quality, economic, and other considerations. This comprehensive framework allows organizations to strategically align their outsourcing decisions with specific objectives, ranging from gaining a competitive edge to addressing managerial challenges, harnessing advanced technologies, ensuring quality standards, realizing economic efficiencies, and addressing various other strategic imperatives (Akbari, 2022; Assaf & Al-Nehmi, 2011; Brown & Wilson, 2005; Douglas, 2009; Slack et al., 2015).

- *Strategic rationales*: One major outsourcing reason is to gain access to a wider talent pool, knowledge, and expertise that is not available in-house. Companies can solve complex problems by outsourcing tasks to experts or specialized suppliers. Outsourcing can also help companies manage risks more effectively by identifying and assessing potential unwanted events and minimizing the likelihood of those risks through resource management.

- *Management rationales*: Effective management is another key driver of outsourcing decisions. By outsourcing certain business functions, companies can improve their capacity management, overcome high turnover and time management failures, and improve the quality of their products and services. Outsourcing can also help firms to address issues that arise from in-house shortages, such as a lack of experienced personnel or a shortage of expertise in emerging technologies.

- *Technology rationales*: Access to in-house operational expertise often poses a challenge for companies. By leveraging external resources, firms can surmount this obstacle and gain competitive advantages without incurring significant costs associated with technology investments and related training. In addition, outsourcing can be used to enhance quality and performance over time, resulting in elevated service levels and increased operational flexibility for companies.

- *Quality rationales*: Executives of a company may opt to outsource a business function if it exhibits poor quality or low performance. This strategic decision is rooted in the potential of outsourcing to drive improvements in both the quality of the function and its overall performance over time, thereby elevating service levels. Additionally, outsourcing can be a catalyst for change and increased flexibility, particularly in cases where companies require third-party expertise for a major technology transformation that they cannot achieve on their own. By outsourcing, companies can access the necessary skills and resources to drive change and increase their agility in responding to market demands.

- *Economic rationales*: Economic factors are also a major driver of outsourcing decisions. Supply chain firms may strategically opt to outsource to achieve an overall reduction in costs and convert fixed costs into variable costs. While cost reduction is frequently highlighted as a primary motivation for outsourcing, companies also prioritize other crucial objectives, including enhancing service levels and effectively managing risk. In essence, the economic rationale for outsourcing extends beyond mere cost-cutting, encompassing a holistic approach to optimizing operational efficiency and achieving strategic goals.

- *Other rationales*: There are other factors involved when considering outsourcing, including gaining access to or expanding business functions across different time zones, responding to customer demands, and even outsourcing the management of contracts. Contracts play a pivotal role for both parties involved, and outsourcing can offer specialized expertise in crafting and managing these essential documents.

2.3.2   Types of Outsourcing

In today's dynamic business landscape, understanding the different types of outsourcing is critical. Oshri et al. (2013) identified four major types of outsourcing that companies can choose from:

- The first type is *total insourcing*, where supply chain firms manage nearly 80% of their business operations/functions in-house while outsourcing the remaining 20%.
- On the other end of the spectrum, *total outsourcing* involves the transfer of over 80% of business functions to an external corporation. However, the company still keeps certain critical functions like customer support and contract management in-house to maintain a high level of control and manage the associated risks.

  A prominent real-world example of total outsourcing is the partnership between Apple Inc. and Foxconn Technology Group. Foxconn, a Taiwanese multinational electronics contract manufacturing company, handles the manufacturing and assembly of various Apple products, including iPhones, iPads, and MacBooks. In this case, Apple has outsourced the entire manufacturing process to Foxconn, transferring more than 80% of its business functions to the external company. While Apple retains control over design, marketing, and other core aspects of its business, the production and assembly of their devices are handled entirely by Foxconn. This type of total outsourcing allows Apple to leverage Foxconn's expertise and production capabilities while focusing on its core competencies. The partnership between Apple and Foxconn exemplifies how total outsourcing can be utilized by companies to streamline their operations, reduce costs, and benefit from the specialized capabilities of external vendors.

- *Selective outsourcing*, the third type, entails entrusting a preferred business function to a third-party company while retaining between 20 and 80% of business functions in-house. This approach, which falls between total insourcing and total outsourcing, is widely adopted for its ability to address challenges associated with extreme outsourcing models. Jones et al. (1998) identified several advantages of selective outsourcing, including lower risks, heightened potential for forming strategic partnerships with third-party entities, and higher control over business functions.

  One example of selective outsourcing is when a company outsources its IT support services while keeping its marketing and sales functions in-house. For instance, a healthcare provider may outsource its IT support services to a third-party company that specializes in managing healthcare IT systems. This way, the healthcare provider can concentrate on its core business functions while relying on the expertise of the third-party company to handle its IT support needs. Another example of selective outsourcing is when a company outsources its customer service department to a third-party provider. For instance, a retail company may outsource its customer service functions to a contact center company that specializes in providing customer support services. By adopting this approach, the retail company can strategically allocate its resources to concentrate on core business functions, all the while guaranteeing that its customers receive top-notch support services.

- Lastly, *transitional outsourcing* represents a temporary outsourcing arrangement that companies opt for during significant transitions, such as implementing new technology. In this scenario, the company outsources the management of the old system to a third party until the transition process is successfully completed.

  In a noteworthy example of transitional outsourcing, Sun Microsystems entered into a 3-year contract with tech consultant CSC. During this period, Sun Microsystems outsourced the management of their IT infrastructure to CSC, illustrating a strategic approach to navigating a transitional phase while benefiting from the specialized expertise of a third-party provider. They decided to outsource their IT infrastructure management to CSC as a temporary solution while they worked on revamping their IT systems. Under the outsourcing agreement, CSC was responsible for managing Sun Microsystems' data centers, servers, storage devices,

and other IT assets. CSC also provided IT support and maintenance services to Sun Microsystems during the contract period. The
contract was worth US$27 million, and it was signed in 2006. It
helped Sun Microsystems to reduce their IT costs and improve their
operational efficiency. The outsourcing arrangement also enabled
Sun Microsystems to focus on their core business activities while
CSC managed their IT infrastructure. The transitional outsourcing
arrangement between Sun Microsystems and CSC ended in 2009,
as per the contract period. Sun Microsystems was then acquired by
Oracle Corporation in 2010, and the outsourcing arrangement with
CSC was not renewed.

Selecting the appropriate outsourcing type can be crucial for companies
to achieve their desired outcomes, and understanding the advantages and
disadvantages of each type is vital. Companies must evaluate their needs
and requirements before deciding on the outsourcing type that fits them
best.

2.3.3   Levels of Outsourcing

Outsourcing is a business practice that allows companies to delegate
their non-core functions to external parties. Depending on operational
requirements, supply chain firms may opt to outsource at various operational levels. These levels include tactical, strategic, and transformational
outsourcing.

- *Tactical outsourcing* is the basic level of outsourcing, where a
  company may choose to outsource a function to overcome a specific
  problem (Mazzawi, 2003). It is a quick approach to tackle problems and create competition between in-house business functions
  and external parties. Success at this level depends on the relationship between the company and the third-party provider(s).
  Non-core business functions are at the heart of tactical outsourcing,
  which helps to share best practices and improve efficiency. Tactical
  outsourcing is simply offloading an internal business function to an
  external party that can perform the same task more efficiently.
    A good example of tactical outsourcing is when a company
  outsources its customer service department to a third-party provider

to overcome a specific problem. For example, suppose a company is facing a sudden surge in customer inquiries due to a new product launch, and their in-house customer service team is overwhelmed. In that case, they may choose to outsource their customer service department temporarily to handle the increased workload. By outsourcing their customer service function, the company can quickly respond to the problem and provide their customers with the support they need without overburdening their internal team. The third-party provider can bring in additional staff and resources to manage the increased call volume and ensure that customers' inquiries are addressed promptly and efficiently. Once the surge in inquiries has subsided, the company can then bring the customer service function back in-house or choose to continue outsourcing it, depending on their long-term needs and goals.

- As companies expand, an awareness of the significance of long-term relationships and the superior values they can yield becomes apparent. *Strategic outsourcing* emerges as a solution enabling managers to retain greater control over business functions and avoid the risk of relinquishing them entirely. This level of outsourcing aims for enduring relationships, with the intention being to collaborate with a select number of third-party providers. Strategic outsourcing represents an advanced approach aligned with the overarching goals of companies and the preservation of their core competencies (Quinn, 1999).

A real-life example of strategic outsourcing is the partnership between Nike and Flex Ltd. (formerly known as Flextronics). Nike is a global leader in athletic footwear and apparel, but it doesn't manufacture its products directly. Instead, it outsources the production of its footwear and apparel to manufacturers located all over the world. However, in 2013, Nike decided to take its outsourcing strategy to the next level by partnering with Flex. The two companies signed a strategic partnership agreement to collaborate on product development, engineering, and manufacturing. The goal of this partnership was to enhance Nike's supply chain capabilities, improve speed to market, and drive innovation. Flex was chosen for this partnership due to its expertise in SCM, engineering, and manufacturing. Nike wanted a long-term relationship with a partner who could provide it with these critical capabilities, while also sharing its commitment to sustainability and ethical business practices.

The partnership between Nike and Flex has been successful in many ways. By working closely together, the two companies have been able to streamline Nike's supply chain, reduce costs, and improve efficiency. They have also developed new manufacturing processes and materials that have helped Nike create more innovative products.

- The most advanced form of outsourcing is referred to as ***transformational outsourcing***. This level is intended to revolutionize the current business or respond to market shifts (Linder, 2004). At this level, companies can potentially benefit from new market opportunities, accelerating companies toward smarter, more flexible, and innovative management. While tactical outsourcing is about quickly solving an existing problem, transformational outsourcing is about creating a competitive advantage.

An example of transformational outsourcing is when a company decides to outsource its entire IT department to a third-party provider to transform its digital capabilities. This decision could be made in response to market shifts, such as a shift toward cloud computing or big data analytics, which the company does not have the expertise to handle in-house. By outsourcing its IT department, the company may benefit from the third-party provider's expertise in the latest technologies, as well as their ability to scale up or down quickly as needed. The company could also reduce costs and improve efficiency by eliminating the need to manage its IT infrastructure. Transformational outsourcing also involves outsourcing core business functions, such as product development or customer service. For example, a company may decide to outsource its product development to a third-party provider with expertise in a particular technology or market segment, allowing the company to bring new products to market faster and more efficiently.

Decisions regarding outsourcing can be evaluated at varying levels of operation, each presenting distinct characteristics and associated benefits. Companies must carefully consider their needs and goals before deciding which level of outsourcing is appropriate for them. With the right approach, outsourcing can be a powerful tool that helps companies achieve their strategic objectives and stay ahead of the competition.

2.3.4   *Success Factors*

The ability to make sound outsourcing decisions can give supply chain firms a significant competitive advantage in today's markets. However, it's not always easy for companies to work together successfully when they outsource. Therefore, it's essential for organizations to understand the fundamentals of outsourcing to help them achieve success. According to studies by Akbari (2022), Brown and Wilson (2005), Koh Ser Mui (2003), Lok et al. (2018), and Rhodes et al. (2016), there are 11 critical success factors to consider when outsourcing:

1. *Preceding need analysis*: Prior to making informed outsourcing decisions, it is crucial to conduct a comprehensive examination of current needs. This includes evaluating the organization's goals, objectives, strategic vision, and business operations. A lack of knowledge in this phase can result in delays in or even failure of the outsourcing process.

2. *Selecting the appropriate provider*: Identifying the right provider is paramount for successful outsourcing. Companies must exercise caution and due diligence when evaluating potential providers. It is particularly crucial to opt for a provider with a proven track record of successful projects and the agility to respond promptly to changes.

3. *Enhancing convention*: A well-written agreement and a contract are crucial factors for successful outsourcing. The contract should provide a clear and comprehensive description of the required services, encompassing service level agreements, timelines, reporting structures, rates, and associated costs. Flexibility to adapt to technological changes is imperative, and a transparent roadmap for both business partners is highly recommended.

4. *Open communication*: Open and transparent communication is a cornerstone of successful outsourcing processes. Establishing clear communication protocols within the organization, especially with affected individuals or groups, helps alleviate employees' fears of job insecurity. Ongoing, continuous management of relationships and communication is imperative, addressing foreseeable dilemmas and facilitating adjustments to foster a successful relationship between the company and third-party providers.

5. *Support and engagement from top management*: Top management's support is crucial to achieving the outsourcing goals and objectives. While formulating strategic goals is within the purview of top management, securing their active support is equally advantageous. It falls on top management to initiate goals and objectives, champion the third-party provider in their achievement, and allocate resources accordingly. Research consistently underscores that top management support stands as the most influential factor contributing to the success of outsourcing endeavors.

6. *Cultural fit*: Often overlooked but critically important, a key success factor in outsourcing is the cultural fit between the company and the outsourcing provider. It is essential that the outsourcing provider aligns with the company's values, culture, and working style to ensure a harmonious collaboration. A strong cultural fit can lead to better communication, collaboration, and a smoother outsourcing process overall.

7. *Continuous improvement*: Companies should strive for continuous improvement when outsourcing. This means that they should continually assess the outsourcing process, identify areas for improvement, and implement changes as needed. This can include streamlining processes, improving communication, or adjusting the service level agreement to reflect changing business needs. By continuously improving the outsourcing process, companies can maximize the benefits of outsourcing and achieve better outcomes.

8. *Risk management*: Outsourcing can come with inherent risks, such as service disruptions, security breaches, or data loss. Companies should have a risk management plan in place to mitigate these risks and ensure business continuity. This plan can include measures such as disaster recovery plans, security protocols, and regular backups of critical data. By proactively managing risks, companies can minimize the negative impact of any potential issues and ensure that the outsourcing process runs smoothly.

9. *Training and development*: Companies should invest in training and development programs for their employees (Akbari et al., 2022), ensuring that they acquire the skills and knowledge essential for effective collaboration with the outsourcing provider. This can include training on the outsourced process or system, cultural awareness training, or communication skills training. By investing in employee development, companies can improve their ability to

work with the outsourcing provider, achieve better outcomes, and foster a positive outsourcing relationship.

10. *Performance measurement*: Companies should establish clear performance metrics to gauge the success of the outsourcing process. This can include metrics such as service level agreements, response times, quality standards, and cost savings. By regularly measuring performance against these metrics, companies can identify areas for improvement, track progress, and ensure that the outsourcing process is delivering the expected benefits.

11. Sustainability is an increasingly important factor in outsourcing decisions, and there are several success factors related to it. Companies should consider the outsourcing provider's environmental policies, social responsibility, and ethical sourcing practices. Selecting a provider whose values align with the company's allows the company to diminish its environmental and social impact while bolstering its reputation as a socially responsible organization. Environmental responsibility, social responsibility, and ethical sourcing are all critical factors that companies should consider when making outsourcing decisions. By taking these factors into account, companies can ensure that their outsourcing decisions align with their values and contribute to a more sustainable future.

Other factors that contribute to successful outsourcing encompass transparency, implementing rewards and penalties, identifying capabilities, and differentiating levels among qualified and skilled in-house personnel/employees. *Transparency* means that both the company and the outsourcing provider should have a clear understanding of each other's expectations, capabilities, and limitations. Transparency is essential to ensure that everyone is on the same page and that the outsourcing process runs smoothly.

Another factor that can impact successful outsourcing is *rewards and penalties*. This means that there should be a system in place to reward the outsourcing provider for meeting or exceeding expectations, and there should be consequences if it fails to do so. This system can motivate the provider to perform well and provide quality services, ultimately leading to better outsourcing outcomes.

Capability identification is another important factor to consider when outsourcing. This means that companies should identify their core competencies and outsource tasks that are not their strengths. By doing so, companies can focus on what they do best and leave the rest to outsourcing providers who have the necessary capabilities and expertise.

Finally, *distinguishing levels of qualified and skilled in-house personnel/ employees* is another factor to consider when outsourcing. Companies should identify their most valuable employees and retain them in-house to ensure that they continue to provide high-quality work. Outsourcing less critical tasks can free up these employees' time and allow them to focus on more strategic initiatives, ultimately leading to better business outcomes.

It's essential to keep in mind these factors when outsourcing to ensure success. By taking these factors into account, companies can ensure that they have a clear and effective outsourcing relationship, maximize the benefits of outsourcing, and achieve better outcomes overall.

To summarize, Table 2.1 and Fig. 2.2 illustrate the outsourcing decisions made within supply chains.

Table 2.1 Summary of outsourcing characteristics and success factors

Characteristics	Elements/Factors
Reasons for outsourcing	Organizations outsource for various reasons, including focusing on core activities, reducing staffing and management issues, gaining flexibility, managing risks, supporting business process reengineering, reducing costs, accessing expert knowledge, and implementing new technologies. Reasons can be categorized into six important factors: strategic, management, technology, quality, economic, and other rationales
Types of outsourcing	Four major types: total insourcing (80% in-house), total outsourcing (more than 80% external), selective outsourcing (20–80% in-house), and transitional outsourcing (temporary during transitions)
Levels of outsourcing	Three levels: tactical outsourcing (basic, addressing specific problems), strategic outsourcing (long-term relationships, control, and values alignment), and transformational outsourcing (revolutionizing business, responding to market shifts)
Success factors	Eleven critical success factors: preceding need analysis, choosing the right provider, enhancing convention through well-written agreements, open communication, support from top management, cultural fit, continuous improvement, risk management, training and development, performance measurement, and sustainability. Additional factors: transparency, implementing rewards and penalties, identifying capabilities, and differentiating levels among qualified and skilled in-house personnel/employees

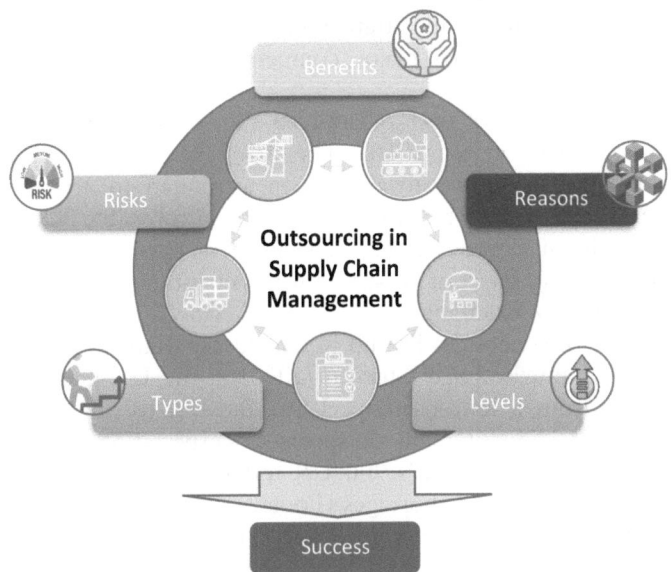

Fig. 2.2 Outsourcing in supply chain management (*Source* Author's own work)

2.4   Emergent Concerns and Future Directions

In the current competitive landscape, supply chain firms are increasingly embracing outsourcing as a strategic approach, enabling them to concentrate on their core competencies while entrusting external entities with the management of non-core processes (Kalinzi, 2016). While outsourcing has numerous benefits, it is important for firms to understand the potential risks that come with the decision to outsource (Yazdani et al., 2021). The risks associated with outsourcing include the potential emergence of competitors, loss of control, and poor vendor performance.

The creation of potential competitors can happen when chosen suppliers/vendors poach customers or start offering the service or product directly to market themselves (Lim & Tan, 2010). The example of Goldstar, Samsung, Kia, and Daewoo in the 1980s illustrates how Original Equipment Manufacturer (OEM) supply contracts with Western companies propelled them to product leadership in their respective domains. Apple's outsourcing strategy has similarly resulted in the inadvertent emergence of two major competitors, namely Samsung and Foxconn (Griffin, 2015).

Relinquishing control over outsourced functions represents another notable risk (Lacity et al., 2010). The Royal Bank of Scotland faced a crash in their banking software system attributed to actions by an unnamed IT vendor, resulting in substantial and irreversible financial and reputational harm (Peston, 2012). The incident persisted for almost a week, underscoring the peril associated with entrusting critical systems to vendors through outsourcing.

The failure of vendors to live up to agreed expectations is also a risk. The case of Kentucky Fried Chicken (KFC) in the UK illustrates how transitioning from a long-term specialist, Bidvest, to other 3PLs like DHL and QSL did not fulfill the promised expectations. This failure resulted in over 560 of KFC's 900 UK restaurants shutting down due to supply deficiencies and shortages (Pooley, 2018; Uddin, 2020). This example underscores the significant impact a business can face due to the underperformance of chosen suppliers or vendors.

In light of these risks, firms should carefully consider their outsourcing decisions and take steps to mitigate these risks. They should identify potential competitors among chosen vendors and consider a non-compete clause in the contract. Additionally, firms should maintain some level of control over outsourced functions and establish a clear set of guidelines for vendors. They should also set clear performance expectations, provide regular feedback, and conduct regular performance evaluations. By taking these steps, firms can maximize the benefits of outsourcing while minimizing the risks.

Another point to consider is that the COVID-19 pandemic has brought about new risks and challenges for outsourcing in supply chains. Restrictions on travel and movement have disrupted the supply chain, causing delays and reduced capacity. The pandemic has underscored the significance of supplier risk management and emphasized the necessity for contingency plans to alleviate disruptions. Given the profound impact of COVID-19 on global supply chains, outsourcing will persist as a crucial strategy for ensuring business continuity and mitigating risks. However, managers will need to exercise greater due diligence in supplier selection and management, as well as consider the potential risks associated with international outsourcing. Additionally, there is an increased focus on nearshoring and reshoring as companies seek to reduce dependence on distant suppliers and ensure greater control over their supply chain operations. The pandemic has underscored the imperative for supply chain resilience and flexibility, and outsourcing will continue to be a key strategy in achieving these goals.

To address these challenges and risks, the future direction of outsourcing in the SCM should focus on strategic partnerships and closer collaboration between the outsourcing firm and the chosen vendor. This means that outsourcing decisions will be made based on long-term strategic considerations, rather than short-term cost savings.

Outsourcing firms will look to develop stronger relationships with their vendors to improve communication and ensure a better alignment of objectives. This will involve the implementation of more comprehensive vendor management programs, which will include regular performance reviews and monitoring key performance indicators (KPIs).

Another important trend in outsourcing in SCM is the increasing use of technology, such as AI, cloud computing, ML, and blockchain, to improve efficiency and transparency. These technologies have the potential to automate repetitive tasks and improve supply chain visibility, which could lead to better decision-making and more efficient operations (Akbari, 2023).

Further, the future direction of outsourcing sustainability is expected to focus on greater transparency, accountability, and collaboration between companies and their outsourcing partners (Zarbakhshnia et al., 2023). There is a growing trend toward incorporating sustainability as a key consideration in the outsourcing decision-making process, with an emphasis on minimizing the environmental impact of supply chain operations. One potential direction for outsourcing sustainability is the implementation of circular economy (CE) principles. The CE is an economic system designed to eliminate waste and encourage the continuous utilization of resources (Geissdoerfer et al., 2017). By applying CE principles to outsourcing, companies can work with their outsourcing partners to design products and services that reduce waste and maximize resource efficiency. This can include strategies such as product design for disassembly, closed-loop material cycles, and the utilization of renewable energy sources.

Finally, collaboration is anticipated to assume a progressively vital role in outsourcing. By working together with outsourcing partners, companies can share knowledge and resources to develop innovative solutions for minimizing the environmental impact of supply chain operations. This can include joint research and development initiatives, sharing best practices, and establishing sustainability-focused supply chain standards and certifications.

2.5   Managerial Implications

To enhance the performance of supply chain companies, practitioners and managers should contemplate outsourcing as a strategic option. Well-designed and effectively implemented outsourcing initiatives can positively impact both the financial and non-financial aspects of companies. However, achieving this requires careful consideration of the trade-offs between outsourcing and insourcing, taking into account the direct and indirect costs associated with delegating certain functions to third-party providers.

The initial step in the outsourcing process involves managers identifying non-core activities and entrusting these tasks to third-party providers, all while retaining control over core activities internally. This approach ensures a concentrated focus on core competencies while leveraging the specialized expertise of external organizations for non-core activities. The subsequent step entails a nuanced understanding of the distinctions between manufacturing and service activities, contributing to enhanced success in the overall outsourcing strategy.

In the context of the globalized logistics industry, opting for international or multinational providers offers distinct advantages over domestic alternatives. Establishing contracts and nurturing long-term relationships with international service providers can be less intricate and offer more consistency compared to domestic counterparts. However, it is imperative for managers to exercise due diligence regarding the resourcing of their suppliers and maintain continuous monitoring throughout the life of their contracts, particularly in light of the ongoing impact of the COVID-19 situation.

To guide supply chain firms in attaining their optimal performance, it is crucial to identify a sound sourcing decision. The outsourcing process can be delineated into seven steps, with the selection of the supplier occurring after the decision to outsource is made and agreements and goals are formulated (see Fig. 2.3) (Schniederjans et al., 2005).

The selection of suppliers should consider multiple criteria, including their capability to leverage technologies for cost-effective production of goods or services, ultimately contributing to the company's competitive

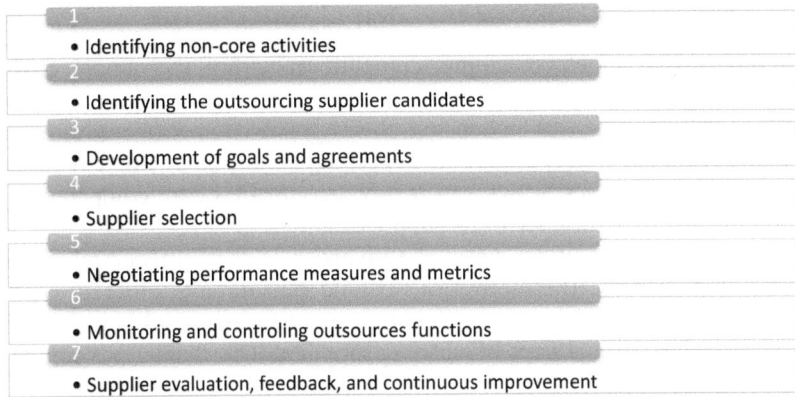

1
- Identifying non-core activities

2
- Identifying the outsourcing supplier candidates

3
- Development of goals and agreements

4
- Supplier selection

5
- Negotiating performance measures and metrics

6
- Monitoring and controling outsources functions

7
- Supplier evaluation, feedback, and continuous improvement

Fig. 2.3 Overview of outsourcing processes (*Source* Author's own work—Adapted from Schniederjans et al. [2005])

advantage (Hoyer et al., 2021). Suppliers should be open to sharing technologies and information, ensuring the delivery of consistent and high-quality products or services. Additionally, they should provide a comprehensive total cost of ownership that covers inventory, quality, technology, logistical, and maintenance costs. Reliability, both in terms of financial stability and lead time, is also a key consideration. An easy ordering system, supplier capacity, communication, and geographic location are also important factors to consider when selecting suppliers.

Ultimately, managers should recognize that the successful implementation of outsourcing efficiency and effectiveness demands a well-planned and phased approach over time. It is crucial for managers to carefully assess the location of providers, their infrastructure, as well as potential cultural and financial disparities, to ensure the success of outsourcing initiatives (Lahiri et al., 2022). In conclusion, supply chain firms should embark on outsourcing their business functions only when they have a comprehensive understanding of the potential benefits and implications associated with such endeavors.

2.6   SUMMARY AND CONCLUSION

In the current global economy, competition within the supply chain has intensified, compelling companies to explore novel approaches for acquiring resources and enhancing their global competitive advantage (Lee, 2021). An effective method to accomplish this is by implementing outsourcing strategies, which can fortify a company's core competencies and enhance the efficiency of its supply chain.

This chapter has underscored the pivotal role that outsourcing plays in SCM, looking at the motivations behind outsourcing, different types and levels of outsourcing, key success factors, the associated benefits and risks, and the essential steps in selecting suppliers. The chapter has empha-sized that outsourcing can provide companies with a range of benefits, including access to specialized expertise and technology, cost savings, and the ability to focus on core competencies. However, outsourcing also involves certain risks, such as loss of control over critical functions and potential damage to a company's reputation.

To mitigate these risks, the chapter has outlined key success factors in outsourcing, such as effective communication and collaboration with suppliers, clear performance metrics, and a well-defined outsourcing strategy aligned with overall business goals. Additionally, this chapter has provided guidance on how to select the right supplier, considering factors such as technology capabilities, product/service quality, total cost of ownership, supplier reliability, ease of ordering, capacity to fulfill orders, communication, and geographic location.

Looking ahead, the next chapter identifies emerging concerns and future directions in outsourcing. This includes the imperative to incor-porate environmental and social sustainability into supplier selection and the escalating significance of digitalization and data analytics. It under-scores the critical need for supply chain firms to comprehend the array of outsourcing options available and to implement effective management practices for navigating risks and realizing benefits.

In conclusion, this chapter has furnished a comprehensive overview of the role of outsourcing in SCM, highlighting its benefits, risks, success factors, and supplier selection steps. It has underscored the importance of considering emerging concerns and future directions in outsourcing to effectively manage risks and capitalize on opportunities. Supply chain firms must remain vigilant and agile in their outsourcing strategies to remain competitive in an ever-evolving global marketplace.

REFERENCES

Akbari, M. (2018). Logistics outsourcing: A structured literature review. *Benchmarking: An International Journal, 25*(5), 1548–1580. https://doi.org/10.1108/BIJ-04-2017-0066

Akbari, M. (2022). Chapter 47—Outsourcing and insourcing in global supply chain. In J. Sarkis (Ed.), *Handbook of supply chain management—A major reference work*. Palgrave. https://doi.org/10.1007/978-3-030-89822-9_47-1

Akbari, M. (2023). Revolutionizing supply chain and circular economy with edge computing: Systematic review, research themes and future directions. *Management Decision* (In-Press). https://doi.org/10.1108/MD-03-2023-0412

Akbari, M., Clarke, S. J., & Maleki Far, S. (2017, July 31–August 5). Outsourcing best practice—The case of large construction firms in Iran. *Proceedings of the Informing Science and Information Technology Education Conference* (pp. 39–50). From: InSITE 2017: Informing Science and Information Technology Education Conference. Ho Chi Minh City, Vietnam. https://doi.org/10.28945/3737

Akbari, M., & Hopkins, J. (2016). The changing business landscape in Iran: Establishing outsourcing best practices. *Operations and Supply Chain Management: An International Journal, 9*(3), 184–197. https://doi.org/10.31387/oscm0250172

Akbari, M., Nguyen, H. M., McClelland, R., & Van Houdt, K. (2022). Design, implementation and academic perspectives on authentic assessment for applied business higher education in a top performing Asian economy. *Education + Training, 64*(1), 69–88. https://doi.org/10.1108/ET-04-2021-0121

Aqlan, F., & Lam, S. S. (2016). Supply chain optimization under risk and uncertainty: A case study for high-end server manufacturing. *Computers & Industrial Engineering, 93*, 78–87. https://doi.org/10.1016/j.cie.2015.12.025

Assaf, S., & Al-Nehmi, A. (2011). Factors affecting outsourcing decisions of maintenance services in Saudi Arabian Universities. *Property Management, 29*(2), 195–212.

Barthélemy, J. (2003). The seven deadly sins of outsourcing. *Academy of Management Perspectives, 17*(2), 87–98. https://doi.org/10.5465/ame.2003.10025203

Beaumont, N., & Sohal, A. (2004). Outsourcing in Australia. *International Journal of Operations and Production Management, 24*(7), 688–700. https://doi.org/10.1108/01443570410541993

Brown, D., & Wilson, S. (2005). *The black book of outsourcing*. Wiley.

Burgess, K., & Singh, P. J. (2006). A proposed integrated framework for analysing supply chains. *Supply Chain Management, 11*(4), 337–344. https://doi.org/10.1108/13598540610671789

Choi, J. J., Ju, M., Kotabe, M., Trigeorgis, L., & Zhang, X. T. (2018). Flexibility as firm value driver: Evidence from offshore outsourcing. *Global Strategy Journal, 8*, 351–376. https://doi.org/10.1002/gsj.1181

Chopra, S., & Meindl, P. (2015). *Supply chain management: Strategy, planning, and operation* (6th ed.). Pearson.

Christopher, M. (2016). *Logistics & supply chain management* (5th ed.). Pearson.

Dong, Y., Xu, K., Xu, Y., & Wan, X. (2016). Quality management in multilevel supply chains with outsourced manufacturing. *Production and Operations Management, 25*, 290–305. https://doi.org/10.1111/poms.12428

Douglas, H. (2009). *The failure of risk management: Why It's broken and how to fix it.* Wiley.

Geissdoerfer, M., Savaget, P., Bocken, N. M. P., & Hultink, R. J. (2017). The circular economy—A new sustainability paradigm? *Journal of Cleaner Production, 143*, 757–768. https://doi.org/10.1016/j.jclepro.2016.12.048

Griffin, M. (2015). *How Apple's outsourcing strategy created two giant competitors.* Retrieved April 12, 2023, from https://www.cio.com/article/2926435/how-apples-outsourcingstrategy-created-two-giant-competitors.html

Ha, N. T., Akbari, M., & Au, B. (2023). Last mile delivery in logistics and supply chain management: A bibliometric analysis and future directions. *Benchmarking: An International Journal, 30*(4), 1137–1170. https://doi.org/10.1108/BIJ-07-2021-0409

Hoyer, C., Gunawan, I., Reaiche, C. H. (2021). Implementing industry 4.0—The need for a holistic approach. In A. Dingli, F. Haddod, & C. Klüver (Eds.), *Artificial intelligence in industry 4.0. Studies in computational intelligence* (Vol. 928). Springer. https://doi.org/10.1007/978-3-030-61045-6_1

Infinit-O Global. (2017). *The best outsourcing success stories of all time.* Retrieved November 19, 2022, from https://resourcecenter.infinit-o.com/blog/outsourcing-success-stories-time/

Iqbal, Z., & Dad, A. M. (2013). Outsourcing: A review of trends, winners & losers and future directions. *International Journal of Business and Social Science, 4*(8), 91–107.

Jones, S., Bebbington, P., & Blanch, G. (1998, Autumn). *Impacts of selective outsourcing of information technology and information services* (Master Thesis, No. 32812). Dept. of Business, and Dept. of Mathematics and Computer Science, University of Technology, Sydney.

Kalinzi, C. (2016). Outsourcing (Logistics) Services and Supply Chain Efficiency-A Critical Review of Outsourcing Function in Mukwano Group of Companies. *Journal of Outsourcing & Organizational Information Management, 2016*, Article ID 937323. https://doi.org/10.5171/2016.937323

Koh Ser Mui, A. (2003). Investigation of IT/IS Outsourcing in Singapore. Dept. of Software Engineering and Computer Science, Master Thesis, June 2003, No. MSE-2003-11, Blekinge Institute of Technology, Sweden.

König, A., & Spinler, S. (2016). The effect of logistics outsourcing on the supply chain vulnerability of shippers: Development of a conceptual risk management framework. *The International Journal of Logistics Management, 27*(1), 122–141. https://doi.org/10.1108/IJLM-03-2014-0043

Kremic, T., Tukel, O. I., & Rom, W. O. (2006). Outsourcing decision support: A survey of benefits, risks, and decision factors. *Supply Chain Management, 11*(6), 467–482. https://doi.org/10.1108/13598540610703864

Lacity, M. C., Khan, S., Yan, A., & Willcocks, L. P. (2010). A review of the IT outsourcing empirical literature and future research directions. *Journal of Information Technology, 25*(4), 395–433. https://doi.org/10.1057/jit.201 0.21

Lacity, M. C., & Willcocks, L. P. (1995). IT outsourcing: Maximize flexibility and control. *Harvard Business Review, 73*(3), 84–93.

Lahiri, S., Karna, A., Chittaranjan Kalubandi, S., & Edacherian, S. (2022). Performance implications of outsourcing: A meta-analysis. *Journal of Business Research, 139*, 1303–1316. https://doi.org/10.1016/j.jbusres.2021.10.061

Lankford, W. M., & Parsa, F. (1999). Outsourcing: A primer. *Management Decision, 37*(4), 310–316. https://doi.org/10.1108/00251749910269357

Lee, J. N., Huynh, M. Q., & Hirschheim, R. (2008). An integrative model of trust on IT outsourcing: Examining a bilateral perspective. *Information Systems Frontiers, 10*, 145–163. https://doi.org/10.1007/s10796-008-9066-7

Lee, R. (2021). The effect of supply chain management strategy on operational and financial performance. *Sustainability, 13*(9), 5138. https://doi.org/10.3390/su13095138

Lim, W. S., & Tan, S. J. (2010). Outsourcing suppliers as downstream competitors: Biting the hand that feeds. *European Journal of Operational Research, 203*(2), 360–369. https://doi.org/10.1016/j.ejor.2009.08.006

Linder, J. C. (2004). Transformational outsourcing. *MIT Sloan Management Review.*

Lok, K. L., Opoku, A., & Baldry, D. (2018). Design of sustainable outsourcing services for facilities management: Critical success factors. *Sustainability, 10*(7), 2292. https://doi.org/10.3390/su10072292

Mazzawi, E. (2003). Transformational outsourcing. *Business Strategy Review, 13*(3), 39–43. https://doi.org/10.1111/1467-8616.00221

McCarthy, E. (1996). To Outsource or Not to Outsource - What's Right for You. *Pension Management, 32*(4), 12–21.

Oshri, I., Kotlarsky, J., & Willcocks, L. P. (2013). *The handbook of global outsourcing and offshoring* (3rd ed.). Palgrave Macmillan.

Peston, R. (2012). *Is outsourcing the cause of RBS debacle?* Retrieved May 5, 2023, from https://www.bbc.com/news/business-18577109

Pooley, C. R. (2018). *KFC runs out of chicken in logistics fiasco.* Retrieved May 3, 2023, from https://www.ft.com/content/223d4df0-1595-11e8-9376-4a6 390addb44

Quinn, J., & Hilmer, F. (1994). Strategic outsourcing. *Sloan Management Review, 35*(4), 43–55.

Quinn, J. B. (1999). Strategic outsourcing: Leveraging knowledge capabilities. *MIT Sloan Management Review.*

Rhodes, J., Lok, P., Loh, W., & Cheng, V. (2016). Critical success factors in relationship management for services outsourcing. *Service Business, 10*, 59–86. https://doi.org/10.1007/s11628-014-0256-8

Schniederjans, M. J., Schniederjans, A. M., & Schniederjans, D. G. (2005). *Outsourcing and insourcing in an international context* (1st ed.). Routledge.

Skipworth, H., Delbufalo, H., & Mena, C. (2020). Logistics and procurement outsourcing in the healthcare sector: A comparative analysis. *European Management Journal, 38*(3), 518–532. https://doi.org/10.1016/j.emj.2020.04.002

Slack, N., Nrandon-Joes, A., Johnston, R., & Betts, A. (2015). *Operations and process management* (4th ed.). Pearson.

Smadi, Z., & Al-Jawazneh, B. (2016). The benefits of the outsourcing strategy as perceived by the industrial companies in Jordan. *Global Journal of Management and Business Research, 16*, 1–13.

Smith, A. D., & Krivacek, S. (2019). Making the case for Global outsourcing: Cases of business complexities and success. *Atlantic Marketing Association Proceedings* (pp. 1–14).

Somjai, S. (2017). Advantages and disadvantages of outsourcing. *The Business and Management Review, 9*(1), 157–160.

Tsay, A. A., Gray, J. V., Noh, I. J., & Mahoney, J. T. (2018). A review of production and operations management research on outsourcing in supply chains: Implications for the theory of the firm. *Production and Operations Management, 27*, 1177–1220. https://doi.org/10.1111/poms.12855

Uddin, S. M. (2020). Operational strategies and management of KFC: An enquiry. *EPRA International Journal of Research and Development (IJRD), 5*(4), 172–179. https://doi.org/10.36713/epra4262

Wagner, B. A., Fillis, I., & Johansson, U. (2003). E-business and e-supply strategy in small and medium sized businesses (SMEs). *Supply Chain Management: An International Journal, 8*(4), 343–354. https://doi.org/10.1108/13598540310490107

Wichmann, P., Brintrup, A., Baker, S., Woodall, P., & McFarlane, D. (2020). Extracting supply chain maps from news articles using deep neural networks.

International Journal of Production Research, 58(17), 5320–5336. https://doi.org/10.1080/00207543.2020.1720925

Williamson, O. E. (2008). Outsourcing: Transaction cost economics and supply chain management. *Journal of Supply Chain Management, 44*, 5–16. https://doi.org/10.1111/j.1745-493X.2008.00051.x

Windrum, P., Reinstaller, A., & Bull, C. (2008). The outsourcing productivity paradox: Total outsourcing, organisational innovation, and long run productivity growth. *Journal of Evolutionary Economics, 19*, 197–229.

Wisner, J. D., Tan, K. C., & Leong, G. K. (2012). *Principles of supply chain management—A balanced approach* (3rd ed.). Cengage Learning.

Yazdani, M., Mohammed, A., Bai, C., & Labib, A. (2021). A novel hesitant-fuzzy-based group decision approach for outsourcing risk. *Expert Systems with Applications, 184*, 115517. https://doi.org/10.1016/j.eswa.2021.115517

Zarbakhshnia, N., Govindan, K., Kannan, D., & Goh, M. (2023). Outsourcing logistics operations in circular economy towards to sustainable development goals. *Business Strategy and the Environment, 32*(1), 134–162. https://doi.org/10.1002/bse.3122

CHAPTER 3

Outsourcing Renaissance: Emergence of the Next Wave with Outsourcing 2.0

3.1 Introduction

Outsourcing, once a straightforward approach to reducing operational costs, has undergone a remarkable transformation in the modern business landscape (Brown & Wilson, 2005). It has transcended its early reputation as a cost-saving strategy and emerged as a dynamic and strategic tool that enables organizations to not only streamline operations but also gain a significant competitive edge (Akbari & Hopkins, 2016). In this chapter, the exploration embarks on a journey through the evolution of outsourcing, exploring how it has matured into a multifaceted and strategic practice. The focus centers on three innovative business models—each representing a unique milestone in this journey—that have redefined the way organizations collaborate with external partners.

Traditionally, outsourcing was primarily adopted to minimize expenses (Akbari, 2013; Aqlan & Lam, 2016). It involved contracting specific tasks or processes to external service providers, often in regions where labor costs were lower (Kotabe & Murray, 2004). While this approach was undeniably effective in cost reduction, it often fell short in addressing other critical aspects of business operations, such as innovation, strategic alignment, and risk management (Akbari et al., 2017).

> The significant problems we face cannot be solved at the same level of thinking we were at when we created them—Albert Einstein. (1879–1955)

© The Author(s), under exclusive license to Springer Nature Singapore Pte Ltd. 2024
M. Akbari, *The Road to Outsourcing 4.0*,
https://doi.org/10.1007/978-981-97-2708-7_3

However, as organizations ventured into the complex and rapidly evolving global marketplace, they began to realize that outsourcing could offer more than just cost savings (Ernst & Kim, 2022). It could serve as a strategic lever to foster growth, gain access to specialized skills, accelerate time-to-market, and enhance customer experiences (Akbari, 2018; Choi et al., 2018). This realization marked the dawn of a new era in outsourcing—an era characterized by innovative models that went beyond the transactional nature of traditional outsourcing (Akbari & Hopkins, 2016).

This chapter explores three groundbreaking business models that have emerged as pivotal milestones in the evolution of Outsourcing 2.0 and Vested Outsourcing (Vitasek & Manrodt, 2012).

The transaction-based model: This model represents a refinement of traditional outsourcing practices. It focuses on specific tasks or processes delegated to external partners, with compensation typically tied to the volume or frequency of these transactions.

The outcome-based business model: Shifting the focus from mere task completion, this model places a premium on achieving predefined outcomes or objectives. Service providers are incentivized to deliver results rather than just perform tasks, aligning their interests with the overarching goals of the organization.

The investment-based model: Going further in fostering collaboration and shared accountability, this model encourages both the client and the service provider to make strategic investments in the outsourcing arrangement. These investments can be financial, intellectual, or resource-based, and they often come with shared risks and rewards.

The exploration of these three models is just the beginning of our journey. As the exploration delves deeper into each model, it uncovers their principles, advantages, and real-world examples that showcase their effectiveness. Moreover, the examination extends to how these models have catalyzed the emergence of a new era in outsourcing, often referred to as outsourcing 2.0 or vested outsourcing. This era represents a significant shift in how organizations approach external collaborations.

Outsourcing 2.0 is characterized by its emphasis on long-term partnerships, innovation, flexibility, and a shared vision for success (Akbari, 2022). It encourages organizations to move beyond the traditional client–service provider relationship toward a more collaborative and strategic alliance. By embracing the principles of outsourcing 2.0, organizations can not only achieve operational excellence but also drive innovation, enhance customer experiences, and gain a competitive edge in an increasingly dynamic and interconnected world (Akbari, 2022).

In the chapters that follow, an in-depth examination unfolds for each of these innovative business models. Their intricacies will be dissected, real-world applications explored, and the transformative impact they can wield on organizations striving to excel in the ever-evolving global marketplace will be revealed. Additionally, the analysis will extend to examine how outsourcing 2.0 serves as a guiding philosophy that underpins these models, driving organizations toward a future where strategic partnerships redefine the boundaries of what is possible through outsourcing.

3.2   OUTSOURCING BUSINESS MODELS

In the evolving landscape of outsourcing, organizations have ventured beyond conventional cost-cutting strategies (Rosenberg, 2005). They now embrace innovative business models that prioritize results, strategic partnerships, and shared risks and rewards (Evan et al., 2017). In this section, an examination unfolds as three distinct business models in outsourcing, each representing a unique milestone in this evolution. The focus extends to exploring the transaction-based, outcome-based business, and investment-based models, providing real-world examples, and highlighting their benefits and challenges.

3.2.1   The Transaction-Based Model in Outsourcing: Delivering Efficiency and Cost Control

The transaction-based model represents a foundational approach to outsourcing, characterized by its simplicity and focus on specific tasks or processes (Mahnke et al., 2005). In this model, organizations delegate well-defined activities to external service providers who, in turn, are compensated based on the volume, frequency, or other agreed-upon metrics of these transactions (Vitasck & Manrodt, 2012). This approach has been a cornerstone of outsourcing for decades and continues to play a crucial role in many business operations (Ayerbe et al., 2014). In this comprehensive exploration, the focus shifts to the transaction-based model in outsourcing, examining its key features, real-world applications, benefits, and challenges. Key features of the transaction-based model are (Vitasek, 2016):

- Task-centric approach: At the heart of the transaction-based model is the concept of breaking down business processes into discrete tasks or activities. These tasks are then outsourced to specialized service providers, who are responsible for their execution.
- Clear compensation structure: Unlike other outsourcing models that may tie compensation to outcomes or shared risks, the transaction-based model has a straightforward payment structure. Service providers are typically compensated for each task they complete or transaction they handle.
- Operational efficiency: This model is well-suited for routine and repetitive tasks that require efficiency and scalability. This approach enables organizations to concentrate on their core competencies while delegating routine functions to external entities.

The transaction-based model finds application across various industries and business functions. Here are a few real-world examples:

- Customer support services: Many companies outsource customer support operations to third-party call centers. These centers are compensated based on the number of customer inquiries or issues they handle, making it a classic example of the transaction-based model.
- Data entry and processing: Organizations often outsource data entry and processing tasks to specialized service providers who are paid per data record entered or processed.
- Payroll processing: Businesses frequently outsource payroll processing to firms that charge on a per-employee or per-payroll run basis.

3.2.1.1   *Benefits of the Transaction-Based Model*
The transaction-based model offers several advantages for organizations (Mahnke et al., 2005; Vitasek & Manrodt, 2012):

- Cost control: The straightforward payment structure allows for predictable budgeting and cost control, particularly for high-volume, repetitive tasks.
- Scalability: Organizations can easily adjust the scale of outsourcing in response to changing workloads or seasonal demands.

- Simplified management: The task-oriented nature of this model simplifies oversight and management since organizations can focus on monitoring the completion of specific tasks.

3.2.1.2 Challenges of the Transaction-Based Model

While the transaction-based model offers notable advantages, it also presents certain challenges (Datta & Roy, 2013; Vitasek & Manrodt, 2012):

- Limited focus: This model tends to prioritize task completion over broader business outcomes. Service providers may focus on meeting quantity targets rather than achieving quality or strategic objectives.
- Potential misalignment: Incentives for service providers may not always align with the organization's overarching goals. This can lead to conflicts of interest if not managed carefully.
- Transaction overload: Overemphasis on transactions can hinder strategic thinking and innovation, as service providers may prioritize efficiency over process improvements.

In summary, the transaction-based model in outsourcing represents a fundamental and effective approach for organizations seeking to streamline specific tasks or processes. It offers operational efficiency, cost control, and scalability advantages, making it a valuable tool in the outsourcing toolkit. However, organizations must carefully consider its limitations, such as potential misalignment and the risk of focusing solely on transactional efficiency, to make informed decisions about its application within their broader outsourcing strategies.

3.2.2 The Outcome-Based Model in Outsourcing: Aligning Success with Results

The outcome-based model in outsourcing stands as a progressive departure from the traditional transaction-based approach (Choi & Cummings, 2016). In this model, the emphasis shifts from merely completing tasks to achieving specific, predefined outcomes or objectives (McLaren, 2022). Service providers are incentivized to deliver measurable results, aligning their interests closely with the broader goals of the client organization (Ng et al., 2009). This comprehensive exploration delves into the outcome-based model in outsourcing, elucidating its key characteristics, real-world applications, benefits, and challenges. Key characteristics of the outcome-based model are (Sjödin et al., 2020; Vitasek & Manrodt, 2012):

- Results-oriented focus: At the core of the outcome-based model is the concept of measuring success by the attainment of predefined outcomes or goals. These outcomes are typically outlined in the service level agreements and are quantifiable and verifiable.
- Incentivized performance: Service providers are motivated by performance-based incentives, which are linked to the achievement of outcomes. This alignment of interests encourages service providers to dedicate their expertise and resources to deliver the desired results.
- Risk-sharing: The outcome-based model often involves sharing risks between the client and the service provider. Both parties share the responsibility for achieving outcomes, fostering a collaborative approach.

The outcome-based model finds application across diverse industries and business functions. Some real-world examples include:

- Healthcare services: Hospitals may contract with external organizations to reduce patient readmission rates. The service provider's compensation is tied to the successful reduction of readmissions.
- IT services: Organizations often outsource IT support services with service level agreements that define specific response times for resolving issues. Service providers earn incentives for meeting or exceeding these response time targets.
- Marketing campaigns: Companies may engage marketing agencies to drive a certain percentage increase in website traffic or conversions. The agency's compensation is linked to the achievement of these measurable goals.

3.2.2.1   Benefits of the Outcome-Based Model

The outcome-based model offers several advantages for organizations (Sjödin et al., 2020; Vitasek & Manrodt, 2012):

- Strategic alignment: By aligning incentives with predefined outcomes, this model ensures that the service provider's efforts are directed toward achieving the organization's strategic goals.
- Quality-focused: It places a strong emphasis on delivering high-quality results, as service providers are motivated to meet or exceed performance targets.
- Risk mitigation: Sharing risks between the client and the service provider mitigates the client's exposure to potential performance shortfalls, fostering a sense of partnership.

3.2.2.2 Challenges of the Outcome-Based Model

While the outcome-based model provides compelling advantages, it also presents certain challenges (Sjödin et al., 2020; Vitasek & Manrodt, 2012):

- Outcome definition and measurement: Clearly defining and measuring outcomes can be complex and may require robust performance-tracking mechanisms.
- Performance variability: The achievement of outcomes may vary over time, impacting cost predictability and requiring adaptive management approaches.
- Potential for disputes: Disagreements may arise between the client and the service provider regarding the successful achievement of outcomes, necessitating effective dispute resolution mechanisms.

In summary, the outcome-based model in outsourcing is a forward-looking approach that elevates the focus from tasks to results. It promotes strategic alignment, quality-driven performance, and risk-sharing between client organizations and service providers. While the model provides clear advantages, its successful implementation requires meticulous outcome definition, robust measurement, and effective governance to ensure that both parties are aligned toward achieving predetermined success metrics. When executed effectively, the outcome-based model can lead to substantial value creation and contribute to achieving strategic business objectives.

3.2.3   The Investment-Based Model in Outsourcing: A Shared Commitment to Success

The investment-based model in outsourcing represents a significant departure from conventional transaction-based approaches (Vitasek & Manrodt, 2012). In this model, both the client organization and the service provider engage in strategic investments as part of the outsourcing arrangement (Vitasek & Ledyard, 2013). These investments can encompass financial resources, intellectual capital, technology, or other critical assets (Vitasek et al., 2013b). Furthermore, the model often involves sharing risks and rewards, cementing a sense of partnership and mutual commitment. Key characteristics of the investment-based model are (Vitasek & Manrodt, 2012):

- Shared commitment: At the core of the investment-based model is a shared commitment to the success of the outsourcing initiative. Both the client and the service provider contribute resources and expertise to jointly achieve predefined goals.
- Strategic investments: Investments made within this model go beyond financial commitments and can include intellectual property, technology assets, infrastructure development, or other strategic resources required to achieve the desired outcomes.
- Risk and reward sharing: Unlike transaction-based models, the investment-based model often entails sharing risks and rewards. Both parties participate in the potential gains or losses associated with the outsourcing endeavor.

The investment-based model finds application across various industries and business functions. Several real-world examples illustrate its versatility (Vitasek & Manrodt, 2012):

- New product development: An automobile manufacturer collaborates with a technology firm to create an innovative electric vehicle. Both organizations invest in research and development, production facilities, and marketing. Profits from the successful product launch are shared between them.
- Supply chain partnerships: Retailers may enter into strategic partnerships with suppliers to optimize supply chain operations. Investments

in inventory management systems, logistics, and demand forecasting are jointly made, with the shared aim of reducing costs and enhancing supply chain efficiency.

- Research consortia: In industries like pharmaceuticals, multiple companies may join forces to fund research consortia focused on developing breakthrough medications. They pool their financial resources and expertise to share the risks and benefits of new drug discoveries.

3.2.3.1 *Benefits of the Investment-Based Model*
The investment-based model offers several compelling benefits for organizations (Keith et al., 2016):

- Strategic alignment: It fosters a high degree of alignment between the client organization and the service provider since both parties are invested in the success of the initiative.
- Innovation catalyst: Joint investments often lead to innovation and the development of cutting-edge solutions, as both organizations bring their expertise and resources to the table.
- Enhanced collaboration: The shared commitment and risk-sharing nature of this model promote open communication and a collaborative approach to problem-solving.

3.2.3.2 *Challenges of the Investment-Based Model*
While the investment-based model presents significant advantages, it also poses certain challenges (Keith et al., 2016):

- Complex negotiations: Arriving at equitable terms for investments and profit-sharing can be intricate and time-consuming, requiring careful negotiation and contractual clarity.
- Shared risks: The model entails sharing risks, which means that both parties may experience losses if the outsourcing initiative does not meet expectations.
- Resource commitment: Significant investments of time, effort, and resources are required, and organizations must be prepared for the associated commitments.

In summary, the investment-based model in outsourcing embodies a collaborative approach that goes beyond financial transactions. It emphasizes a shared commitment to success, strategic investments, and aligning interests between client organizations and service providers. While it presents challenges in negotiation and resource commitment, it offers the potential for substantial value creation and innovation. When implemented effectively, the investment-based model can result in mutually beneficial partnerships that drive success and propel organizations toward their strategic objectives.

3.3   The Hybrid Model of Outsourcing 2.0: A New Era of Collaborative Partnership

There are multiple interpretations of outsourcing 2.0. According to Casale (2007), outsourcing 2.0 signifies an evolved approach to managing relationships, emphasizing heightened collaboration, shared stability, and efficient communication. This approach leads to enhanced access to supply chain information. Other terms linked to this concept include strategic impact, mature relationships, multi-sourcing, multi-language capabilities, risk-sharing, transitioning from a focus on cost and efficiency to highlighting value and innovation, BPO, and ultimately moving toward knowledge process outsourcing.

Vitasek et al., (2013a) refer to this as "vested outsourcing", highlighting relationships as the focal point in the generation of business value, with mutual investments in success from both suppliers and companies. Linden, Schmidt, and Rosenkranz (2017) link outsourcing 2.0 to IT outsourcing by introducing a relationship process model comprising five stages (see Fig. 3.1):

- The process begins with the initiation and evaluation of the outsourcing strategy to meet the business needs.
- In the second stage, the focus shifts to establishing the necessary outsourcing services and selecting suitable suppliers, leading to the formulation of outsourcing contracts.
- The third stage involves the transition of the chosen services to the supplier or vendor and the establishment of supply capabilities.

Fig. 3.1 IT outsourcing relationship model of processing (*Source* Author's own work—Adapted from Linden et al. [2017])

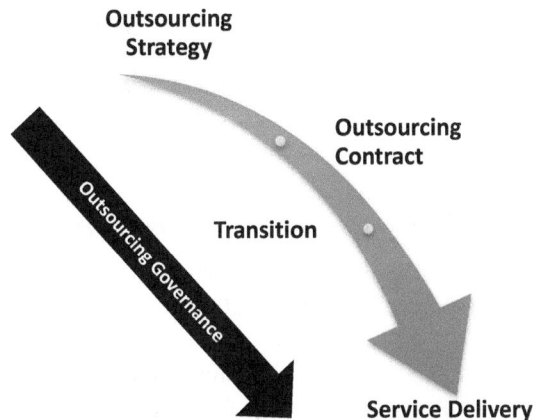

- The fourth stage is centered on maintaining the value of the outsourced function between the company and the supplier or vendor.
- Finally, the fifth stage represents the comprehensive step of the entire procedure, referred to as outsourcing governance. This phase facilitates collaborative leadership to make effective decisions in response to any required business changes.

Additionally, Kaushik (2009) suggested the integration of Web 2.0 into offshoring outsourcing 2.0 through several key elements:

a. leveraging offshore capabilities as a platform
b. coordinating global delivery networks
c. enhancing user experience, measuring success through human relationships and interactions, and promoting co-creation as a main engagement mode.

In the ever-evolving landscape of outsourcing, a hybrid model has emerged as a transformative approach that blends the best elements of traditional outsourcing practices with the principles of outsourcing 2.0 (Vitasek & Manrodt, 2012). Outsourcing 2.0 represents a paradigm shift, emphasizing long-term partnerships, innovation, flexibility, and a shared vision for success (Curley & Salmelin, 2017). This hybrid model harnesses the power of strategic collaboration while incorporating the efficiencies of established outsourcing practices (Vitasek, 2016). In the following subsections, there will be an exploration of the hybrid model of outsourcing 2.0, elucidating its key characteristics, real-world applications, benefits, and challenges.

3.3.1   Key Characteristics of the Hybrid Model of Outsourcing 2.0

The hybrid model of outsourcing 2.0 is defined by several key characteristics (Vitasek & Ledyard, 2013):

- Collaborative partnership: The hybrid model places a strong emphasis on fostering a true partnership between the client organization and the service provider. It goes beyond the traditional client–service provider relationship and encourages open communication, trust, and mutual respect.
- Shared objectives and goals: Unlike transaction-based outsourcing, where tasks are clearly defined, the hybrid model focuses on shared objectives and goals. These objectives are often dynamic, allowing for adaptation in response to changing business environments.
- Innovation and flexibility: Innovation is a cornerstone of the hybrid model. It encourages both parties to contribute their expertise and ideas, fostering a culture of continuous improvement. Flexibility is also paramount, allowing for agility in addressing evolving challenges and opportunities.

3.3.2   Real-World Applications of the Hybrid Model of Outsourcing 2.0

The hybrid model of outsourcing 2.0 finds applications across various industries and business functions, where the emphasis is on building strategic alliances and creating shared value. Real-world examples illustrate its versatility:

- IT services: A global technology company collaborates with a software development firm under a vested outsourcing agreement. They share the risks and rewards of developing a cutting-edge software product. This hybrid approach allows for innovation and risk mitigation.

- Manufacturing and supply chain: An automotive manufacturer forms a long-term partnership with a key supplier to optimize the production process. The supplier invests in advanced production technology, and both parties share the benefits of increased efficiency and cost savings.
- Research and development consortia: In industries like pharmaceuticals, multiple companies pool their resources and expertise to form research consortia. They collectively invest in cutting-edge research to develop breakthrough medications and share the resulting intellectual property and profits.

3.3.3 Benefits and Challenges of the Hybrid Model of Outsourcing 2.0

The hybrid model of outsourcing 2.0 offers several compelling benefits for organizations (Vitasek & Ledyard, 2013):

- Strategic partnerships: It promotes the development of strategic partnerships that foster trust, collaboration, and mutual benefit. These partnerships are characterized by a shared commitment to success. An example of this benefit can be seen in the collaboration between a leading technology company and a software development firm. Both organizations enter into a long-term strategic partnership under a vested outsourcing agreement. They share the risks and rewards of developing a groundbreaking software product. This partnership is characterized by trust, mutual commitment, and a shared vision of success, where both parties are equally invested in the outcome.
- Adaptability and innovation: The hybrid model encourages adaptability to changing market conditions and the development of innovative solutions. Both parties are incentivized to continually enhance processes and drive innovation. Consider a global pharmaceutical company that engages in a hybrid outsourcing model with a contract research organization for drug development. In response to evolving regulatory requirements, the partnership allows for rapid

adjustments to research protocols and the adoption of innovative technologies, enabling the organization to stay at the forefront of drug discovery.

- Risk mitigation: By sharing risks and rewards, organizations can better manage uncertainties and mitigate potential losses. This shared risk approach promotes a sense of partnership and collaboration. An illustrative example of risk mitigation in the hybrid model can be found in supply chain partnerships. An automotive manufacturer forms a long-term partnership with a key supplier. Both entities invest in advanced production technology and logistics systems. In the event of unexpected supply chain disruptions, such as natural disasters or geopolitical issues, the shared risk approach facilitates collaborative problem-solving and mitigates the impact on production.

- Long-term focus: The hybrid model is inherently long-term in nature, allowing organizations to develop enduring relationships that transcend transactional objectives. A financial institution partnering with a specialized outsourcing provider for customer service operations exemplifies the long-term focus of the hybrid model. Beyond the transactional scope of handling customer inquiries, the partnership extends to improving customer experience, developing future service enhancements, and cultivating a loyal customer base over the years.

While the hybrid model of outsourcing 2.0 offers significant advantages, it also poses certain challenges (Vitasek & Ledyard, 2013):

- Cultural shift: Embracing a partnership-oriented, innovation-focused culture can be a substantial change for organizations accustomed to transactional outsourcing. Successfully navigating this shift requires leadership and change management. For instance, a traditional manufacturing company adopting a hybrid model for its supply chain may face challenges in aligning the organization's culture with that of its innovative and technology-driven partner.

- Complex agreements: Developing and managing intricate partnerships can be challenging. Clear contractual frameworks and governance structures are essential to avoid misunderstandings. An example could be a multinational corporation collaborating with multiple technology startups. Coordinating the various contractual elements, governance committees, and dispute resolution mechanisms can be a demanding task.

- Investment risks: The hybrid model often involves substantial financial and resource commitments. Organizations must be prepared for the associated investments and risks. Suppose a pharmaceutical company enters into an investment-based hybrid model with a biotechnology startup to develop a new drug. Both parties invest substantial financial resources and intellectual property in the project. If the drug does not receive regulatory approval, both organizations may face significant losses, highlighting the inherent investment risks of the hybrid model.
- Performance evaluation: Measuring the success of a hybrid outsourcing partnership can be more nuanced than traditional transaction-based metrics. Organizations may need to develop customized performance evaluation criteria. For instance, a retail giant engaging in an ecosystem collaboration with multiple startups and research institutions for product innovation must allocate resources for research, development, and ongoing collaboration efforts.

The hybrid model of outsourcing 2.0 represents a dynamic and strategic approach to outsourcing that combines the best elements of traditional practices with the principles of collaboration, innovation, and flexibility. It encourages organizations to move beyond transactional relationships and cultivate true partnerships. While it presents challenges, the potential for mutual benefit, innovation, and long-term success makes it a compelling choice for organizations seeking to thrive in an ever-evolving and interconnected global marketplace. The hybrid model of outsourcing 2.0 epitomizes the future of strategic outsourcing, where collaboration and shared vision redefine the boundaries of what is possible through external partnerships (see Table 3.1).

3.4   Emergent Concerns and Future Directions

As organizations continue to embrace outsourcing 2.0, a dynamic landscape is evolving, marked by emerging concerns and exciting future directions (Akbari, 2022). This strategic evolution of outsourcing emphasizes long-term partnerships, innovation, flexibility, and a shared vision for

Table 3.1   Outsourcing 2.0 characteristics, applications, benefits, and challenges

Aspect	Description
Characteristics	Collaborative partnership, shared objectives and goals, innovation and flexibility
Applications	IT services: vested outsourcing, manufacturing and supply chain optimization, R&D consortia
Benefits	Strategic partnerships, adaptability and innovation, risk mitigation, long-term focus
Challenges	Cultural shift, complex agreements, investment risks, performance evaluation

success. In this section, the exploration extends to the emergent concerns faced by organizations in the realm of outsourcing 2.0, as well as the promising future directions that shape the trajectory of this transformative approach.

3.4.1   Emergent Concerns in Outsourcing 2.0

- Cybersecurity and data privacy: With an increasing reliance on technology and data sharing in outsourcing 2.0, concerns about cybersecurity and data privacy have risen to the forefront (Böhm et al., 2011). Organizations are grappling with safeguarding sensitive information while fostering collaboration with external partners. Addressing these concerns requires robust security measures, data encryption, and strict adherence to regulatory compliance.
- Complex governance and contract management: The shift toward long-term strategic partnerships has given rise to more complex governance structures and contractual agreements (Böhm et al., 2011). Organizations are challenged with effectively managing these intricate partnerships, ensuring that both parties remain aligned with shared objectives, and resolving disputes swiftly. Advanced contract management technologies and strong governance frameworks are essential to mitigate these concerns.
- Cultural alignment: Building a collaborative and innovative culture across organizations, regardless of geographical location, remains a concern in outsourcing 2.0. Effective communication, cultural sensitivity training, and fostering a shared sense of purpose are critical to overcoming this challenge.

- Talent management: In an increasingly competitive global marketplace, securing and retaining top talent within outsourcing partnerships is crucial (Akbari, 2022). Organizations must devise strategies to attract and retain skilled professionals while addressing issues such as remote work, talent shortages, and cultural diversity.
- Ethical sourcing: The ethical dimension of outsourcing, including labor practices, environmental impact, and supply chain ethics, is gaining prominence (Akbari, 2022). Organizations must consider the ethical implications of their outsourcing decisions and work with partners who share their commitment to responsible business practices.

3.4.2   Future Directions in Outsourcing 2.0

- Advanced analytics and AI: The integration of advanced analytics and AI is poised to transform outsourcing 2.0. Predictive analytics can help organizations anticipate issues and optimize operations, while AI-powered automation can streamline routine tasks, freeing up human talent for higher-value activities.
- Blockchain for transparency: Blockchain technology offers transparency and traceability, making it a promising tool for addressing concerns related to data privacy and supply chain ethics. It can enhance trust in outsourcing relationships by ensuring the integrity of shared data.
- Green outsourcing: Environmental sustainability is becoming a strategic consideration. Future directions in outsourcing 2.0 may involve partnerships with service providers who adopt eco-friendly practices, reducing the carbon footprint of outsourcing operations.
- Resilience and risk management: Outsourcing 2.0 is likely to emphasize resilience and risk management as organizations face unforeseen disruptions. Business continuity planning, risk mitigation strategies, and the ability to quickly adapt to changing circumstances will be crucial.
- Skills development and training: As technology evolves, there will be an increasing emphasis on continuous skills development and training for both client organizations and service providers. A skilled workforce is essential to harness the full potential of innovative technologies.

- Regulatory compliance and data localization: With evolving data privacy regulations, organizations may see a shift toward data localization, which could impact how data is managed and shared in outsourcing relationships. Future directions may include strategies to navigate these regulatory complexities.
- Ecosystem collaboration: Outsourcing 2.0 is moving beyond traditional client–service provider relationships to encompass a broader ecosystem of partners. Organizations may collaborate with multiple stakeholders, including startups, research institutions, and industry consortia, to drive innovation and competitiveness.

These examples illustrate the benefits and challenges associated with the hybrid model of outsourcing 2.0, emphasizing the dynamic nature of these partnerships and the need for organizations to carefully navigate the complexities while harnessing the potential for long-term success and innovation.

Furthermore, outsourcing 2.0 is not merely a reflection of the present state of outsourcing; it's a strategic leap into the future of collaboration between organizations and their external partners. While it presents emergent concerns, including those related to cybersecurity, governance, and cultural alignment, it's crucial to recognize that these challenges are integral to the process of reshaping and advancing the outsourcing landscape. Additionally, as organizations adapt to this evolving landscape, they should consider not only the challenges but also the promising future directions in outsourcing 2.0. These directions not only offer exciting opportunities for innovation, sustainability, and growth but also underscore the need for organizations to be agile, technologically adept, and ethically and environmentally conscious in their outsourcing strategies. Ultimately, as outsourcing 2.0 matures, it carries with it the potential to instigate transformative change and redefine the traditional boundaries of what can be achieved through strategic external partnerships.

3.5   Managerial Implications in the Era of Outsourcing 2.0

The adoption of outsourcing 2.0 represents a profound shift in the way organizations engage with external partners. As this transformative approach emphasizes long-term strategic partnerships, innovation, and shared success, it also brings about significant managerial implications. To navigate the complexities and maximize the benefits of outsourcing 2.0, managers must adapt their approaches and strategies. Here are several key managerial implications in the era of outsourcing 2.0:

- Embrace a partnership mindset: Managers must foster a culture of collaboration and partnership within their organizations. The traditional client–service provider relationship is evolving into a more collaborative and mutually beneficial alliance (Meneguel et al., 2022). This shift requires a mindset that prioritizes shared objectives, open communication, and a commitment to the success of both parties.
- Invest in relationship building: Building and nurturing long-term relationships with external partners (Michalakopoulou et al., 2022; Wagner & Zanger, 2023) is paramount in outsourcing 2.0. Managers should allocate time and resources to cultivating robust relationships built on trust, shared values, and a commitment to mutual growth. Effective relationship management is a strategic imperative.
- Focus on shared objectives and outcomes: Managers should work closely with their outsourcing partners to define and measure shared objectives and outcomes (Navarro-Paule et al., 2023). This involves setting clear expectations, developing KPIs, and establishing performance metrics that align with the organization's broader goals.
- Navigate complex governance structures: The shift toward strategic partnerships often results in more complex governance structures and contractual agreements (Khan et al., 2022). Managers must have a clear understanding of these structures and be prepared to navigate them effectively. This includes establishing governance committees, dispute resolution mechanisms, and performance review processes.
- Cultural sensitivity and alignment: Cultural differences can pose challenges in collaborative outsourcing relationships. Managers should promote cultural sensitivity and awareness within their teams and facilitate cross-cultural training for employees working with global partners (Thapliyal & Joshi, 2022). Cultural alignment and effective cross-cultural communication are vital for success.
- Innovation and continuous improvement: Outsourcing 2.0 places a strong emphasis on innovation and continuous improvement. Managers should encourage their teams to contribute innovative

ideas, explore new technologies, and seek opportunities for process optimization (Akbari et al., 2023). This culture of innovation can lead to competitive advantages and enhanced value creation.

- Mitigate risks and ensure compliance: Managers must proactively identify and mitigate risks associated with outsourcing partnerships. This includes assessing cybersecurity risks, data privacy concerns, legal compliance, and regulatory requirements (Duong et al., 2023). Developing risk management strategies and ensuring compliance are essential responsibilities.
- Invest in skills development: As outsourcing relationships become more strategic and technology-driven, managers should invest in the skills development of their teams (Akbari et al., 2022). This includes providing training in areas such as data analytics, digital technologies, project management, and cross-functional collaboration.
- Ethical sourcing and sustainability: Managers should prioritize ethical sourcing practices and sustainability in their outsourcing decisions. This involves conducting due diligence to ensure that partners adhere to responsible business practices, environmental standards, and labor regulations (Akbari, 2022).
- Adaptability and resilience: The business landscape is dynamic, and managers must cultivate adaptability and resilience within their organizations (Akbari & Hopkins, 2022). Being prepared to respond to unforeseen disruptions, market shifts, and changing customer preferences is crucial in maintaining outsourcing relationships.
- Performance evaluation and metrics: Managers should develop robust performance evaluation processes and metrics tailored to the specific objectives of outsourcing partnerships (Baid & Jayaraman, 2022). Regular performance reviews and feedback sessions help identify areas for improvement and reinforce alignment with strategic goals.
- Ecosystem collaboration: In the era of outsourcing 2.0, managers should explore opportunities for collaboration within broader ecosystems (Choi et al., 2023). This may involve partnerships with startups, research institutions, industry consortia, and other stakeholders to drive innovation and competitiveness.

The transition to outsourcing 2.0 presents both challenges and opportunities for managers. Embracing a partnership mindset, focusing on shared objectives, navigating complex governance structures, and prioritizing innovation and sustainability are essential elements of successful managerial strategies in this evolving landscape (Vitasek & Ledyard, 2013). By adapting to the changing dynamics of outsourcing, managers can position their organizations for long-term success, innovation, and growth in the era of outsourcing 2.0.

3.6 Summary and Conclusion

This chapter has taken us on a journey through the evolution and profound impact of outsourcing 2.0, a paradigm shift that has reshaped the outsourcing landscape. What was once viewed primarily as a cost-saving tactic has matured into a strategic tool for organizations aiming to secure a competitive edge in the dynamic global market. Three distinct business models were reviewed within the outsourcing 2.0 framework—the transaction-based, outcome-based, and investment-based models—each with its own set of characteristics, real-world applications, advantages, and challenges.

The transaction-based model, deeply rooted in traditional outsourcing practices, centers on outsourcing specific tasks or processes to external service providers. Compensation in this model is structured around transaction volume or frequency. It offers benefits such as cost control and scalability but can potentially limit strategic alignment and innovation.

In contrast, the outcome-based business model shifts the focus from mere task completion to achieving specific, measurable outcomes or objectives. Service providers are incentivized to deliver tangible results, aligning their interests with the client organization's overarching goals. This model highlights strategic alignment, quality-focused performance, and risk-sharing, albeit with complexities in outcome definition and measurement.

The investment-based model elevates outsourcing partnerships by encouraging both clients and service providers to make strategic investments in the outsourcing arrangement. These investments span financial, intellectual, or resource-based commitments and often involve shared risks and rewards. The investment-based model fosters strategic alignment, innovation, and enhanced collaboration, though it requires adept navigation of complex negotiations and shared risks.

At the heart of these models lies the essence of outsourcing 2.0, advocating long-term partnerships, innovation, adaptability, and shared success. Real-world illustrations demonstrated how organizations leverage outsourcing 2.0 to drive strategic growth, foster innovation, and establish sustainable competitive advantages. Collaborative partnerships and a shared commitment to success form the bedrock of outsourcing 2.0, steering organizations toward a future where strategic alliances redefine the boundaries of outsourcing possibilities.

However, as one contemplate the emerging concerns and future trajectories in outsourcing 2.0, it is apparent that this transformative journey is not devoid of challenges. Issues such as cybersecurity, data privacy, intricate governance structures, and cultural alignment necessitate proactive strategies and innovative solutions. Organizations must skillfully navigate these intricacies while embracing promising future directions like advanced analytics, blockchain for transparency, environmentally responsible outsourcing, and an unwavering focus on resilience and risk management.

In closing, the evolution of outsourcing into the era of outsourcing 2.0 signifies a strategic renaissance that transcends mere cost-cutting measures. It empowers organizations to cultivate collaborative, innovative, and mutually beneficial partnerships with external service providers. The managerial considerations delineated in this chapter underscore the significance of adaptability, ethical sourcing, skills development, and a shared vision of objectives.

Outsourcing 2.0 charts an auspicious course for organizations seeking to thrive in an interconnected global arena. By embracing this paradigm shift, organizations can fortify their positions for enduring success, innovation, and resilience in a continually shifting business landscape. As outsourcing 2.0 continues to mature, it will undoubtedly mold the future of strategic external collaborations and redefine how organizations confront the challenges and opportunities of a swiftly evolving world.

References

Akbari, M. (2013). *Factors affecting outsourcing decisions in Iranian industries* (Doctoral thesis). Victoria University, Melbourne, Australia. https://vuir.vu.edu.au/22299/1/Mohammadreza%20Akbari.pdf

Akbari, M. (2018). Logistics outsourcing: A structured literature review. *Benchmarking: An International Journal, 25*(5), 1548–1580. https://doi.org/10.1108/BIJ-04-2017-0066

Akbari, M. (2022). Chapter 47—Outsourcing and insourcing in global supply chain. In J. Sarkis (ed.), *Handbook of supply chain management—A major reference work*, Palgrave. https://doi.org/10.1007/978-3-030-89822-9_47-1

Akbari, M., & Hopkins, J. (2016). The changing business landscape in Iran: Establishing outsourcing best practices. *Operations and Supply Chain Management: An International Journal, 9*(3), 184–197. https://doi.org/10.31387/oscm0250172

Akbari, M., & Hopkins, J. L. (2022). Digital technologies as enablers of supply chain sustainability in an emerging economy. *Operations Management Research, 15,* 689–710. https://doi.org/10.1007/s12063-021-00226-8

Akbari, M., Clarke, S.J., & Maleki Far, S. (2017). Outsourcing best practice— The case of large construction firms in Iran. *Proceedings of the Informing Science and Information Technology Education Conference.* 39–50. From: InSITE 2017: Informing Science and Information Technology Education Conference, 31 July–5 August 2017, Ho Chi Minh City, Vietnam. https://doi.org/10.28945/3737

Akbari, M., Kok, S.K., Hopkins, J., Frederico, G.F., Nguyen, H., & Alonso, A.D. (2023). The changing landscape of digital transformation in supply chains: Impacts of industry 4.0 in Vietnam. *The International Journal of Logistics Management,* (In-press). https://doi.org/10.1108/IJLM-11-2022-0442

Akbari, M., Nguyen, H.M., McClelland, R., & Van Houdt, K. (2022). Design, implementation and academic perspectives on authentic assessment for applied business higher education in a top performing Asian economy. *Education + Training, 64*(1), 69–88. https://doi.org/10.1108/ET-04-2021-0121

Aqlan, F., & Lam, S. S. (2016). Supply chain optimization under risk and uncertainty: A case study for high-end server manufacturing. *Computers & Industrial Engineering, 93,* 78–87. https://doi.org/10.1016/j.cie.2015.12.025

Ayerbe, C., Lazaric, N., Callois, M., & Mitkova, L. (2014). The new challenges of organizing intellectual property in complex industries: A discussion based on the case of Thales. *Technovation, 34*(4), 232–241. https://doi.org/10.1016/j.technovation.2014.01.001

Baid, V., & Jayaraman, V. (2022). Amplifying and promoting the "S" in ESG investing: The case for social responsibility in supply chain financing. *Managerial Finance, 48*(8), 1279–1297. https://doi.org/10.1108/MF-12-2021-0588

Böhm, M., Leimeister, S., Riedl, C., & Krcmar, H. (2011). Cloud computing– outsourcing 2.0 or a new business model for IT provisioning? *Application management: Challenges–service creation–strategies,* 31–56. https://doi.org/10.1007/978-3-8349-6492-2_2

Brown, D., & Wilson, S. (2005). *The black book of outsourcing.* John Wiley & Sons.

Casale, F. (2007). *Outsourcing 2.0: The new outsourcing and what it means to you.* The Outsourcing Institute.

Choi, J., & Cummings, M.L. (2016). Outcome-based contract model for IT outsourcing: A system dynamics approach. *Issues in Information Systems, 17*(2). https://doi.org/10.48009/2_iis_2016_93-104

Choi, J. J., Ju, M., Kotabe, M., Trigeorgis, L., & Zhang, X. T. (2018). Flexibility as firm value driver: Evidence from offshore outsourcing. *Global Strategy Journal., 8*, 351–376. https://doi.org/10.1002/gsj.1181

Choi, T. Y., Hofmann, E., Templar, S., Rogers, D. S., Leuschner, R., & Korde, R. Y. (2023). The supply chain financing ecosystem: Early responses during the COVID-19 crisis. *Journal of Purchasing and Supply Management, 100836*. https://doi.org/10.1016/j.pursup.2023.100836

Curley, M., & Salmelin, B. (2017). *Open innovation 2.0: The new mode of digital innovation for prosperity and sustainability*. Springer.

Datta, P. P., & Roy, R. (2013). Incentive issues in performance-based outsourcing contracts in the UK defence industry: A simulation study. *Production Planning & Control, 24*(4–5), 359–374. https://doi.org/10.1080/095 37287.2011.648488

Duong, A. T. B., Hoang, T.-H., Nguyen, T. T. B., Akbari, M., Hoang, T. G., & Truong, H. Q. (2023). Supply chain risk assessment in disruptive times: Opportunities and challenges. *Journal of Enterprise Information Management, 36*(5), 1372–1401. https://doi.org/10.1108/JEIM-02-2023-0104

Ernst, D., & Kim, L. (2002). Global production networks, knowledge diffusion, and local capability formation. *Research Policy, 31*(8–9), 1417–1429. https://doi.org/10.1016/S0048-7333(02)00072-0

Evans, S., Vladimirova, D., Holgado, M., Van Fossen, K., Yang, M., Silva, E. A., & Barlow, C. Y. (2017). Business model innovation for sustainability: Towards a unified perspective for creation of sustainable business models. *Business Strategy and the Environment, 26*(5), 597–608. https://doi.org/10.1002/bse.1939

Kaushik, A. (2009). Outsourcing 2.0: Does that really mean anything? *Computer World*. Retrieved September 11, 2023, from https://www.computerworld.com/article/2530365/outsourcing-2-0%2D%2Ddoes-that-really-mean-anything-.html

Keith, B., Vitasek, K., Manrodt, K., Kling, J., Keith, B., Vitasek, K., Manrodt, K., & Kling, J. (2016). Investment-based sourcing models. *Strategic sourcing in the new economy: Harnessing the potential of sourcing business models for modern procurement, 159–188*. https://doi.org/10.1007/978-1-137-552 20-4_8

Khan, G. M., Khan, S. U., Khan, H. U., & Ilyas, M. (2022). Challenges and practices identification in complex outsourcing relationships: A systematic literature review. *PLoS ONE, 17*(1), e0262710. https://doi.org/10.1371/journal.pone.0262710

Kotabe, M., & Murray, J. Y. (2004). Global procurement of service activities by service firms. *International Marketing Review, 21*(6), 615–633. https://doi. org/10.1108/02651330410568042

Linden, R., Schmidt, N., & Rosenkranz, C. (2017). Outsourcing 2.0: Towards an innovation-driven process model for client-vendor relationships in information technology outsourcing. In I. Oshri, J. Kotlarsky, & L. P. Willcocks (Eds.), *Global sourcing of digital services: Micro and macro perspectives*, LNBIP 306 (pp. 39–64). https://doi.org/10.1007/978-3-319-70305-3_3

Mahnke, V., Overby, M. L., & Vang, J. (2005). Strategic outsourcing of IT services: Theoretical stocktaking and empirical challenges. *Industry & Innovation, 12*(2), 205–253. https://doi.org/10.1080/13662710500087958

McLaren, S. (2022). *Outsourcing government: The use of outcome-based payments in UK social policy* (Doctoral dissertation, Birkbeck, University of London). https://eprints.bbk.ac.uk/id/eprint/47929

Meneguel, C. R. D. A., Hernández-Rojas, R. D., & Mateos, M. R. (2022). The synergy between food and agri-food suppliers, and the restaurant sector in the World Heritage City of Córdoba (Spain). *Journal of Ethnic Foods, 9*(1), 11. https://doi.org/10.1186/s42779-022-00126-7

Michalakopoulou, K., Nikitas, A., Njoya, E. T., & Johnes, J. (2022). Innovation in the legal service industry: Examining the roles of human and social capital, and knowledge and technology transfer. *The International Journal of Entrepreneurship and Innovation, 14657503221119668*. https://doi.org/10. 1177/14657503221119667

Navarro-Paule, A. J., Romerosa-Martínez, M. M., & Lloréns-Montes, F. J. (2023). IT vendor integration as catalyst of IT outsourcing success. *Journal of Business & Industrial Marketing*. https://doi.org/10.1108/JBIM-10-2021-0491

Ng, I., Williams, J., & Neely, A. (2009). Outcome-based contracting. *Changing the boundaries of B2B customer relationships: an executive summary. London: Advanced Institute of Management Research.* https://citeseerx.ist.psu.edu/document?repid=rep1&type=pdf&doi=0c919186d34cdb23e060f2a0caf9fe9ad4a4c61f

Rosenberg, M. J. (2005). *Beyond e-learning: Approaches and technologies to enhance organizational knowledge, learning, and performance.* John Wiley & Sons.

Sjödin, D., Parida, V., Jovanovic, M., & Visnjic, I. (2020). Value creation and value capture alignment in business model innovation: A process view on outcome-based business models. *Journal of Product Innovation Management, 37*(2), 158–183. https://doi.org/10.1111/jpim.12516

Thapliyal, K., & Joshi, M. (2022). Cross-cultural management: Opportunities and challenges. *Integrating new technologies in international business: Opportunities challenges*, 31–53.

Vitasek, K. (2016). Strategic sourcing business models. *Strategic Outsourcing: An International Journal, 9*(2), 126–138. https://doi.org/10.1108/SO-02-2016-0003

Vitasek, K., & Manrodt, K. (2012). Vested outsourcing: A flexible framework for collaborative outsourcing. *Strategic Outsourcing: An International Journal, 5*(1), 4–14. https://doi.org/10.1108/17538291211221924

Vitasek, K., & Ledyard, M. (2013). *Vested outsourcing: Five rules that will transform outsourcing.* Springer.

Vitasek, K., Ledyard, M., & Manrodt, K. (2013a). *Vested outsourcing: Five rules that will transform outsourcing* (2nd ed.). Palgrave Macmillan.

Vitasek, K., Ledyard, M., Manrodt, K., Vitasek, K., Ledyard, M., & Manrodt, K. (2013b). Chapter 4 Changing the game: The rise of vested outsourcing. *Vested outsourcing: Five rules that will transform outsourcing,* 41–66. https://doi.org/10.1057/9781137321183_5

Wagner, S. M., & Zanger, I. (2023). Supply chain capabilities and new venture growth. *International Journal of Logistics Research and Applications, 1–26.* https://doi.org/10.1080/13675567.2023.2175802

The Impact of Crowdsourcing on Innovation and Decision-Making

4.1 Introduction

Crowdsourcing has emerged as a promising approach to open innovation in recent years, empowering organizations to harness the collective intelligence and creativity of a diverse group of individuals for problem-solving, generating new ideas, and driving innovation (Martinez-Torres, 2013). The term "crowdsourcing" was coined in 2006 by Jeff Howe, a contributing editor at *Wired* magazine, to describe the practice of outsourcing tasks to a large and undefined group of people, typically through an online platform (Howe, 2006).

Since then, crowdsourcing has evolved into a powerful tool for innovation (Howe, 2008), with applications ranging from product development and marketing to scientific research and social activism (Kieffer & Romanek, 2019). Crowdsourcing has also become increasingly relevant in the context of the COVID-19 pandemic (Mariani & Chatterjee, 2023; Vermicelli et al., 2021), with numerous examples of crowdsourcing initiatives aimed at addressing the many challenges posed by the pandemic.

Crowdsourcing can be an advantageous tool in SCM, as it offers several benefits (Li et al., 2021). First, it can help reduce costs by enabling businesses to source products, services, or transportation at a lower cost than traditional methods (Nassar & Karray, 2019). This is achieved by tapping into a larger pool of potential suppliers, giving businesses access to more competitive pricing (Perera & Perera, 2014). Second, it can provide flexibility by allowing businesses to quickly scale up or down their operations as needed, without investing in additional resources or infrastructure (Ernst et al., 2017). This is particularly useful in industries with fluctuating demand or in response to unforeseen circumstances. Third, crowdsourcing can drive innovation by enabling businesses to identify new products or services or find creative solutions to problems (Palacios et al., 2016). By leveraging the collective intelligence of a diverse group of individuals, businesses can generate new and fresh ideas. Lastly, it can enhance speed by allowing businesses to quickly identify and address supply chain issues such as delays or quality problems (Wu et al., 2013). With a larger pool of potential solutions, businesses can quickly find the most effective one (Ghezzi et al., 2018). Nevertheless, it's crucial to acknowledge that crowdsourcing also presents potential challenges, including quality control, intellectual property concerns, transparency and accountability issues, and language and cultural barriers. Therefore, businesses need to take appropriate steps to mitigate these risks and maximize the benefits of crowdsourcing.

The objective of this chapter is to furnish an overview of crowdsourcing as an open innovation mechanism, exploring its potential benefits and challenges, as well as its applications in different domains. I will begin by defining crowdsourcing and describing its various forms, including crowdfunding, crowdvoting, and crowdcasting. I will also examine the different types of crowdsourcing—task-, idea-, and knowledge-based crowdsourcing—and discuss their strengths and limitations.

Next, I will review the potential benefits of crowdsourcing, such as access to a diverse pool of talent and expertise, faster and more cost-effective innovation, and the ability to engage with customers and stakeholders in new and innovative ways. I will also examine the challenges of crowdsourcing, including the difficulty of managing and motivating large and diverse groups of participants, ensuring the quality and relevance of contributions, and protecting intellectual property rights.

The chapter will then highlight some of the most prominent applications of crowdsourcing in different domains, such as product design, marketing, scientific research, and social activism. I will review specific examples of crowdsourcing initiatives, such as the development of low-cost ventilators during the COVID-19 pandemic, the design of innovative and stylish face masks, and the use of crowdsourcing to identify new drug targets and treatments for diseases.

Finally, the chapter will be concluded by examining some of the emerging trends and future directions in crowdsourcing, such as the increasing utilization of AI and ML to analyze and interpret crowdsourced data, the integration of crowdsourcing with other open innovation mechanisms, and the potential for crowdsourcing to drive social and environmental impact.

4.2 Background and Current Practices

In the contemporary landscape, SCM has gained heightened importance as businesses grapple with novel challenges and disruptions brought about by the COVID-19 pandemic, climate change, and geopolitical instability (Akbari, 2023). One of the main challenges facing SCM today is ensuring resilience and agility in the face of unforeseen disruptions (Ha et al., 2022; Queiroz et al., 2022). The pandemic, for example, has disrupted supply chains by causing border closures, production shutdowns, and labor shortages (De Beukelaer, 2021). To manage these disruptions, businesses need to have contingency plans in place, diversify their supplier base, and build more flexible and adaptable supply chains (Akbari et al., 2022).

> Businesses that grow by development and improvement do not die—Henry Ford. (1863–1947)

A supply chain refers to the interconnected network of businesses, individuals, and activities that are involved in the production, distribution, and delivery of a product/service to the end consumer (Akbari, 2018; Cohen & Russel, 2013). It involves the transfer of goods and services from suppliers to manufacturers, distributors, retailers, and ultimately to the end user (Konig & Spinler, 2016). An effective supply chain is critical for ensuring the timely and efficient delivery of products and services to customers (Christopher, 2016).

Crowdsourcing is becoming increasingly important in SCM, as it supports businesses to tap into the collective intelligence and resources of a large group of individuals (Li et al., 2021). This helps businesses to identify new suppliers, products, or services, find innovative solutions to supply chain problems, and respond more quickly and effectively to changes in demand.

Crowdsourcing is a process of obtaining services, ideas, or content by soliciting contributions from a large group of people, often through an online platform (Howe, 2008). The contributors may be employees, customers, or members of the public, and the goal of crowdsourcing is to leverage the collective knowledge, skills, and creativity of the crowd to solve problems or generate new ideas (Nguyen et al., 2016).

Crowdsourcing comes in many forms, including crowdfunding, crowdvoting, and crowdcasting. Crowdfunding involves raising funds from a large group of people to support a project or business venture (Belleflamme et al., 2015), while crowdvoting allows people to vote on a particular idea or proposal (Chen et al., 2020). Crowdcasting, on the other hand, involves outsourcing a task or project to a large group of people, who then compete to provide the best solution (Obal, 2012).

Task-based crowdsourcing is one of the most common types, and it involves outsourcing specific tasks to a large group of people (Brehmer et al., 2019), often referred to as "microtasking". Microtasking platforms, such as Amazon Mechanical Turk (MTurk), allow businesses to outsource small and repetitive tasks, such as data entry, image labeling, and content moderation, to a large and distributed workforce.

Idea-based crowdsourcing, on the other hand, involves soliciting ideas or proposals from a large group of people to solve a particular problem or challenge (Wang et al., 2023). Idea-based crowdsourcing is a type of crowdsourcing that involves gathering ideas from a diverse group of individuals to solve a problem or generate new ideas (Holzmann et al., 2014). This type of crowdsourcing is often used by companies and organizations to tap into the collective intelligence of a broader community to come up with innovative solutions or ideas (Martinez-Torres, 2013). In idea-based crowdsourcing, individuals are invited to submit their ideas, which are then evaluated by either the crowd or a panel of judges. The best ideas are then selected and potentially implemented by the organization. Idea-based crowdsourcing can be either open or closed, with open crowdsourcing allowing anyone to submit an idea, while closed crowdsourcing is limited to a specific group of individuals (Harland & Nienaber, 2014).

Knowledge-based crowdsourcing is another form of crowdsourcing, which involves tapping into the expertise and knowledge of a large group of individuals to solve complex problems (Kim & Chung, 2017). Knowledge-based crowdsourcing platforms, such as InnoCentive and Kaggle, enable organizations to leverage the collective expertise of a diverse group of individuals, often including scientists, engineers, and data analysts, to solve challenging problems and drive innovation.

Crowdsourcing has numerous potential benefits, including access to a diverse pool of talent and expertise, faster and more cost-effective innovation, and the ability to engage with customers and stakeholders in new and innovative ways (Nguyen et al., 2016). Crowdsourcing also helps organizations to tap into the collective intelligence of the crowd, generating a wide range of ideas and solutions that may not have been possible through traditional methods (Holzmann et al., 2014).

The utilization of crowdsourcing offers a bright prospect for supply chain companies in resolving intricate issues, and there are numerous trends that will shape its future applications (Akbari, 2022).

One such trend is *decentralization*, by delegating responsibilities to lower-level and mid-level management, top management can concentrate on more crucial tasks. Various fintech corporations have already embraced this model—Blockchain, Uber, and Lyft are prime examples of decentralized technology (Li et al., 2018).

An alternative crowdsourcing method that has the potential to enhance brand awareness is *user-generated* content (Feng & Yan, 2019). Supply chain firms can leverage this strategy by encouraging audiences to create branded content and share it on social media using pertinent hashtags (Kache & Seuring, 2017). By monitoring these hashtags, businesses can keep track of the generated content.

Co-creation is yet another way that supply chain firms can leverage their network's skills, connections, and resources (Akbari, 2022). It marks a departure from conventional R&D and offers substantial opportunities, thanks to the constantly changing and dynamic nature of technology. By giving customers a voice, co-creation has the potential to engage them in supporting the development of diverse business models and products.

However, crowdsourcing also presents several challenges, including the difficulty of managing and motivating large and diverse groups of participants, ensuring the quality and relevance of contributions, cultural and language barriers, and protecting intellectual property rights (Phuttharak & Loke, 2018; Seltzer & Mahmoudi, 2013). Organizations must also carefully consider the potential ethical implications of crowdsourcing, such as the fair compensation of contributors and the potential exploitation of vulnerable populations.

Despite these challenges, crowdsourcing has become increasingly prevalent in recent years, with numerous examples of successful crowdsourcing initiatives across different domains (Bastardo et al., 2023; Herter et al., 2023; Moghaddam et al., 2023). From the highly popular online encyclopedia, Wikipedia, to the innovative protein folding game, Foldit, crowdsourcing has become an integral part of many industries and fields. In the following examples, I will explore some of the most prominent examples of crowdsourcing, including Wikipedia, Foldit, Galaxy Zoo, Kickstarter, MTurk, and the New Zealand flag design competition. I will examine the benefits and challenges of crowdsourcing, as well as the different methods and platforms used to engage and mobilize a diverse community of participants.

Example 1 (knowledge-based crowdsourcing): Wikipedia

Wikipedia is an online encyclopedia that is based on crowdsourcing. It is one of the most popular and largest crowdsourcing projects in the world. The platform relies on contributions from volunteers from around the globe to write and edit articles on an extensive range of topics.

Wikipedia is an example of knowledge-based crowdsourcing, where individuals contribute their expertise and knowledge to create a shared resource. The platform allows anyone to contribute, edit, or modify articles, and the articles are then reviewed and monitored by other volunteers to ensure the accuracy and quality of the information provided.

Wikipedia has become an essential resource for information seekers worldwide, and it has a significant impact on the way people access and consume information. According to the Wikimedia Foundation, which manages Wikipedia, the platform has over 50 million articles in more than 300 languages, and it attracts over 1.5 billion unique visitors per month.

The success of Wikipedia is due to the principles of crowdsourcing, which allow for the collective wisdom of the crowd to contribute to the creation of a valuable resource. The platform's openness, transparency, and accessibility have enabled individuals from diverse backgrounds and locations to contribute to the project.

However, Wikipedia is not without its challenges. The platform faces issues concerning the quality and reliability of the information prepared by its contributors. The platform has a strict policy for monitoring and verifying the accuracy of the articles, but mistakes and inaccuracies can still occur.

The platform also faces challenges related to the motivation and retention of contributors. Wikipedia relies on the voluntary contributions of its users, and maintaining a large and engaged community of contributors is crucial for the platform's success. The Wikimedia Foundation has implemented various strategies to encourage participation and increase retention, such as gamification and recognition programs.

Example 2 (knowledge-based crowdsourcing): Foldit

Foldit is an online puzzle game that challenges players to fold virtual proteins in the most efficient way possible. The game's creators hope to use players' insights to develop new treatments for diseases. Foldit is another example of knowledge-based crowdsourcing.

Proteins are essential molecules that perform a wide range of functions in the body, from helping to digest food to fighting off infections. However, the way that proteins fold and interact with other molecules is complex and not entirely comprehended. This is where Foldit comes in.

The game was created by researchers at the University of Washington who wanted to harness the power of crowdsourcing to solve complex scientific problems. Players are presented with a series of puzzles that involve folding a virtual protein into the most stable and efficient configuration possible. The game's scoring system rewards players for creating the most efficient protein structures.

While Foldit is a game, it has real-world implications. The game's creators hope to use the insights gained from players' solutions to develop new treatments for diseases. For example, by understanding how proteins fold and interact, researchers may be able to develop new drugs that can target specific proteins and treat diseases more effectively.

Foldit has been highly successful in engaging players and generating valuable insights. In 2011, Foldit players made headlines when they helped to solve the structure of a protein that had stumped scientists for over a decade. This breakthrough resulted in an improved comprehension of the protein's involvement in diseases such as AIDS and cancer.

Example 3 (knowledge-based crowdsourcing): Galaxy Zoo

Galaxy Zoo is an online citizen science project that was launched in 2007 by a team of astronomers from the University of Oxford, the University of Portsmouth, and Johns Hopkins University. Over 400,000 volunteers have participated in Galaxy Zoo and completed over 11 million galaxy classification tasks. The project's goal is to classify millions of galaxies based on their shapes and structures, which can help scientists better understand the evolution of the universe.

The project uses images of galaxies that have been taken by telescopes such as the Sloan Digital Sky Survey and the Hubble Space Telescope. Volunteers are asked to look at these images and classify the galaxies into different types based on their shapes, including elliptical, spiral, and irregular.

To participate in Galaxy Zoo, volunteers create an account on the project's website and are presented with a series of images of galaxies. They are then asked to classify the galaxies based on their shapes and structures using a set of simple questions and tools. The classifications provided by volunteers are then used by scientists to study the properties of galaxies, such as their sizes, shapes, and orientations.

Galaxy Zoo has been incredibly successful as a knowledge-based crowdsourcing project, with hundreds of thousands of volunteers from around the world contributing to it. The classifications provided by volunteers have led to numerous scientific discoveries, including the identification of a new type of galaxy known as a "green pea" galaxy and the discovery of a rare class of galaxies known as "Hanny's Voorwerp".

The project has also been instrumental in helping scientists better understand how galaxies form and evolve over time and has led to the development of new computer algorithms that can automatically classify galaxies based on their shapes. Galaxy Zoo continues to be one of the most successful and popular citizen science projects in the world and has inspired similar projects in fields such as biology, chemistry, and physics.

Example 4 (idea-based crowdsourcing): Kickstarter

Kickstarter is primarily an idea-based crowdsourcing platform and a popular crowdfunding platform that enables creators to pitch their ideas and raise money from backers. The platform has become a vital tool for entrepreneurs, innovators, and artists to bring their ideas to life by securing the necessary funding to develop their projects.

On Kickstarter, creators post their project proposals and set a funding goal and deadline. Interested backers can then contribute to the project in exchange for various rewards, such as early access to the product, special edition versions, or recognition on the project's website.

The Kickstarter platform offers several benefits to both creators and backers. For creators, Kickstarter provides a straightforward and accessible way to fund their projects without relying on traditional investors or bank loans. It also allows creators to test the market demand for their products and validate their ideas before investing significant time and resources. Moreover, Kickstarter can help creators build a loyal community of supporters and generate buzz around their projects.

For backers, Kickstarter offers a chance to support innovative projects and help bring them to life. It provides an opportunity to be part of the creative process and get exclusive rewards and benefits. Supporters can directly influence the project's success by disseminating information and sharing the project within their networks.

Since its launch in 2009, Kickstarter has become a popular platform for crowdfunding and has helped fund a wide range of projects. The platform has supported the development of new gadgets, software, games, films, music albums, and more.

Kickstarter has also played a significant role in enabling independent creators to bypass traditional gatekeepers and gain access to funding and support. This trend has given rise to a new generation of entrepreneurs and artists who can pursue their passions and ideas without depending on traditional sources of funding.

However, Kickstarter also faces some challenges related to the quality and reliability of the projects posted on the platform. The platform has implemented several guidelines and policies to prevent fraudulent or low-quality projects, but some still slip through the cracks. Backers must carefully evaluate the projects and creators before contributing to ensure that they are supporting a legitimate and high-quality project.

Example 5 (idea-based crowdsourcing): New Zealand flag project

The process of designing a new flag for New Zealand involved elements of crowdsourcing, as the public was invited to submit designs and provide feedback throughout the process. This is an idea-based crowdsourcing project.

In 2014, the New Zealand government launched a flag design competition that allowed anyone in the country to submit their own design for consideration. The competition received over 10,000 entries, which were then narrowed down to a shortlist of four designs.

The shortlisted designs were put to a public vote in 2015, which was also open to all New Zealanders. This vote was also considered a form of crowdsourcing, as it allowed the general public to have a say in the final design of the flag.

However, the final outcome of the vote was somewhat controversial, as many critics argued that the process was too heavily influenced by political agendas and lacked true public engagement. Some also argued that the selection of the four shortlisted designs was too limited and did not represent the full range of design possibilities.

Despite the controversy surrounding the flag design process, it is an example of how crowdsourcing can be used to engage the public in decision-making and allow a wider range of ideas to be considered. By opening up the design process to the public and allowing feedback and input, the government was able to tap into the creativity and expertise of the wider community, and ensure that the final design was a reflection of the country's diverse perspectives and values.

Example 6 (task-based crowdsourcing): Amazon Mechanical Turk

MTurk is an online task-based crowdsourcing platform that connects businesses with a global workforce of freelancers who can perform a wide range of tasks, from data entry to content creation. The platform is considered the pioneering crowdsourcing platform and has become a popular way for businesses to get work done quickly and efficiently.

MTurk is an online marketplace that enables businesses to post tasks, known as Human Intelligence Tasks (HITs), and pay workers to complete them. HITs can range from simple tasks, such as data entry or image tagging, to more complex tasks, such as writing product descriptions or conducting surveys.

One of the key advantages of MTurk is its large and diverse pool of workers, who come from around the world and have a wide range of skills and expertise. This enables businesses to tap into a global workforce and get work done quickly and efficiently, without the need to hire full-time employees or outsource work to expensive contractors.

MTurk also provides businesses with a flexible and scalable way to get work done. Businesses can post as many HITs as they need and pay workers only for the completed work.

MTurk offers several benefits to workers, including the flexibility to work on their own terms and schedule, the ability to work from anywhere with an internet connection, and the opportunity to earn money in their spare time.

However, MTurk also faces some challenges related to the quality and reliability of the work performed by its workers. The platform has implemented several measures to ensure the quality of work, such as worker ratings and qualifications, but some businesses still face issues with low-quality work or fraudulent activity.

Example 7 (task-based crowdsourcing): Clickworker

Clickworker is a task-based crowdsourcing (crowdworking) platform that connects businesses with workers from all over the world who perform small online tasks. The platform's tasks can range from data entry, content creation, image and video tagging, website testing, and more.

Clickworkers can choose from a variety of tasks available on the platform and work on them at their own pace and schedule. The platform uses advanced algorithms and quality control measures to ensure that the tasks are completed accurately and efficiently.

Businesses can use Clickworker to access a large pool of workers to complete tasks that are time-consuming, repetitive, or require human intelligence. Clickworker provides a cost-effective and flexible solution for businesses to scale their operations and get work done quickly.

For example, a company may want to gather data on the prices of products in different regions. They can use Clickworker to crowdsource this task by having workers search for the product prices in different regions and report them back to the company. The company can then use this data to inform their pricing strategy and market research.

Overall, task-based crowdsourcing platforms like Clickworker provide a scalable and efficient solution for businesses to get work done quickly and cost-effectively, while also providing workers with flexible job opportunities.

4.3   Emergent Concerns and Future Directions

The concept of crowdsourcing has evolved from being a simple business process or routine to a full-fledged business model archetype that organizations are increasingly utilizing to attain a competitive advantage in the market. As stated by Massa et al. (2017), the traditional approach of using in-house teams or external contractors to complete tasks and projects has now shifted toward leveraging the collective intelligence and expertise of a diverse and global crowd through digital platforms and tools. The benefits of crowdsourcing include increased innovation, improved efficiency, reduced costs, and greater flexibility (Herter et al., 2023). With the rise of technology and digital platforms, organizations are now able to tap into a broader pool of talent and resources, leading to more effective problem-solving, idea-generation, and decision-making processes (Bastardo et al., 2023). As such, it is no surprise that more and more firms are embracing crowdsourcing as a practical and operational business model to drive success in their industries.

The COVID-19 pandemic has undeniably highlighted the substantial potential of crowdsourcing as a powerful tool for open innovation in addressing complex challenges (Mariani & Chatterjee, 2023; Vermicelli et al., 2021). Crowdsourcing is the practice of utilizing the knowledge, expertise, and innovation of a varied group of people to tackle challenges or generate fresh concepts (Martinez-Torres, 2013). During the pandemic, many organizations and governments have turned to crowdsourcing to seek innovative solutions to a range of challenges, including the development of low-cost ventilators, the design of protective face masks, and the development of new treatments and vaccines for COVID-19.

Ennomotive organized a crowdsourcing challenge that required participants to develop a low-cost and easy-to-build ventilator to meet the urgent need of hospitals (Gurca et al., 2023). This challenge was launched in response to the shortage of ventilators during the initial stages of the COVID-19 pandemic. The challenge was open to a wide range of participants, including engineers, designers, and innovators, who were invited to submit their ideas for low-cost ventilators. The goal of the challenge was to leverage the collective expertise of the crowd to develop a solution that could be quickly produced and distributed to hospitals in need. The winning solution was a low-cost ventilator that could be built using off-the-shelf components and was designed to be easy to use and maintain.

An additional illustration of crowdsourcing was the reinvention of protective face masks used to curb the spread of COVID-19 that enhanced their comfort, functionality, accessibility, and style (Gurca et al., 2023). This challenge was launched to address the issue of mask fatigue, where people were becoming tired of wearing uncomfortable and unappealing masks. The challenge was open to designers, artists, and other creative individuals who were invited to submit their ideas for innovative and stylish face masks. The goal was to leverage the creativity and diverse perspectives of the crowd to develop masks that people would be more willing to wear. The winning solutions included masks with innovative designs, such as masks that resembled jewelry or scarves, masks made from sustainable materials, and masks with added features such as air filters and built-in fans. These solutions aimed to make wearing masks more comfortable and appealing, while still providing effective protection against COVID-19.

As the field of crowdsourcing continues to evolve, there are several emergent concerns and future directions that should be considered. One of the key concerns is the issue of ethical and legal implications of crowdsourcing (Standing et al., 2018). Given the increasing popularity of crowdsourcing, it is crucial to ensure that participants are treated fairly and that their rights and privacy are protected. Additionally, there is a need to establish clear guidelines and regulations to govern the use of crowdsourcing, particularly in areas such as intellectual property and data privacy (à Campo et al., 2019).

Another emerging concern is the need to ensure that the crowd is diverse and representative (Clark & Brudney, 2019). The success of crowdsourcing initiatives is often dependent on the diversity of the crowd, which can bring a range of perspectives and expertise to the innovation process (Clark et al., 2017). However, there is a risk that certain groups may be excluded or underrepresented, leading to a lack of diversity in the outcomes of the process. To address this, there is a need to develop strategies to ensure that the crowd is diverse and representative, including incentives for outreach programs and underrepresented groups to participate.

Looking to the future, there are several exciting directions for crowdsourcing. One potential area is the utilization of AI and ML to augment the efficiency and effectiveness of crowdsourcing (Sheng & Zhang, 2019). These technologies can be used to identify patterns and insights from large datasets and improve the accuracy and speed of the innovation process.

Another direction is the development of new tools and platforms to support crowdsourcing initiatives (Taeihagh, 2017). There is a growing need for more user-friendly and accessible platforms that can be used by a wide range of individuals and organizations. These platforms should be designed to facilitate collaboration, communication, and feedback, allowing participants to work together more effectively (Nguyen et al., 2022).

Finally, there is a need to consider the broader societal impacts of crowdsourcing (Dolmaya, 2012; Kohler & Chesbrough, 2019). As crowdsourcing becomes more prevalent, it holds the potential to revolutionize the way we work and innovate. This transformation could bring significant benefits, such as increased collaboration and creativity, but it may also have unintended consequences, such as the displacement of traditional employment. As such, there is a need to carefully consider the societal implications of crowdsourcing and develop strategies to mitigate any negative impacts.

4.4   Managerial Implications

Crowdsourcing has a range of managerial implications for businesses. By understanding the managerial implications of academic research, managers and leaders can make more informed decisions, optimize business performance, and drive innovation and growth. In this context, it is essential to examine some of the key managerial implications that arise from various research studies and explore how these can be applied to real-world business situations to achieve better outcomes. Here are some key considerations:

- *Clear objectives and guidelines:* To ensure that crowdsourcing efforts are productive, it is important to have clear objectives and guidelines. Organizations must define what they hope to achieve through crowdsourcing and how they will evaluate the results. Participants should be given clear guidelines to ensure a comprehensive understanding of what is expected from them.
- *Incentives and rewards:* Offering incentives and rewards can motivate participants and increase the quality and quantity of contributions. Rewards can take many forms, including monetary compensation, recognition, and exclusive access to products or services.
- *Communication and engagement:* Effective communication and engagement are essential to successful crowdsourcing. Organizations must provide regular updates and feedback to participants and be open to dialogue and collaboration. Engaging with participants can also help organizations to identify potential collaborators or partners.

- *Intellectual property rights:* Intellectual property rights can be a complex issue in crowdsourcing. It is important for organizations to clarify ownership of any contributions and to ensure that all parties involved agree to the terms of use. Organizations may need to consider licensing agreements or other legal arrangements to protect their interests.
- *Risk management:* Crowdsourcing can involve risks, such as the disclosure of confidential information or the potential for reputational damage. Organizations must carefully manage these risks by implementing appropriate security measures and monitoring contributions.
- *Integration with existing processes:* Crowdsourcing can be integrated with existing processes to enhance innovation and problem-solving. For example, crowdsourcing can be used to generate ideas for new products/services or to identify potential improvements to existing processes.
- *Collaboration and partnerships:* Crowdsourcing can also be used to build collaboration and partnerships. By engaging with a diverse range of individuals and organizations, businesses can build new networks and relationships that can lead to future opportunities.

Overall, crowdsourcing can be a powerful tool for businesses and organizations seeking to tap into the collective intelligence and creativity of a broader community. By carefully considering the managerial implications of crowdsourcing, organizations can maximize the potential benefits while mitigating the risks.

4.5 Summary and Conclusion

Crowdsourcing has emerged as a powerful tool for innovation and problem-solving in recent years. With the advent of technology, it has become easier to harness the collective intelligence of a diverse group of individuals to achieve a common goal. This book chapter has discussed various examples of crowdsourcing, including Wikipedia, Kickstarter, MTurk, and Foldit, among others.

The chapter has also highlighted the emergence of crowdsourcing to address the COVID-19 pandemic, where it has been used to solve complex challenges such as developing low-cost ventilators and reimagining protective face masks.

The managerial implications of crowdsourcing are significant, as organizations can leverage it to develop new products, improve processes, and solve problems. However, it is important to note that successful crowdsourcing requires careful planning, management, and coordination. Organizations must be clear about the problem they are trying to solve or the ideas they want to generate, and they must be willing to invest time and resources into managing the crowdsourcing process effectively.

The chapter has also highlighted some of the potential challenges and concerns with crowdsourcing, including issues of intellectual property, quality control, and ethical considerations. Organizations need to address these concerns and implement appropriate safeguards to ensure that crowdsourcing is used effectively and ethically.

Looking ahead, the future of crowdsourcing is promising, as advances in technology are making it easier to engage larger and more diverse groups of individuals in the crowdsourcing process. However, it is important for organizations to continue to explore and experiment with different crowdsourcing models to find the most effective approaches for their specific needs.

REFERENCES

à Campo, S., Khan, V.J., Papangelis, K., & Markopoulos, P. (2019). Community heuristics for user interface evaluation of crowdsourcing platforms. *Future Generation Computer Systems, 95*, 775–789. https://doi.org/10.1016/j.fut ure.2018.02.028

Akbari, M. (2018). Logistics outsourcing: a structured literature review. *Benchmarking: An International Journal, 25*(5), 1548–1580. https://doi.org/10. 1108/BIJ-04-2017-0066

Akbari, M. (2022). Chapter 47—Outsourcing in Supply Chain Management. In J. Sarkis (ed.), *Handbook of supply chain management—A major reference work*, Palgrave. https://doi.org/10.1007/978-3-030-89822-9_47-1

Akbari, M. (2023). Data-driven review of additive manufacturing on supply chains: Regionalization, key research themes and future directions. *Computers & Industrial Engineering, 184*, 109600. https://doi.org/10. 1016/j.cie.2023.109600

Akbari, M., Clarke, S. J., & Maleki Far, S. (2017). Outsourcing best practice— The case of large construction firms in Iran. *Proceedings of the Informing Science and Information Technology Education Conference.* 39–50. From: InSITE 2017: Informing Science and Information Technology Education

Conference, 31 July–5 August 2017, Ho Chi Minh City, Vietnam. https://doi.org/10.28945/3737

Akbari, M., Ha, N., & Kok, S. (2022). A systematic review of AR/VR in operations and supply chain management: Maturity, current trends and future directions. *Journal of Global Operations and Strategic Sourcing, 15*(4), 534–565. https://doi.org/10.1108/JGOSS-09-2021-0078

Bastardo, R., Pavão, J., & Rocha, N. P. (2023). Crowdsourcing technologies to promote citizens' participation in smart cities, a scoping review. *Procedia Computer Science, 219*, 303–311. https://doi.org/10.1016/j.procs.2023.01.294

Belleflamme, P., Omrani, N., & Peitz, M. (2015). The economics of crowdfunding platforms. *Information Economics and Policy, 33*, 11–28. https://doi.org/10.1016/j.infoecopol.2015.08.003

Brehmer, M., Lee, B., Isenberg, P., & Choe, E. K. (2019). Visualizing ranges over time on mobile phones: A task-based crowdsourced evaluation. *IEEE Transactions on Visualization and Computer Graphics, 25*(1), 619–629. https://doi.org/10.1109/TVCG.2018.2865234

Xu., Chen, & P., & Liu, D. (2020). Effect of crowd voting on participation in crowdsourcing contests. *Journal of Management Information Systems, 37*(2), 510–535. https://doi.org/10.1080/07421222.2020.1759342

Christopher, M. (2016). *Logistics and supply chain management* (5th ed.). Pearson.

Clark, B. Y., & Brudney, J. L. (2019). Citizen representation in city government-driven crowdsourcing. *Computer Supported Cooperative Work (CSCW), 28*, 883–910. https://doi.org/10.1007/s10606-018-9308-2

Clark, B.Y., Zingale, N., & Logan, J. (2017). Intelligence and information gathering through deliberative crowdsourcing. Clark, BY, Zingale, N., & Logan, J. (2017). Intelligence and information gathering through deliberative crowdsourcing. *Journal of Public and Nonprofit Affairs, 3*(1), 55–78. https://doi.org/10.20899/jpna.3.1.55-78

Cohen, S., & Roussel, J. (2013). *Strategic supply chain management: The five core disciplines for top performance* (2nd ed.). McGraw-Hill.

De Beukelaer, C. (2021). COVID-19 border closures cause humanitarian crew change crisis at sea. *Marine Policy, 132*, 104661. https://doi.org/10.1016/j.marpol.2021.104661

Dolmaya, J. M. (2012). Analyzing the crowdsourcing model and its impact on public perceptions of translation. *The Translator, 18*(2), 167–191. https://doi.org/10.1080/13556509.2012.10799507

Ernst, C., Mladenow, A., & Strauss, C. (2017). Collaboration and crowdsourcing in emergency management. *International Journal of Pervasive Computing and Communications, 13*(2), 176–193. https://doi.org/10.1108/IJPCC-03-2017-0026

Feng, W., & Yan, Z. (2019). MCS-Chain: Decentralized and trustworthy mobile crowdsourcing based on blockchain. *Future Generation Computer Systems, 95,* 649–666. https://doi.org/10.1016/j.future.2019.01.036

Ghezzi, A., Gabelloni, D., Martini, A., & Natalicchio, A. (2018). Crowdsourcing: A review and suggestions for future research. *International Journal of Management Reviews, 20*(2), 343–363. https://doi.org/10.1111/ijmr.12135

Gurca, A., Bagherzadeh, M., & Velayati, R. (2023). Aligning the crowdsourcing type with the problem attributes to improve solution search efficacy. *Technovation, 119,* 102613. https://doi.org/10.1016/j.technovation.2022.102613

Ha, N.T., Akbari, M., & Au, B. (2022). Last mile delivery in logistics and supply chain management: A bibliometric analysis and future directions. *Benchmarking: An International Journal, 30*(4), 1137–1170. https://doi.org/10.1108/BIJ-07-2021-0409

Harland, P. E., & Nienaber, A. M. (2014). Solving the matchmaking dilemma between companies and external idea contributors. *Technology Analysis & Strategic Management, 26*(6), 639–653. https://doi.org/10.1080/09537325.2014.919378

Herter, M.M., Shuqair, S., Pinto, D.C., Mattila, A.S., & Zandonai Pontin, P. (2023). Does crowdsourcing necessarily lead to brand engagement? The role of crowdsourcing cues and relationship norms on customer-brand relationships. *Journal of Product & Brand Management* (In-Press). https://doi.org/10.1108/JPBM-06-2022-4020

Holzmann, T., Sailer, K., & Galbraith, B. (2014). Matchmaking for open innovation—Theoretical perspectives based on interaction, rather than transaction. *Technology Analysis & Strategic Management, 26*(6), 595–599. https://doi.org/10.1080/09537325.2014.913344

Howe, J. (2006). The Rise of Crowdsourcing. *Wired Magazine,* (14.06). Retrieved from http://www.wired.com/wired/archive/14.06/crowds_pr.html. Accessed 3 April 2023.

Howe, J. (2008). *Crowdsourcing: How the power of the crowd is driving the future of business.* Century.

Kache, F., & Seuring, S. (2017). Challenges and opportunities of digital information at the intersection of big data analytics and supply chain management. *International Journal of Operations & Production Management, 37*(1), 10–36. https://doi.org/10.1108/IJOPM-02-2015-0078

Kieffer, C. L., & Romanek, D. (2019). Crowdsourcing a current events exhibition on community activism against DAPL. *Curator, 62,* 135–150. https://doi.org/10.1111/cura.12302

Kim, J. C., & Chung, K. (2017). Depression index service using knowledge based crowdsourcing in smart health. *Wireless Personal Communications, 93,* 255–268. https://doi.org/10.1007/s11277-016-3923-3

Kohler, T., & Chesbrough, H. (2019). From collaborative community to competitive market: The quest to build a crowdsourcing platform for social innovation. *R&D Management, 49*, 356–368. https://doi.org/10.1111/radm.12372

Konig, A., & Spinler, S. (2016). The effect of logistics outsourcing on the supply chain vulnerability of shippers. *The International Journal of Logistics Management, 27*(1), 122–141. https://doi.org/10.1108/IJLM-03-2014-0043

Li, J., Yu, Y., & Liu, C. (2021). Product design crowdsourcing in a dual-channel supply chain: Joint reviews from manufacturer and consumers. *International Transactions in Opertaional Research, 28*, 784–808. https://doi.org/10.1111/itor.12749

Li, M., Weng, J., Yang, A., Lu, W., Zhang, Y., Hou, L., Liu, J. N., Xiang, Y., & Deng, R. H. (2018). CrowdBC: A blockchain-based decentralized framework for crowdsourcing. *IEEE Transactions on Parallel and Distributed Systems, 30*(6), 1251–1266. https://doi.org/10.1109/TPDS.2018.2881735

Massa, L., Tucci, C., & Afuah, A. (2017). A critical assessment of business model research. *Academy of Management Annals, 11*(1), 73–104. https://doi.org/10.5465/annals.2014.0072

Mariani, M., & Chatterjee, S. (2023). Examining the influence of trustworthiness, financial rewards, and admiration for crowdsourcing in the post COVID-19 period. *IEEE Transactions on Engineering Management.* https://doi.org/10.1109/TEM.2023.3246115

Martinez-Torres, M. R. (2013). Application of evolutionary computation techniques for the identification of innovators in open innovation communities. *Expert Systems with Applications, 40*(7), 2503–2510. https://doi.org/10.1016/j.eswa.2012.10.070

Moghaddam, E. N., Aliahmadi, A., Bagherzadeh, M., Markovic, S., Micevski, M., & Saghafi, F. (2023). Let me choose what I want: The influence of incentive choice flexibility on the quality of crowdsourcing solutions to innovation problems. *Technovation, 120*, 102679. https://doi.org/10.1016/j.technovation.2022.102679

Nassar, L., & Karray, F. (2019). Overview of the crowdsourcing process. *Knowledge and Information Systems, 60*, 1–24. https://doi.org/10.1007/s10115-018-1235-5

Nguyen, H. T., Antunes, A., & Johnstone, D. (2016). Factors influencing the decision to crowdsource: A systematic literature review. *Information Systems Frontiers, 18*, 47–68. https://doi.org/10.1007/s10796-015-9578-x

Nguyen, H., Onofrei, G., Akbari, M., & McClelland, R. (2022). Enhancing quality and innovation performance: The role of supplier communication and knowledge development. *Total Quality Management & Business Excellence, 33*(3–4), 410–433. https://doi.org/10.1080/14783363.2020.1858711

Obal, D. (2012). Crowdcasting: A platform fostering open innovation. In *Handbook of research on business social networking: Organizational, managerial, and technological dimensions* (pp. 786–804). IGI Global.

Palacios, M., Martinez-Corral, A., Nisar, A., & Grijalvo, M. (2016). Crowdsourcing and organizational forms: Emerging trends and research implications. *Journal of Business Research, 69*(5), 1834–1839. https://doi.org/10.1016/j. jbusres.2015.10.065

Perera, I., & Perera, A. P. (2014). Developments and leanings of crowdsourcing industry: Implications of China and India. *Industrial and Commercial Training, 46*(2), 92–99. https://doi.org/10.1108/ICT-06-2013-0038

Phuttharak, J., & Loke, S. W. (2018). A review of mobile crowdsourcing architectures and challenges: Toward crowd-empowered internet-of-things. *IEEE Access, 7*, 304–324. https://doi.org/10.1109/ACCESS.2018.2885353

Queiroz, M. M., Ivanov, D., Dolgui, A., Dolgui, A., & Wamba, S. F. (2022). Impacts of epidemic outbreaks on supply chains: Mapping a research agenda amid the COVID-19 pandemic through a structured literature review. *Annals of Operations Research, 319*, 1159–1196. https://doi.org/10.1007/s10479-020-03685-7

Seltzer, E., & Mahmoudi, D. (2013). Citizen participation, open innovation, and crowdsourcing: Challenges and opportunities for planning. *Journal of Planning Literature, 28*(1), 3–18. https://doi.org/10.1177/0885412212469112

Sheng, V. S., & Zhang, J. (2019). Machine learning with crowdsourcing: A brief summary of the past research and future directions. *Proceedings of the AAAI Conference on Artificial Intelligence, 33*(01), 9837–9843. https://doi.org/10.1609/aaai.v33i01.33019837

Standing, S., & Standing, C. (2018). The ethical use of crowdsourcing. *Business Ethics: A European Review, 27*(1), 72–80. https://doi.org/10.1111/beer.12173

Taeihagh, A. (2017). Crowdsourcing: A new tool for policy-making? *Policy Sciences, 50*, 629–647. https://doi.org/10.1007/s11077-017-9303-3

Vermicelli, S., Cricelli, L., & Grimaldi, M. (2021). How can crowdsourcing help tackle the COVID-19 pandemic? An explorative overview of innovative collaborative practices. *R&D Management, 51*, 183–194. https://doi.org/10.1111/radm.12443

Wang, K., Dong, B., & Ma, J. (2023). Testing computational assessment of idea novelty in crowdsourcing. *Creativity Research Journal* (In-Press). https://doi.org/10.1080/10400419.2023.2187544

Wu, C. C., Chen, K. T., Chang, Y. C., & Lei, C. L. (2013). Crowdsourcing multimedia QoE evaluation: A trusted framework. *IEEE Transactions on Multimedia, 15*(5), 1121–1137. https://doi.org/10.1109/TMM.2013.2241043

CHAPTER 5

Current Trends in Reshoring, Nearshoring, Rightshoring, and Emerging Strategies

5.1 Introduction

For decades, companies have utilized outsourcing and offshoring as key strategies which have drawn attention from operations, logistics, and SCM scholars (Albertoni et al., 2017; Foerstl et al., 2016). Many companies have chosen to offshore their operations to reduce costs and transfer risks and responsibilities to suppliers in countries with lower labor costs (Bals et al., 2016). This has resulted in significant cost savings for businesses as globalization has led to an increase in the offshoring and outsourcing of products and services to low-cost countries (Akbari, 2013, 2018).

However, recent events such as the COVID-19 pandemic, natural disasters, geopolitical tensions, and trade disputes have exposed the vulnerabilities of global supply chains, leading to disruptions in the flow of goods, services, and information, and highlighting the importance of supply chain resilience and risk management (Akbari, 2023; Duong et al., 2023). This has prompted many firms to reevaluate their offshoring and outsourcing strategies and to consider reshoring or nearshoring as ways to reduce their reliance on distant suppliers and increase their supply chain resilience.

> Whenever you see a successful business, someone once made a courageous decision.—Peter Drucker (1909–2005)

© The Author(s), under exclusive license to Springer Nature Singapore Pte Ltd. 2024
M. Akbari, *The Road to Outsourcing 4.0*,
https://doi.org/10.1007/978-981-97-2708-7_5

In response to these challenges, many businesses have been rethinking their supply chain strategies and considering alternatives such as reshoring, backshoring, and nearshoring. These terms refer to the practice of bringing products and services back to the home country, relocating them to nearby countries, or moving them to a new location within the home country, respectively (Akbari, 2022).

Research on reshoring has been conducted across various fields, including strategic and operations management, international business, and the role of institutions (Srai & Ané, 2016). This literature covers several topics, such as defining different types of reshoring (Ellram et al., 2013; Gray et al., 2013), the reasons behind reshoring, including the failures and shortcomings of offshoring (Albertoni et al., 2017; Fratocchi et al., 2016), the impact of consumer behavior on reshoring (Grappi et al., 2018), and changes in the offshore country environment, such as rising labor and energy costs (Tate et al., 2014). Understanding the reasons why companies choose to reshore provides valuable insights into the location of their activities, the activities themselves, and their governance (Benito, 2015). With the growing trend of multinational enterprises reversing offshore outsourcing decisions, reshoring serves as a useful context for merging knowledge from location decisions and governance literature (Kedia & Mukherjee, 2009).

5.2   CURRENT PRACTICES

In recent decades, companies have widely adopted offshoring to reap cost advantages (Akbari & Hopkins, 2016). Jahns et al. (2006) defined offshoring as the operation or location outside a country's borders, and Mol (2007) described it as procuring inputs from or supplying them to foreign countries. Casson and Wadeson's (2013) later research emphasized that offshoring is purely a location decision based on cost differentials between locations and the willingness to leverage such differences. Offshoring is a business strategy that involves relocating certain business functions or activities to another country to take advantage of cost advantages, such as lower labor costs, favorable tax policies, or other economic incentives. Companies typically use offshoring to remain competitive in a global market, reduce production costs, and increase profits.

Offshoring can be divided into two models: "offshore insourcing", in which a company locates its production activities in a foreign country, regardless of previous ownership decisions, as described by Schniederjans et al. (2005); and "offshore outsourcing", in which manufacturing activities are outsourced through foreign suppliers, as described by Duening and Click (2005).

Despite its potential benefits, offshoring can also have some downsides, such as cultural and language barriers, differences in legal and regulatory frameworks, and potential quality control issues. Additionally, offshoring can lead to job losses in the home country, which can have economic and social implications.

Therefore, companies need to weigh the potential benefits and risks of offshoring before deciding to implement this business strategy (Akbari, 2022). Companies that opt to offshore should carefully consider their specific business needs and objectives, as well as the potential risks and benefits of offshoring to determine which approach to offshoring (insourcing or outsourcing) is most appropriate for their situation. The most appropriate strategy may vary depending on the company's industry, customer base, and other factors (Akbari et al., 2017).

5.2.1   Reshoring and Backshoring

Recent research has highlighted the challenges associated with outsourcing and offshoring, leading to the emergence of insourcing and backshoring strategies (Stentoft et al., 2016). Insourcing involves bringing activities previously outsourced back in-house, while backshoring involves relocating foreign activities back to the parent company's location. These pairwise opposite movements of manufacturing locations are often referred to as globalization strategies (Arlbjørn & Lüthje, 2012).

Various factors drive companies to reverse their offshoring decision and pursue backshoring (Ellram et al., 2013). These include an increase in local labor costs, unfulfilled savings, lack of quality, unavailability of a qualified workforce, proximity to R&D resources, and the utilization of new technology and automation (Gylling et al., 2015; Leibl et al., 2011). Other terms used in the literature to describe this phenomenon include onshoring (Kazmer, 2014), reshoring (Ancarani et al., 2015), and back-reshoring (Fratocchi et al., 2014). Additionally, the concepts of nearshoring and near-reshoring have been introduced for moving activities within the region or neighboring countries and relocating previously offshored activities back close to the parent company's headquarters, respectively (Ellram et al., 2013).

While backshoring has not been extensively discussed in the literature, Kinkel and Maloca (2009) estimated that between one-sixth and one-quarter of companies that previously turned offshore have turned to backshoring again, based on German data.

Reshoring and backshoring have become more attractive to many companies as a result of the COVID-19 pandemic, as they seek to minimize supply chain risks and ensure greater control over their operations. The disruptions caused by the pandemic have highlighted the vulnerability of global supply chains, and many companies are now considering bringing back certain business functions to their home country to ensure greater resilience.

Example I

One of the most famous cases of reshoring in the world is Apple's decision to bring back some of its manufacturing operations to the US. In 2012, Apple announced that it would invest $100 million to bring the production of some of its Mac computers back to the US from China. This move was seen as a significant departure from the company's long-standing strategy of outsourcing manufacturing to low-cost countries.

Apple's decision to reshore some of its manufacturing operations was driven by a combination of factors, including rising labor costs in China, concerns about supply chain disruptions, and a desire to improve the speed and flexibility of its operations. By bringing some of its manufacturing operations back to the US, Apple was able to reduce lead times, increase the speed of innovation, and improve the quality of its products.

However, reshoring was not without its challenges. One of the biggest challenges that Apple faced was finding a skilled workforce to handle the complex manufacturing processes involved in making its products. To address this challenge, Apple partnered with local community colleges and universities to develop training programs that would provide workers with the skills needed to work in its manufacturing facilities.

Apple's decision to reshore some of its manufacturing operations was seen as a positive development by many stakeholders, including US politicians, labor unions, and consumers. It was also seen as a sign that reshoring could be a viable strategy for companies looking to bring jobs back to the US and support local communities. Today, many other companies are also exploring the potential benefits of reshoring, including reduced supply chain risks, increased agility, and a stronger connection to local customers.

Example II

One example of a company that has engaged in reshoring due to the COVID-19 pandemic is the US medical device manufacturer, Boston Scientific.

In early 2020, the company faced supply chain disruptions and shortages due to the pandemic, as many of its suppliers were located in China and other countries that were hit hard by the virus. In response, Boston Scientific began to explore reshoring certain parts of its supply chain to reduce its dependence on offshore suppliers and ensure greater supply chain resilience.

In May 2020, the company announced that it would be investing US$60 million to expand its operations in its home state of Minnesota, including adding manufacturing lines for medical devices that were previously manufactured in China. This decision was driven by the need to ensure a more secure and reliable supply chain, as well as by the company's commitment to supporting local jobs and communities.

Boston Scientific's reshoring efforts have been supported by government incentives, including a grant from Minnesota's Department of Employment and Economic Development. The grant will help to fund the expansion of the company's operations and create up to 1,000 new jobs in the region.

Overall, Boston Scientific's decision to reshore certain parts of its supply chain is a response to the disruptions and uncertainties caused by the COVID-19 pandemic. By bringing certain manufacturing activities closer to home, the company aims to ensure greater supply chain resilience and minimize the risk of future disruptions.

5.2.2   *Nearshoring*

Relocating facilities and services back to the home country is often a short-term solution to address the drawbacks of offshoring and to enhance proximity to the firm's sphere of influence. Such movements can be classified as either backshoring or nearshoring, based on the distance of relocation (Bals et al., 2016).

Nearshoring emerged as a strategic solution for firms that, upon deciding to backshore, found that bringing production facilities back to their home country was not cost-effective due to significant gaps in production costs (Piatanesi & Arauzo-Carod, 2019). Moreover, in some cases, keeping facilities in offshored countries was not practical due to drawbacks related to competitiveness. Therefore, an intermediate solution was necessary, which gave rise to nearshoring. This term was most likely coined by Softtek, a Mexican IT solutions firm, in 1997 (Purkayastha & Samad, 2014). Nearshoring involves relocating previous overseas activities to countries that are closer to the home country, leading to greater control, reduced coordination costs, and shorter time-to-market. The aim is to reduce geographical, cultural, and linguistic distances, making it an intermediate strategy between moving back production facilities and keeping them in the destination country (Piatanesi & Arauzo-Carod, 2019).

Example I

Over the last few decades, the automotive industry has witnessed a noteworthy instance of nearshoring through the relocation of production to Mexico. Renowned automakers like General Motors, Ford, and Volkswagen have set up their production facilities in Mexico, leveraging the benefits of its proximity to the US, affordable labor costs, and favorable trade policies. Moreover, the COVID-19 pandemic has left a significant impact on the global economy and has expedited various strategic trends, including the inclination toward nearshoring.

Mexico's strategic location, just south of the US border, allows automakers to transport finished vehicles and components quickly and efficiently to their primary market, the US. Additionally, Mexico's labor costs are significantly lower than those of the US, while still offering a skilled and experienced workforce. Mexico has also signed several free trade agreements, including the North American Free Trade Agreement and the US-Mexico-Canada Agreement, which have facilitated trade and investment between the three countries.

The shift toward nearshoring in the automotive industry has been driven by several factors, including rising labor costs in traditional manufacturing centers like the US, Europe, and Japan, as well as increasing competition from emerging economies like China and India. By establishing production facilities in Mexico, automakers can reduce their costs while still maintaining close proximity to their primary market and taking advantage of favorable trade agreements.

The automotive industry's move toward nearshoring in Mexico has had a significant impact on the country's economy, creating jobs and driving growth in key regions. It has also helped to strengthen economic ties between Mexico and the US, as well as other countries in the region. While there have been some concerns about the impact of nearshoring on jobs and wages in the US, overall the trend toward nearshoring has been seen as a positive development for the automotive industry and the global economy as a whole.

Example II

One notable case of nearshoring is the decision by electronics giant Samsung to shift some of its manufacturing operations from China to Vietnam. This move was prompted by several factors, including rising labor costs in China and the trade tensions between China and the US.

Samsung has been a major player in the electronics industry for decades and has relied heavily on China for its manufacturing operations. However, as wages in China have increased in recent years, Samsung has faced pressure to reduce costs and maintain its competitiveness.

The company recognized that Vietnam, with its lower labor costs and favorable geographic location, offered a compelling alternative to China. Vietnam is located near major markets in Southeast Asia and has a growing economy that is attracting increasing amounts of foreign investment.

Samsung began investing in Vietnam in the late 2000s and has since expanded its operations significantly. In 2013, the company opened a US$2 billion smartphone factory in the northern province of Thai Nguyen. The factory, which covers an area of over 500,000 square meters, is one of Samsung's largest and most advanced manufacturing facilities.

The shift to Vietnam has not been without its challenges, however. Vietnam's infrastructure is not as well developed as China's, which has made it more difficult for Samsung to transport goods and raw materials. The country's legal system is also less mature, which has created uncertainty for foreign investors.

Despite these challenges, Samsung's nearshoring strategy has been successful thus far. The company has been able to reduce its labor costs while maintaining quality and improving time-to-market. Samsung has also benefited from the favorable business environment in Vietnam, including government incentives and a young, skilled workforce.

The COVID-19 pandemic has also highlighted the benefits of nearshoring for Samsung. As global supply chains were disrupted by the pandemic, the company's manufacturing operations in Vietnam were able to continue without major interruptions. This has given Samsung greater resilience in the face of future disruptions.

Overall, Samsung's nearshoring strategy in Vietnam has been a significant success story. The company has been able to reduce costs, improve efficiency, and maintain its competitive edge in the electronics industry. As other companies consider their own nearshoring strategies, Samsung's experience offers valuable lessons for success in this area.

5.2.3   Rightshoring

Since the 1980s, there have been documented instances of offshoring processes being reversed (Fratocchi et al., 2014). In recent years, there has been a significant push, particularly in the US, to reshore products and services. This has largely been driven by a political platform focused on bringing jobs back home (Tate, 2014). However, research on the location decision has also been conducted in many other countries. Some of this research focuses on bringing jobs back to high-cost environments, which offers an interesting perspective on the issue. As decision-makers weigh the benefits and risks of offshoring, nearshoring, and reshoring, they are finding that the most important factor is to focus on "rightshoring" (Tate & Bals, 2017).

Rightshoring is a strategic approach to SCM that involves determining the optimal location for each step of the production and distribution process based on factors such as cost, quality, efficiency, and customer service. It is a balancing act between offshoring, nearshoring, and reshoring (Hilletofth et al., 2019).

The goal of rightshoring is to achieve the best possible balance between cost and quality by locating production and distribution activities in the most appropriate locations (Joubioux & Vanpoucke, 2016). This may involve offshoring some activities to take advantage of lower labor costs, nearshoring some activities to reduce transportation costs and improve responsiveness, or reshoring some activities to ensure better quality control and intellectual property protection.

The key to successful rightshoring is to carefully analyze the specific requirements of each product or service and determine the best combination of locations and suppliers to meet those requirements (Hilletofth et al., 2019). This requires a deep understanding of the supply chain and the specific factors that affect each step of the process, as well as the ability to adapt to changing market conditions and customer demands.

By focusing on rightshoring, companies can optimize their supply chain operations and gain a competitive advantage in the marketplace (Tate & Bals, 2017). They can reduce costs, improve quality, increase flexibility, and enhance customer service by positioning production and distribution activities in the most appropriate locations. Ultimately, rightshoring helps companies achieve their goals of maximizing profitability and delivering value to customers.

Example I

One of the most famous cases of rightshoring is the decision by Lenovo, the Chinese multinational technology company, to acquire IBM's personal computer business in 2005. This acquisition allowed Lenovo to rightshore its manufacturing and supply chain operations by consolidating its production facilities in China with IBM's facilities in Mexico, Brazil, and Scotland.

Lenovo's decision to rightshore was driven by several factors, including rising labor costs in China, increasing competition from other Asian manufacturers, and a desire to expand its global footprint and customer base. By acquiring IBM's PC business, Lenovo was able to tap into IBM's established global sales and distribution network, while also gaining access to advanced manufacturing technologies and expertise.

Lenovo's rightshoring strategy allowed it to leverage the strengths of each region in its supply chain, while also optimizing costs and improving efficiency. For example, the company continued to manufacture most of its low-end and mid-range products in China, where labor costs were lower, while shifting its higher-end and more complex products to its facilities in Mexico and Brazil, where labor costs were higher but skilled labor was more readily available. In addition, Lenovo was able to take advantage of Scotland's expertise in engineering and design to develop new products and technologies.

Overall, Lenovo's rightshoring strategy has been highly successful, allowing the company to become the world's largest PC manufacturer and expand into new markets around the world. By leveraging the strengths of different regions and optimizing its supply chain operations, Lenovo has been able to stay competitive and drive growth in an increasingly complex and dynamic global business environment.

Example II

One example of rightshoring can be seen in the case of the American appliance manufacturer, Whirlpool Corporation. In 2010, Whirlpool closed down its production facility in Evansville, Indiana, and shifted its production to a plant in Mexico. This decision was made to take advantage of the lower labor costs in Mexico and to remain competitive in the global market.

However, in 2012, Whirlpool decided to rightshore its production back to the US. The company invested US$200 million to retool and expand its facility in Clyde, Ohio, and created 1,000 new jobs in the process. The decision to rightshore was based on several factors, including rising transportation costs, increasing wage rates in Mexico, and the need for quicker response times to customer demands.

By rightshoring, Whirlpool was able to benefit from the advantages of both offshoring and reshoring. The company was able to take advantage of the lower labor costs in Mexico when it needed to but could also bring production back to the US when it made sense to do so. This strategy allowed Whirlpool to remain competitive in the global market while also supporting domestic manufacturing and job creation.

Additionally, rightshoring also allowed Whirlpool to reduce its carbon footprint by reducing the amount of transportation needed to move products from Mexico to the US. This not only reduced transportation costs but also aligned with Whirlpool's sustainability goals.

The case of Whirlpool Corporation demonstrates how rightshoring can be an effective strategy for companies looking to remain competitive in the global market while also supporting domestic manufacturing and job creation. By strategically balancing the advantages of offshoring and reshoring, companies like Whirlpool can achieve greater flexibility, cost savings, and sustainability.

Table 5.1 provides a concise summary of each strategy, its definition, factors driving adoption, and examples of companies implementing the respective strategies.

Table 5.1 Strategies in manufacturing location decision-making

Strategy	Definition	Factors driving adoption	Examples
Reshoring and backshoring	Reversal of offshoring decisions; insourcing and backshoring strategies	• Increase in local labor costs • Unfulfilled savings • Lack of quality • Unavailability of a qualified workforce • Proximity to R&D resources • Utilization of new technology and automation	• Apple's decision to bring back Mac production to the US • Boston Scientific's reshoring efforts due to the COVID-19 pandemic
Nearshoring	Relocating overseas activities to countries closer to the home country	• Cost-effectiveness due to significant gaps in production costs • Drawbacks related to competitiveness in offshored countries	• Automotive industry's nearshoring to Mexico for proximity, labor costs, and trade policies • Samsung's shift from China to Vietnam for lower costs and favorable location
Rightshoring	Strategic approach to SCM; optimal location based on cost, quality, efficiency	• Balancing offshoring, nearshoring, and reshoring • Analyzing product-specific requirements	• Lenovo's acquisition of IBM's PC business for global consolidation • Whirlpool's shift from Mexico to the US for cost savings, flexibility, and sustainability

5.3   Other Emerging Trends

5.3.1   Intelli-sourcing

The term "intelli-sourcing" has recently emerged to describe how companies with the most intelligent sourcing teams achieve the greatest success (Fine, 2013). With a focus on intelli-sourcing, companies need to shift from an either/or approach to offshoring, outsourcing, and reshoring to a both/and decision-making attitude (Arlbjørn & Mikkelsen, 2014; Foerstl et al., 2016). Essential capabilities in an intelli-sourcing framework include local knowledge, access to global partner networks, and the ability to build competitive business relationships (Fine, 2013). The concept of "rightshoring" is related to this approach and refers to achieving the right balance of manufacturing activities between domestic and foreign locations (Stentoft et al., 2016).

5.3.2   Friendshoring

"Friendshoring" is a term used to describe a supply chain strategy where companies seek to partner with suppliers who share a close relationship with them, often characterized by personal connections, shared values, and mutual trust (Gordon, 2023). Friendshoring goes beyond traditional supply chain relationships, which are primarily focused on transactional efficiency and cost savings.

In a friendshoring model, the emphasis is on collaboration, flexibility, and innovation. Companies and their suppliers work together to identify and address challenges, develop new products, and improve processes (Rojas et al., 2022). Friendshoring also involves sharing risk and reward, as companies and their suppliers collaborate to achieve common goals.

While friendshoring provides several benefits, such as improved collaboration and a deeper understanding of supplier capabilities, it may also pose some risks (Gordon, 2023). For example, a close relationship with a supplier may make it challenging to maintain objectivity and negotiate effectively. Additionally, relying on personal connections may limit opportunities to identify new and potentially more competitive suppliers.

5.3.3   Homeshoring

Homeshoring, also known as home-based outsourcing or flexible workforce, is a relatively new alternative to offshoring that involves sending work to low-wage areas within a company's own country, rather than to another country (Crane et al., 2007). This practice is also known as home-based outsourcing or onshoring. Unlike traditional domestic sourcing, homeshoring involves a new relationship between companies and government economic development agencies, which work together to promote economic growth and development in low-wage areas within the country (Crane et al., 2007).

In homeshoring, a process is decoupled from a company's main operations, just as it would be if it were offshored (Duran, 2004). However, instead of outsourcing the work to a foreign country, it is sent to remote workers who work from their homes or other locations within the same country. This allows companies to take advantage of lower labor costs and other advantages without having to deal with the challenges of outsourcing work to another country, such as language barriers, time zone differences, and cultural differences (Crane et al., 2007).

Homeshoring represents a new type of relationship between companies and local economic development agencies that work together to create jobs and support economic growth in low-wage areas (Crane et al., 2007). These agencies provide incentives and support to companies that are willing to invest in these areas, such as tax breaks, infrastructure improvements, and workforce training programs. In return, companies can tap into a skilled and motivated workforce that is eager to work from home and help drive economic growth in their local communities.

Homeshoring can offer several benefits for both employees and companies (Crane et al., 2007). For employees, it can provide greater flexibility in terms of work–life balance, reduced commuting time and expenses, and increased autonomy over their work environment. For companies, homeshoring can lead to cost savings on office space and other overhead expenses, as well as access to a wider pool of talent from around the world.

However, homeshoring also presents some challenges that companies must address to ensure its success (Crane et al., 2007). For example, companies must establish effective communication channels to maintain team cohesion and productivity. Additionally, managers must provide clear guidance and expectations for employees working from home and ensure that they have access to the necessary tools and resources to perform their jobs effectively.

5.3.4   Other Emerging Terms

Numerous terms reflect the evolving landscape of outsourcing and the diverse range of strategies and practices that companies can use to achieve their business objectives. Some additional emerging terms are listed here:

- Co-sourcing: This is a type of outsourcing where companies work with an external partner to share responsibility for a specific business function or process (Koçağa et al., 2015). Co-sourcing provides access to specialized expertise and resources while still allowing companies to retain control over key business operations.
- Multi-sourcing: This is the practice of outsourcing work or services to multiple suppliers, rather than relying on a single supplier (Junjian et al., 2019). Multi-sourcing helps to mitigate risk, increase competition, and provide access to a wider range of expertise and resources (O'Connor et al., 2022).
- Cloud sourcing: This is a type of outsourcing where companies use cloud-based platforms and services to manage and perform key business operations (Schneider & Sunyaev, 2016). Cloud sourcing offers scalability, cost savings, and flexibility, as well as access to advanced technologies and tools.
- Rural sourcing: This is a practice of outsourcing work or services to suppliers located in rural areas within the same country, typically those with lower labor costs and favorable tax incentives (Lacity & Rottman, 2012). Rural sourcing can provide access to a skilled workforce and cost savings while supporting economic development in rural areas.
- Smart sourcing: This is a strategic approach to outsourcing that involves selecting suppliers based on a range of criteria, such as their capabilities, performance, risk profile, and alignment with the company's goals and values (Koulopoulos, 2020). Smart sourcing supports companies to optimize their outsourcing arrangements and achieve better outcomes.

5.4   Emergent Concerns and Future Directions

Emergent concerns and future directions for outsourcing and offshoring trends are shaped by various factors, including the ongoing COVID-19 pandemic, the geopolitical environment, and sustainability considerations.

One of the major emergent concerns for these trends is the impact of the pandemic on global supply chains. The disruptions caused by lockdowns, travel restrictions, and border closures have highlighted the vulnerability of global supply chains and the risks of relying on distant suppliers. As a result, many companies are rethinking their sourcing strategies and exploring alternative options such as nearshoring and rightshoring (Alicke et al., 2021).

Another emerging concern is the geopolitical environment, particularly the growing tensions between the US and China. The trade war and increasing protectionism have led to rising costs and uncertainties for businesses operating in China. This has prompted some companies to consider shifting their production to other countries or reshoring to their home countries.

Sustainability considerations are also becoming more important for reshoring, nearshoring, and rightshoring (Fernández-Miguel et al., 2022). As companies seek to reduce their carbon footprint and minimize the environmental impact of their operations, they are looking for ways to shorten their supply chains and source materials locally. This has led to a growing interest in rightshoring as a way to balance the benefits of offshoring with the environmental and social benefits of sourcing locally.

The future directions for these offshoring trends will likely depend on several factors. First, the ongoing COVID-19 pandemic has shown the vulnerabilities of global supply chains, leading to increased interest in more localized production and supply networks. This interest is likely to continue, with companies looking to shorten their supply chains and increase resilience to disruptions.

Second, technological advancements such as automation and digitalization are likely to continue to play a significant role in shaping these trends (Ha et al., 2022). Companies may increasingly adopt technologies that enable more flexible and efficient production processes, which could reduce the need for outsourcing and offshoring.

Third, sustainability concerns are likely to drive companies to adopt more environmentally-friendly practices, including reducing transportation-related emissions by sourcing materials and producing goods closer to their end markets (Fernández-Miguel et al., 2022).

Fourth, geopolitical factors such as trade policies and regulations will continue to shape the direction of these trends (Roscoe et al., 2022). Changes in trade policies, tariffs, and regulations could either encourage or discourage companies from reshoring or nearshoring.

Finally, changing consumer preferences and demands may also influence the direction of these trends. For example, consumers may increasingly prefer locally produced goods or those with a smaller carbon footprint, which could lead companies to adopt more localized production models.

5.5   MANAGERIAL IMPLICATIONS

The recent trends of reshoring, nearshoring, and rightshoring have significant managerial implications for companies. Here are some of the key implications:

- *Cost considerations*: These trends are often driven by cost considerations, such as rising wages in offshore locations or disruptions in the supply chain due to geopolitical events or natural disasters. Therefore, companies need to carefully analyze the cost structures of their operations and supply chains to determine whether reshoring, nearshoring, or rightshoring is the best option.
- *Emerging technologies*: The implementation of Industry 4.0 technologies such as automation, AI, and the IoT can significantly impact offshoring and outsourcing trends (Akbari et al., 2022). The ability to digitize and streamline operations can make it more cost-effective and efficient to keep production local, leading to a potential decrease in offshoring. However, outsourcing opportunities may still exist for companies that lack the necessary skills and capabilities to implement Industry 4.0 technologies in-house. Therefore, managers must carefully evaluate their company's readiness for Industry 4.0 (Hoyer et al., 2020) and assess how it will impact their offshoring and outsourcing decisions.
- *Flexibility*: The COVID-19 pandemic has highlighted the importance of flexibility in supply chains. Companies need to be able to quickly adapt to changing circumstances, such as disruptions in

transportation, changes in demand, or shifts in government policies. Reshoring, nearshoring, and rightshoring can help companies achieve greater flexibility and reduce their dependence on a single offshore location.

- *Risk management*: Companies need to carefully manage the risks associated with reshoring, nearshoring, and rightshoring. For example, if a company is heavily dependent on a single offshore location, it may face significant risks in the event of a natural disaster or geopolitical event. Therefore, companies need to diversify their operations and supply chains to mitigate these risks.

- *Talent management*: Reshoring, nearshoring, and rightshoring can have implications for talent management. For example, companies may need to hire new employees in different locations or train existing employees to work in new locations. Therefore, companies need to carefully manage their talent pipelines to ensure that they have the skills and expertise needed to succeed in the new location.

- *Regulatory compliance*: Companies need to ensure that they are compliant with local regulations and laws when reshoring, nearshoring, or rightshoring. This can include issues related to taxes, labor laws, environmental regulations, and intellectual property. Therefore, companies need to carefully analyze the regulatory environment in the new location and ensure that they are compliant with all relevant laws and regulations.

The latest trends related to outsourcing and offshoring have far-reaching implications for supply chain firms. As these trends involve significant changes in the location and management of products and services, companies must be careful in evaluating the potential costs, risks, and benefits of adopting them. For example, reshoring may involve higher production costs but may improve quality control, while nearshoring may reduce logistical costs but may require additional efforts to manage cultural and language differences. Similarly, rightshoring may require careful analysis of production costs and market demand to determine the optimal location for production.

These trends highlight the importance of a strategic approach to SCM that considers a range of factors beyond mere cost savings. This requires careful analysis of the firm's internal operations, supply chain partners, and the broader business environment to identify opportunities for optimization and improvement. By taking a holistic approach and considering all available options, firms can achieve a more resilient and efficient supply chain that is better able to adapt to changing market conditions and customer needs.

5.6   SUMMARY AND CONCLUSION

The globalization of the economy has led to the emergence of outsourcing and offshoring as key strategies for businesses to remain competitive. However, recent trends such as reshoring, nearshoring, and rightshoring have challenged the traditional models of outsourcing and offshoring. Reshoring involves bringing back production facilities to the home country, nearshoring involves relocating overseas activities to countries closer to the home country, and rightshoring involves selecting the optimal location for each activity within the global supply chain. These trends have significant managerial implications for supply chain firms.

Reshoring allows firms to increase their geographical proximity to their area of influence, but it can be more costly than traditional offshoring. Nearshoring provides an intermediate solution for firms that are struggling with the disadvantages of wages and production costs in the offshored countries, but it can also have its own drawbacks in terms of cultural and linguistic differences. Rightshoring allows firms to select the optimal location for each activity within the global supply chain based on factors such as cost, quality, and time-to-market, but it requires a thorough analysis of the costs, risks, and opportunities associated with each location.

The COVID-19 pandemic has accelerated these trends, as firms have faced disruptions in their supply chains and have re-evaluated the risks associated with offshoring. Additionally, geopolitical tensions and changing trade policies have made it more difficult for firms to rely on traditional models of offshoring and outsourcing. As a result, firms must carefully analyze the costs and benefits of each option and consider factors such as flexibility, control, and resilience in their supply chains.

References

Akbari, M. (2013). *Factors affecting outsourcing decisions in Iranian industries* (Doctoral thesis). Victoria University, Melbourne, VIC. https://vuir.vu.edu.au/22299/1/Mohammadreza%20Akbari.pdf

Akbari, M. (2018). Logistics outsourcing: A structured literature review. *Benchmarking: An International Journal, 25*(5), 1548–1580. https://doi.org/10.1108/BIJ-04-2017-0066

Akbari, M. (2022). Outsourcing in supply chain management. In J. Sarkis (Ed.), *Handbook of supply chain management—A major reference work* (Chapter 47). Palgrave. https://doi.org/10.1007/978-3-030-89822-9_47-1

Akbari, M. (2023, in press). Revolutionizing supply chain and circular economy with edge computing: Systematic review, research themes and future directions. *Management Decision.* https://doi.org/10.1108/MD-03-2023-0412

Akbari, M., Clarke, S. J., & Maleki Far, S. (2017). *Outsourcing best practice— The case of large construction firms in Iran.* Proceedings of the Informing Science and Information Technology Education Conference, pp. 39–50. From: InSITE 2017: Informing Science and Information Technology Education Conference, 31 July–5 August 2017, Ho Chi Minh City, Vietnam. https://doi.org/10.28945/3737

Akbari, M., Ha, N., & Kok, S. (2022). A systematic review of AR/VR in operations and supply chain management: Maturity, current trends and future directions. *Journal of Global Operations and Strategic Sourcing, 15*(4), 534–565. https://doi.org/10.1108/JGOSS-09-2021-0078

Akbari, M., & Hopkins, J. (2016). The changing business landscape in Iran: Establishing outsourcing best practices. *Operations and Supply Chain Management: An International Journal, 9*(3), 184–197. https://doi.org/10.31387/oscm0250172

Albertoni, F., Elia, S., Massini, S., & Piscitello, L. (2017). The reshoring of business services: Reaction to failure or persistent strategy? *Journal of World Business, 52*(3), 417–430. https://doi.org/10.1016/j.jwb.2017.01.005

Alicke, K., Barriball, E. D., & Trautwein, V. (2021). *How COVID-19 is reshaping supply chains.* McKinsey and Company, 2011 2020. https://www.mckinsey.com/~/media/mckinsey/business%20functions/operations/our%20insights/how%20covid-19%20is%20reshaping%20supply%20chains/how-covid-19-is-reshaping-supply-chains_final.pdf. Accessed 31 March 2023.

Ancarani, A., Mauro, C. D., Fratocchi, L., Orzes, G., & Sartor, M. (2015). Prior to reshoring: A duration analysis of foreign manufacturing ventures. *International Journal of Economics, 169*, 141–155. https://doi.org/10.1016/j.ijpe.2015.07.031

Arlbjørn, J. S., & Lüthje, T. (2012). Global operations and their interaction with supply chain performance. *Industrial Management & Data Systems, 112*(7), 1044–1064. https://doi.org/10.1108/02635571211255014

Arlbjørn, J. S., & Mikkelsen, O. S. (2014). Backshoring manufacturing: Notes on an important but under-researched theme. *Journal of Purchasing & Supply Management, 20*(1), 60–62. https://doi.org/10.1016/j.pursup.2014.02.003

Bals, L., Kirchoff, J. F., & Foerstl, K. (2016). Exploring the reshoring and insourcing decision making process: Toward an agenda for future research. *Operations Management Research, 9*, 102–116. https://doi.org/10.1007/s12063-016-0113-0

Benito, G. R. (2015). Why and how motives (still) matter. *The Multinational Business Review, 23*(1), 15–24. https://doi.org/10.1108/MBR-02-2015-0005

Casson, M., & Wadeson, N. (2013). The economic theory of international supply chains: A systems view. *International Journal of the Economics of Business, 20*(2), 163–186. https://doi.org/10.1080/13571516.2013.783514

Crane, D., Stachura, J., Dalmat, S., King-Matters, K., & Metters, R. (2007). International sourcing of services: The "Homeshoring" alternative. *Service Business, 1*, 79–91. https://doi.org/10.1007/s11628-006-0008-5

Duening, T. N., & Click, R. L. (2005). *Essentials of business process outsourcing.* John Wiley & Sons.

Duong, A. T. B., Hoang, T. H., Nguyen, T. T. B., Akbari, M., Hoang, T. G., & Truong, H. Q. (2023). Supply chain risk assessment in disruptive times: Opportunities and challenges. *Journal of Enterprise Information Management, 36*(5), 1372–1401. https://doi.org/10.1108/JEIM-02-2023-0104

Duran, A. (2004). Lean potential of network-enabled remote service outsourcing: Spatio-temporal decoupling and resource flexibility. *International Journal of Services Technology and Management, 5*(5–6), 448–464. https://doi.org/10.1504/IJSTM.2004.006277

Ellram, L. M., Tate, W. L., & Petersen, K. J. (2013). Offshoring and reshoring: An update on the manufacturing location decision. *Journal of Supply Chain Management, 49*(2), 14–22. https://doi.org/10.1111/jscm.12019

Fernández-Miguel, A., Riccardi, M. P., Veglio, V., García-Muiña, F. E., Fernández del Hoyo, A. P., & Settembre-Blundo, D. (2022). Disruption in resource-intensive supply chains: Reshoring and nearshoring as strategies to enable them to become more resilient and sustainable. *Sustainability, 14*(17), 10909. https://doi.org/10.3390/su141710909

Fine, C. H. (2013). Intelli-sourcing to replace offshoring as supply chain transparency increases. *Journal of Supply Chain Management, 49*(2), 6–7. https://doi.org/10.1111/jscm.2013.49.issue-2

Foerstl, K., Kirchoff, J. F., & Bals, L. (2016). Reshoring and insourcing: Drivers and future research directions. *International Journal of Physical Distribution & Logistics Management, 46*, 492–515. https://doi.org/10.1108/IJPDLM-02-2015-0045

Fratocchi, L., Ancarani, A., Barbieri, P., Di Mauro, C., Nassimbeni, G., Sartor, M., Vignoli, M., & Zanoni, A. (2016). Motivations of manufacturing reshoring: An interpretative framework. *International Journal of Physical Distribution & Logistics Management, 46*(2), 98–127. https://doi.org/10.1108/IJPDLM-06-2014-0131

Fratocchi, L., Di Mauro, C., Barbieri, P., Nassimbeni, G., & Zanoni, A. (2014). When manufacturing moves back: Concepts and questions. *Journal of Purchasing & Supply Management, 20*(1), 54–59. https://doi.org/10.1016/j.pursup.2014.01.004

Gordon, J. (2023). *What friendshoring means for global supply chains.* Raconteur. https://www.raconteur.net/global-business/what-friendshoring-means-for-global-supply-chains/. Accessed 31 March 2023.

Grappi, S., Romani, S., & Bagozzi, R. P. (2018). Reshoring from a demand-side perspective: Consumer reshoring sentiment and its market effects. *Journal of World Business, 53*(2), 194–208. https://doi.org/10.1016/j.jwb.2017.11.001

Gray, J. V., Skowronski, K., Esenduran, G., & Rungtusanatham, M. J. (2013). The reshoring phenomenon: What supply chain academics ought to know and should do. *Journal of Supply Chain Management, 49*(2), 27–33. https://doi.org/10.1111/jscm.12012

Gylling, M., Heikkilä, J., Jussila, K., & Saarinen, M. (2015). Making decisions on offshore outsourcing and backshoring: A case study in the bicycle industry. *International Journal of Production Economics, 162*, 92–100. https://doi.org/10.1016/j.ijpe.2015.01.006

Ha, N. T., Akbari, M., & Au, B. (2022). Last mile delivery in logistics and supply chain management: A bibliometric analysis and future directions. *Benchmarking: An International Journal, 30*(4), 1137–1170. https://doi.org/10.1108/BIJ-07-2021-0409

Hilletofth, P., Eriksson, D., Tate, W., & Kimkel, S. (2019). Right-shoring: Making resilient offshoring and reshoring decisions. *Journal of Purchasing and Supply Management, 25*(3), 100540. https://doi.org/10.1016/j.pursup.2019.100540

Hoyer, C., Gunawan, I., & Reaiche, C. H. (2020). The implementation of Industry 4.0—A systematic literature review of the key factors. *System Research & Behavioral Science, 37*, 557–578. https://doi.org/10.1002/sres.2701

Jahns, C., Hartmann, E., & Bals, L. (2006). Offshoring: Dimensions and diffusion of a new business concept. *Journal of Purchasing and Supply Management, 12*(4), 218–231. https://doi.org/10.1016/j.pursup.2006.10.001

Joubioux, C., & Vanpoucke, E. (2016). Towards right-shoring: A framework for off-and re-shoring decision making. *Operations Management Research, 9*, 117–132. https://doi.org/10.1007/s12063-016-0115-y

Junjian, W., Haiyan, W., & Jennifer, S. (2019). Multi-sourcing and information sharing under competition and supply uncertainty. *European Journal of Operational Research, 278*(2), 658–671. https://doi.org/10.1016/j.ejor.2019.04.039

Kazmer, D. O. (2014). Manufacturing outsourcing, onshoring, and global equilibrium. *Business Horizons, 57*(4), 463–472. https://doi.org/10.1016/j.bushor.2014.03.005

Kedia, B. L., & Mukherjee, D. (2009). Understanding offshoring: A research framework based on disintegration, location and externalization advantages. *Journal of World Business, 44*(3), 250–261. https://doi.org/10.1016/j.jwb.2008.08.005

Kinkel, S., & Maloca, S. (2009). Drivers and antecedents of manufacturing offshoring and backshoring—A German perspective. *Journal of Purchasing & Supply Management, 15*(3), 154–165. https://doi.org/10.1016/j.pursup.2009.05.007

Koçağa, Y. L., Armony, M., & Ward, A. R. (2015). Staffing call centers with uncertain arrival rates and co-sourcing. *Production and Operations Management, 24*, 1101–1117. https://doi.org/10.1111/poms.12332

Koulopoulos, T. (2020). *Reimagining healthcare: How the smartsourcing revolution will drive the future of healthcare and refocus it on what matters most, the patient*. Post Hill Press.

Lacity, M. C., & Rottman, J. (2012). Rural sourcing and impact sourcing. In *Advanced outsourcing practice*. Technology, Work and Globalization. Palgrave Macmillan. https://doi.org/10.1057/9781137005588_7

Leibl, P., Morefield, R., & Pfeiffer, R. (2011). A study of effects of backshoring in the EU. *Journal of Business and Behavioural Science, 23*(2), 72–79. https://www.academia.edu/download/8143019/asbbs_%20proceedings_13th_intl_meeting.pdf#page=72

Mol, M. J. (2007). *Outsourcing: Design, process and performance*. Cambridge University Press.

O'Connor, N. G., Du, Y., Yang, Z., & Akbari, M. (2022). Managing from a distance in international purchasing and supply. *Operations Management Research, 16*, 594–619. https://doi.org/10.1007/s12063-022-00291-7

Piatanesi, B., & Arauzo-Carod, J. M. (2019). Backshoring and nearshoring: An overview. *Growth and Change., 50*, 806–823. https://doi.org/10.1111/grow.12316

Purkayastha, D., & Samad, S. A. (2014). Mexico's Softtek: Success through nearshoring. *The IUP Journal of Operations Management, XIII*(2), 31–52. https://ssrn.com/abstract=2531233

Rojas, M., Routh, A., Sherwood, J., Buckley, J., & Keyal, A. (2022). *Reshoring and "friendshoring" supply chains—Reshaping supply chains to improve economic resilience*. Delloite. https://ibestuur.nl/file_download/618/del oitte-nl-ps-government-trends-2022-executive-summary_compressed+%281% 29.pdf#page=21. Accessed 31 March 2023.

Roscoe, S., Aktas, E., Petersen, K. J., Skipworth, H. D., Handfield, R. B., & Habib, F. (2022). Redesigning global supply chains during compounding geopolitical disruptions: The role of supply chain logics. *International Journal of Operations & Production Management, 42*(9), 1407–1434. https://doi. org/10.1108/IJOPM-12-2021-0777

Schneider, S., & Sunyaev, A. (2016). Determinant factors of cloud-sourcing decisions: Reflecting on the IT outsourcing literature in the era of cloud computing. *Journal of Information Technology, 31*(1), 1–31. https://doi.org/ 10.1057/jit.2014.25

Schniederjans, M. J., Schniederjans, A. M., & Schniederjans, D. G. (2005). *Outsourcing and insourcing in an international context* (1st ed.). Routledge. https://doi.org/10.4324/9781315701936

Srai, J. S., & Ané, C. (2016). Institutional and strategic operations perspectives on manufacturing reshoring. *International Journal of Production Research, 54*(23), 7193–7211. https://doi.org/10.1080/00207543.2016.1193247

Stentoft, J., Mikkelsen, O. S., & Jensen, J. K. (2016). Offshoring and back-shoring manufacturing from a supply chain innovation perspective. *Supply Chain Forum: An International Journal, 17*(4), 190–204. https://doi.org/ 10.1080/16258312.2016.1239465

Tate, W. L. (2014). Offshoring and reshoring: US insights and research challenges. *Journal of Purchasing and Supply Management, 20*(1), 66–68. https://doi.org/10.1016/j.pursup.2014.01.007

Tate, W. L., & Bals, L. (2017). Outsourcing/offshoring insights: Going beyond reshoring to rightshoring. *International Journal of Physical Distribution & Logistics Management, 47*(2/3), 106–113. https://doi.org/10.1108/ IJPDLM-11-2016-0314

Tate, W. L., Ellram, L. M., Schoenherr, T., & Petersen, K. J. (2014). Global competitive conditions driving the manufacturing location decision. *Business Horizons, 57*(3), 381–390. https://doi.org/10.1016/j.bushor.2013.12.010

CHAPTER 6

Sustainable Outsourcing: Managing Global Responsibilities

6.1 Introduction

In the ever-evolving landscape of modern business, the imperative for sustainability is increasingly evident, placing substantial pressure on supply chains to operate responsibly across environmental, economic, and societal dimensions (Kane et al., 2021). Sustainability is defined as the "ability to meet the needs of the present without compromising the ability of future generations to meet their own needs" (World Commission on Environment and Development [WCED], 1987, p. 43). Sustainability in the supply chain seamlessly integrates environmentally conscious and socially responsible practices from sourcing to distribution. This involves selecting ethically sound suppliers and materials, optimizing energy usage with eco-friendly technologies, reducing waste through recycling and responsible packaging, ensuring fair labor practices and community engagement, maintaining transparency in product origins and impacts, adhering to regulations, and conducting thorough life cycle assessments (Akbari & McClelland, 2020). This comprehensive approach aims to create a responsible, well-balanced supply chain that not only meets current needs but also safeguards the environment and society, fostering a commitment to minimizing adverse impacts while promoting long-term resilience and vitality (Kane et al., 2021).

The supply chain is compelled to integrate sustainable practices into its business processes due to new regulations, heightened competition,

M. Akbari, *The Road to Outsourcing 4.0*, https://doi.org/10.1007/978-981-97-2708-7_6

and substantial pressure from stakeholders (Fiorini & Jabbour, 2017). Numerous studies highlight an increased emphasis on and adoption of sustainable codes of conduct for performance measurement purposes, as illustrated in Fig. 6.1 (Akbari & McClelland, 2020; Dubey et al., 2017). These developments underscore a growing recognition of the imperative to incorporate sustainability metrics as a critical aspect of SCM.

Recognizing the complexities and potential limitations within their own capabilities, numerous firms opt to outsource sustainability efforts to external organizations. This strategic move is not only a pragmatic response to a dynamic global market but also a recognition that sustainability cannot be singularly achieved within the confines of individual companies (Adams et al., 2016).

> Only if we treat nature with respect & care can we, as a society, survive in the long term.—Hans Carl von Carlowitz (1645–1714)

The outsourcing landscape's acknowledgment of sustainability as a competitive necessity is underscored by the realization that supply chain companies cannot afford to operate devoid of eco-friendly and socially responsible practices (Ma et al., 2023). Stakeholders, be they customers, investors, or the wider public, are increasingly vocal about their expectations regarding ethical, environmental, and social considerations (Kane

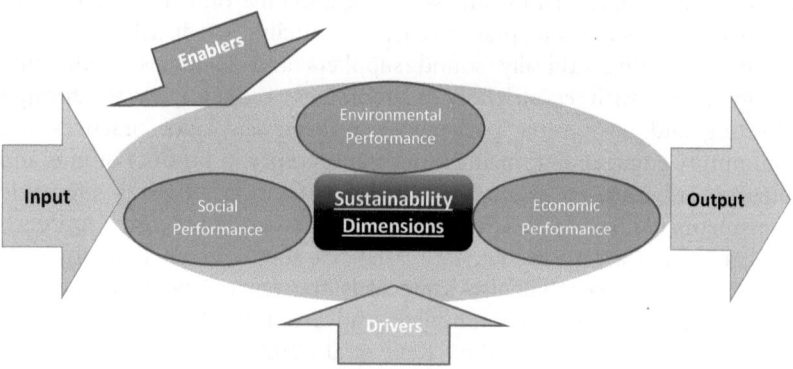

Fig. 6.1 Sustainable practices in supply chain management (*Source* Author's own work—Adapted from Akbari and McClelland [2020] and Dubey et al. [2017])

et al., 2021). This has led to a scenario where sustainability becomes a corporate initiative and a shared responsibility spanning the entire supply chain (Akbari & McClelland, 2020).

A compelling illustration of this symbiotic relationship between sustainability and outsourcing can be found in the case of tech giant Apple. In 2012, Apple faced substantial pressure to confront working conditions in its suppliers' plants, particularly at Foxconn, due to concerns raised by stakeholders through social media (Mendoza & Clemen, 2013). Demonstrating a proactive stance on sustainability, Apple forged a partnership with the Fair Labor Association for a voluntary review, signaling a pivotal moment where sustainability became an integral aspect of stakeholder expectations.

This trend is not unique to Apple; other industry giants such as Walmart, Nike, and Adidas have also embarked on journeys to enhance their sustainability performances (Plambeck et al., 2012). The outsourcing of sustainability efforts, in these instances, reflects a strategic response to the evolving demands of a socially and environmentally conscious consumer base.

The incorporation of environmental measures introduces an additional layer of complication to the already intricate global supply chain dynamics (Yang et al., 2021). The intricate nature of regulatory environmental policies becomes apparent when considering divergent approaches, as exemplified by measures like the carbon tax. Governments worldwide, starting with Finland in 1990, have been imposing carbon taxes on companies, aiming to offset greenhouse gas emissions (Carl & Fedor, 2016). Consequently, manufacturers facing higher local carbon taxes often choose to outsource certain functions, thereby reducing emissions within their home countries. The interplay between government policies, corporate strategies, and outsourcing decisions highlights the need for a comprehensive and collaborative approach to sustainability (Akbari, 2022).

Moreover, as customer awareness of sustainable practices grows, their preferences become pivotal in shaping the decisions of both businesses and governments (Yang et al., 2021). Governments, as such, carry the responsibility of implementing strategic measures, such as targeted campaigns promoting low-carbon practices, to elevate customer awareness and drive sustainable practices across industries (Yang et al., 2021).

In essence, the symbiotic relationship between sustainability and outsourcing is reshaping the landscape of global supply chains (Akbari &

Hopkins, 2022). As stakeholders increasingly demand responsible practices, companies are not only outsourcing sustainability efforts but also recognizing the intrinsic value of integrating sustainability into their core business strategies. This evolution is not only a response to market dynamics but a testament to the fundamental shift toward a more responsible and sustainable future (Adams et al., 2016).

Within the context of this chapter, a comprehensive exploration unfolds regarding the evolving dynamics between sustainability and outsourcing in the global business ecosystem. As supply chains grapple with heightened expectations from stakeholders to operate responsibly, the intricate interplay between economic considerations, social responsibility, and environmental stewardship is delved into. The outsourcing landscape takes center stage, not only for operational efficiency but as a strategic avenue for companies to navigate the complexities of sustainability initiatives. Real-world examples are drawn upon to analyze the symbiotic relationship between outsourcing decisions and the growing demands of an increasingly conscious consumer base. Additionally, an examination is conducted into the incorporation of environmental measures and regulatory policies, such as carbon tax, showcasing how these factors contribute to the evolving complexity of global supply chains. Ultimately, this chapter unfolds as a journey through the intricate intersections of business strategy, stakeholder expectations, and the imperative for sustainability, offering insights into how organizations can navigate this landscape to forge a responsible and resilient future.

6.2   Current Practices

As organizations increasingly recognize the imperative of sustainability, the realm of outsourcing has become a strategic frontier for navigating the complex interplay between economic efficiency, social responsibility, and environmental stewardship (Montiel & Delgado-Ceballos, 2014). In this exploration of current practices in sustainable outsourcing, we delve into real-world examples that highlight the evolving landscape and showcase how companies strategically respond to the demands of stakeholders and the imperative for sustainability.

6.2.1 Economic Efficiency and Sustainable Outsourcing

Economic efficiency has long been a cornerstone of outsourcing strategies, focusing on optimizing costs and operational processes (Stevens & Johnson, 2016). In the contemporary business landscape, however, the lens through which economic efficiency is viewed has broadened to encompass a more holistic understanding that integrates sustainability principles. Companies recognize that economic viability cannot be divorced from environmental and social considerations (Akbari & Hopkins, 2022).

Example I

Unilever, a pioneering force in sustainable business practices, exemplifies the integration of economic efficiency and sustainability. Through its Sustainable Living Plan, Unilever commits to sourcing raw materials responsibly, reducing its environmental footprint, and improving the social impact of its operations. In the context of outsourcing, Unilever strategically partners with suppliers who align with these sustainability goals. This integration not only enhances economic efficiency by ensuring a resilient and responsible supply chain but also contributes to the company's overall commitment to sustainable business practices.

Example II

IKEA, a global leader in the furniture retail sector, has taken economic efficiency in outsourcing a step further by investing in renewable energy for its suppliers. Recognizing that energy costs are a significant component of the overall production expenses, IKEA's strategic move not only optimizes economic efficiency but also aligns with broader sustainability objectives. By fostering a supply chain powered by renewable energy, the company contributes to reducing its carbon footprint while fortifying the economic sustainability of its operations.

In essence, the integration of economic efficiency and sustainable outsourcing represents a paradigm shift, where companies leverage responsible business practices not as an added cost but as a strategic investment in long-term operational resilience and environmental stewardship (Settembre-Blundo et al., 2021). This approach recognizes that economic success is intertwined with sustainability, with the two serving as mutually reinforcing pillars of organizational resilience and success.

6.2.2   Social Responsibility in Outsourcing

In the landscape of contemporary business, the integration of social responsibility into outsourcing practices has emerged as a critical imperative. Social responsibility encompasses a commitment to ethical and fair treatment of workers, community engagement, and a broader recognition of the societal impact of business operations (Taghipour et al., 2022). Companies are increasingly attuned to the fact that their outsourcing decisions can have profound social ramifications, and stakeholders, ranging from customers to investors, are demanding greater accountability in this regard (Taghipour et al., 2022).

Example I

Nike, a global leader in the sportswear industry, provides a poignant example of a company actively addressing social responsibility within its outsourcing practices. In response to intense scrutiny over labor conditions in its supply chain, particularly at suppliers like Foxconn, Nike initiated comprehensive measures to improve working conditions. By collaborating closely with outsourcing partners and emphasizing fair wages and safe working environments, Nike not only addressed ethical concerns but also positioned itself as a socially responsible corporate entity. This strategic alignment with social responsibility is not just a reactive response to public scrutiny; it is a proactive stance toward fostering a supply chain that respects human rights and fair labor practices.

Example II

H&M, a prominent fashion retailer, similarly underscores the integration of social responsibility into outsourcing decisions. Committed to fair living wages for workers within its supply chain, H&M actively engages with its outsourcing partners to ensure compliance with ethical labor standards. This exemplifies a broader trend where companies recognize that social responsibility is not merely a corporate responsibility but a fundamental aspect of sustainable outsourcing. By embedding ethical considerations into their outsourcing practices, these companies contribute to creating a more equitable and socially conscious global business environment.

Essentially, social responsibility in outsourcing extends beyond compliance with regulations; it represents a strategic commitment to fostering positive social impact all over the supply chain network (Stahl et al., 2020). As companies increasingly prioritize ethical considerations in their outsourcing decisions, they not only mitigate risks associated with labor practices but also contribute to developing a more socially equitable and responsible global business ecosystem.

6.2.3   Environmental Stewardship and Outsourcing

Environmental stewardship within the realm of outsourcing has evolved into a paramount consideration for businesses seeking to align their operations with sustainability principles (Fisher et al., 2012). Acknowledging the profound impact that supply chains can have on the environment, companies are integrating eco-friendly practices and initiatives into their outsourcing strategies (Khan et al., 2023). This entails not only minimizing the environmental footprint of their operations but actively contributing to broader ecological goals and conservation efforts.

Example I

Google, a trailblazer in technology, exemplifies a commitment to environmental stewardship in its outsourcing practices. The company has set ambitious sustainability goals, vowing to operate entirely on renewable energy. This commitment extends to its outsourcing partnerships, where Google prioritizes suppliers that adhere to green practices. By doing so, Google not only fulfills its environmental responsibilities but also fosters a supply chain that is in harmony with broader ecological objectives. This integration of environmental stewardship into outsourcing decisions reflects a proactive approach to sustainability that goes beyond mere compliance.

Example II

Walmart, a global retail giant, has embarked on sustainable sourcing practices, setting ambitious goals to achieve zero net emissions across its supply chain by 2040. This initiative underscores a comprehensive commitment to environmental stewardship in outsourcing. Walmart actively engages with suppliers, fostering a collaborative approach to reduce the carbon footprint associated with its products. This exemplifies how environmental considerations are woven into the fabric of outsourcing decisions, shaping not only immediate operational concerns but also long-term sustainability objectives.

Fundamentally, incorporating environmental stewardship into outsourcing practices represents a paradigm shift toward recognizing that business operations must align with ecological sustainability (Fisher et al., 2012). Companies are not only reducing their own environmental impact but leveraging their influence to catalyze the establishment of a more sustainable and ecologically conscious supply chain (Khan et al., 2023). This strategic alignment with environmental goals positions businesses as responsible stewards of the planet, contributing to a collective effort to address pressing environmental challenges.

6.2.4   Collaborative Initiatives and Industry Standards

Collaborative initiatives and adherence to industry standards have become integral to shaping responsible business practices. Recognizing that sustainability is a collective endeavor that extends beyond individual companies, collaborative efforts bring together industry stakeholders to establish common frameworks, share best practices, and foster a collective commitment to ethical, social, and environmental responsibilities (Voegtlin & Scherer, 2017).

Example I

The Sustainable Apparel Coalition (SAC) stands out as a powerful example of industry collaboration. Comprising major apparel and footwear companies, including Adidas and Levi Strauss, SAC's mission is to improve supply chain sustainability collectively. Members collaborate on developing standardized assessment tools, best practices, and industry benchmarks. Through the SAC, companies pool resources and expertise to address shared challenges, fostering a united front toward sustainable outsourcing practices. This collaborative approach not only benefits individual companies but contributes to raising sustainability standards across the entire industry.

Example II

In the technology sector, the Responsible Business Alliance (RBA) serves as a conduit for industry-wide collaboration. Members, such as Apple and Intel, unite under the RBA to promote responsible business practices, including ethical labor and environmental sustainability. The RBA facilitates sharing insights, tools, and strategies to enhance responsible outsourcing practices. This collaborative initiative ensures a more comprehensive and consistent approach to sustainability across the technology industry.

Fundamentally, collaborative initiatives in sustainable outsourcing underscore the recognition that the challenges of sustainability are best tackled collectively (Voegtlin & Scherer, 2017). By aligning with industry standards and engaging in collaborative efforts, companies not only benefit from shared knowledge but contribute to establishing a collective ethos of responsibility. This collaborative paradigm is fundamental to raising the bar for sustainability practices, fostering innovation, and driving positive change throughout the outsourcing ecosystem (Sardá & Pogutz, 2018).

6.2.5   Technological Innovation and Sustainable Outsourcing

In the dynamic landscape of contemporary business, technological innovation has emerged as a transformative force in the realm of sustainable outsourcing. Businesses are increasingly leveraging cutting-edge technologies to not only optimize operational efficiency but also integrate sustainability principles into their core strategies (Garg & Sharma, 2020). This fusion of technology and sustainability is reshaping outsourcing practices, introducing innovative solutions that minimize environmental impact, enhance transparency, and foster responsible business operations (Kantaros et al., 2022).

Example I

Cloud computing for sustainable operations: A prominent example of technological innovation in sustainable outsourcing is the widespread adoption of cloud computing. Companies such as Amazon Web Services (AWS) have pioneered sustainable cloud solutions. AWS, a major player in cloud computing, has committed to operating its data centers entirely on renewable energy. By choosing cloud providers with robust sustainability practices, organizations not only optimize their operations but also contribute to the broader goal of reducing the carbon footprint associated with data storage and processing.

Example II

Blockchain for enhanced transparency: Blockchain technology has emerged as a catalyst for enhancing transparency in supply chains. IBM, a global technology company, has harnessed blockchain to provide end-to-end visibility into supply chain processes. This innovation ensures traceability and accountability, particularly in industries like food and fashion, where consumers increasingly demand information about the origin and sustainability of products. By leveraging blockchain in outsourcing relationships, companies promote transparency and ethical sourcing practices.

In the realm of sustainable outsourcing, technological innovation is more than just a tool for operational efficiency; it is a transformative force. Companies at the forefront of adopting these innovations aren't just securing the future of their operations—they are actively sculpting a technological landscape that champions environmental responsibility and ethical business practices.

6.2.6　Regulatory Compliance and Risk Management

In the intricate tapestry of sustainable outsourcing, regulatory compliance and robust risk management practices stand as linchpins, ensuring that organizations navigate the complex landscape with ethical integrity and operational resilience (Tafti, 2005). The regulatory environment, characterized by a myriad of laws and standards, necessitates a strategic approach to compliance, while risk management becomes imperative in mitigating potential disruptions and safeguarding the long-term viability of outsourcing relationships (Dhillon et al., 2017).

Example I

General Data Protection Regulation (GDPR) compliance in data processing: The GDPR in the European Union serves as a prominent illustration of the critical intersection between regulatory compliance and outsourcing practices. Companies engaging in outsourcing relationships that involve processing personal data must meticulously adhere to GDPR guidelines. Robust compliance mechanisms not only shield organizations from legal ramifications but also fortify the privacy rights of individuals. This strategic alignment with regulatory standards showcases a proactive approach to ethical outsourcing practices.

Example II

California Transparency in Supply Chains Act: For companies with global supply chains, regulatory compliance extends to addressing issues of social responsibility. The California Transparency in Supply Chains Act requires businesses to disclose efforts aimed at eradicating slavery and human trafficking from their direct supply chains. Intel, a technology giant, exemplifies a commitment to compliance by implementing comprehensive due diligence processes. By actively engaging in risk management strategies, Intel ensures that its outsourcing relationships align with regulatory standards, mitigating the risk of unethical practices in the supply chain.

At its core, the collaboration between regulatory compliance and risk management forms the bedrock of sustainable outsourcing practices (Tafti, 2005). This partnership not only shields organizations from legal complexities but also nurtures a business culture where ethical considerations hold utmost importance. Companies that place equal emphasis on compliance and risk management lay a sturdy groundwork for responsible outsourcing, underscoring their unwavering commitment to ethical conduct and resilience in the face of potential challenges (Dhillon et al., 2017).

6.2.7 Global Supply Chain Resilience

In today's global business, the concept of supply chain resilience has risen to prominence, underscored by the recognition that disruptions are inevitable and that a robust supply chain must withstand and adapt to unforeseen challenges (Herold et al., 2021). This resilience is not merely about bouncing back from disruptions but entails proactively building capacities to navigate uncertainties, ensuring continuity, and fostering adaptability in the face of global dynamics (Aldrighetti et al., 2021).

Example I

Apple's diversification strategy: The disruptions affected by the COVID-19 pandemic highlighted the significance of global supply chain resilience. Apple, a technology giant, responded by diversifying its sourcing strategies. Recognizing the vulnerability of a concentrated supply chain, Apple strategically invested in local suppliers to reduce dependencies on specific regions. This proactive approach not only mitigated disruptions but also exemplified a commitment to building a resilient and diversified supply chain capable of navigating unforeseen challenges.

Example II

Automotive industry's agility: The automotive industry provides another compelling example of global supply chain resilience. The sector faced disruptions due to semiconductor shortages, impacting production schedules. Automotive companies responded by fostering agility within their supply chains. Rather than being solely reliant on a fixed set of suppliers, they embraced a more flexible approach, identifying alternative sources for critical components. This adaptive strategy showcased the industry's commitment to resilience, preventing disruptions in the supply chain from causing a chain reaction of problems.

To summarize, Fig. 6.2 delineates the prevailing trends in sustainable outsourcing.

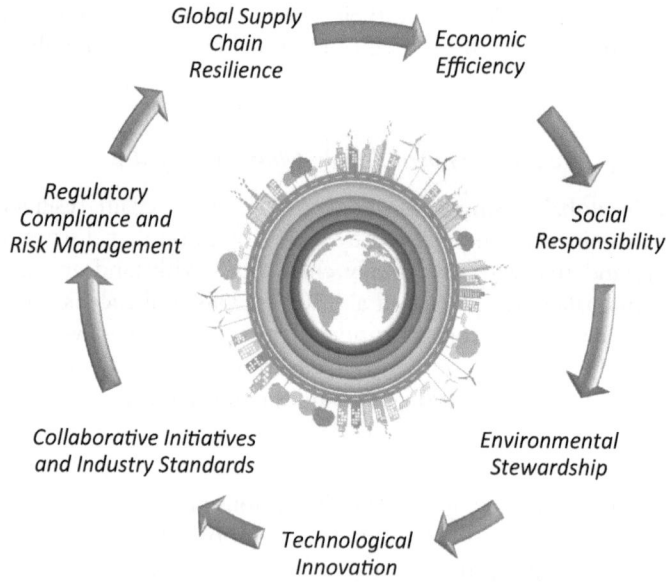

Fig. 6.2   Current trends in sustainable outsourcing (*Source* Author's own work)

Essentially, global supply chain resilience extends beyond merely enduring disruptions; it necessitates strategic planning, adaptability, and a forward-thinking mindset (Herold et al., 2021). Companies prioritizing resilience understand that disruptions are not anomalies but intrinsic elements of the global business landscape. Nurturing a resilient supply chain enables organizations not just to weather shocks but to prosper amid uncertainty, showcasing a steadfast commitment to sustained success in a constantly evolving world (Aldrighetti et al., 2021).

6.3   Other Emerging Trends

As the landscape of sustainable outsourcing continues to evolve, several emerging trends are reshaping the way businesses approach and implement their outsourcing strategies. These trends not only respond to the pressing challenges of the present but also anticipate the future demands of an increasingly complex and interconnected global business environment.

6.3.1   Circular Economy Integration

One of the emerging trends in sustainable outsourcing is the integration of circular economy principles. Traditionally, the linear economy model, characterized by a take-make-dispose approach, dominated business practices. However, the circular economy promotes the idea of a closed-loop system, where resources are reused, refurbished, remanufactured, and recycled (Akbari, 2023). This trend is gaining traction as companies recognize the potential to minimize waste and maximize resource efficiency throughout the entire product life cycle (Awan et al., 2021).

In the realm of outsourcing, businesses are beginning to demand circularity from their partners. This includes not only sustainable sourcing of raw materials but also a commitment to designing products for longevity, facilitating ease of repair, and ensuring responsible end of life disposal (Kiørboe, 2015; Rissman et al., 2020). By integrating circular economy principles into outsourcing practices, companies contribute to a more sustainable and resilient supply chain while meeting the expectations of environmentally conscious consumers (Akbari, 2022).

6.3.2   *Artificial Intelligence for Sustainable Decision-Making*

The advent of AI is transforming various aspects of business operations, and sustainable outsourcing is no exception (Di Vaio et al., 2020). AI technologies, including ML and data analytics, are increasingly being employed to optimize decision-making processes in the outsourcing domain (Tetrick, 2023). From SCM to vendor selection, AI-driven algorithms can analyze vast datasets to identify patterns, predict outcomes, and recommend sustainable practices (Akbari & Do, 2021).

For instance, AI can assist in assessing the environmental impact of different sourcing options, helping organizations make decisions that align with their sustainability goals (Zhao & Gómez Fariñas, 2023). Additionally, AI-powered analytics can enhance transparency by tracking and reporting key sustainability metrics throughout the supply chain (Attaran, 2020). This data-driven approach not only facilitates better decision-making but also enables companies to demonstrate and communicate their sustainability efforts more effectively.

6.3.3   *Ethical AI in Outsourcing*

As AI becomes more integrated into outsourcing processes, there is a growing emphasis on ensuring that these technologies are deployed ethically (Lo Piano, 2020). Ethical AI in outsourcing involves considering the social and environmental implications of AI applications. This includes addressing concerns related to bias, transparency, accountability, and the ethical treatment of workers in the development and deployment of AI technologies.

Companies engaged in sustainable outsourcing are increasingly incorporating ethical considerations into their AI strategies. This includes conducting ethical impact assessments, promoting diversity and inclusion in AI development teams, and ensuring that AI applications align with broader ethical and sustainability principles (Ryan & Stahl, 2020). By championing ethical AI in outsourcing, organizations not only mitigate potential risks but also contribute to developing responsible and socially conscious AI technologies.

6.3.4   *Reshoring and Nearshoring Strategies*

The disruptions caused by events such as geopolitical tensions, natural disasters, pandemic, and economic recessions have prompted a re-evaluation of global supply chain strategies (Akbari & Hopkins, 2022). A trend emerging in response to these disruptions is the reconsideration of offshoring in favor of reshoring and nearshoring (Akbari, 2022). Reshoring involves bringing production and sourcing activities back to the domestic or nearby markets, reducing dependence on distant and potentially vulnerable suppliers.

Reshoring and nearshoring strategies align with sustainability goals by minimizing the environmental impact associated with long-distance transportation and reducing the overall carbon footprint of the supply chain (Millar, 2015). Proximity to suppliers also facilitates better oversight of ethical and environmental practices. While reshoring and nearshoring may not be suitable for every industry, businesses are increasingly exploring these strategies as a means of enhancing supply chain resilience and sustainability (Choudhary et al., 2023).

6.3.5   *Blockchain for Transparency and Traceability*

Blockchain technology continues to gain prominence as a robust tool for enhancing transparency and traceability in supply chains (Nguyen et al., 2023). In the context of sustainable outsourcing, blockchain can provide an immutable and transparent record of every transaction and interaction within the supply chain (Aslam et al., 2021). This level of transparency is crucial for verifying the authenticity of sustainable practices, ensuring responsible sourcing, and building trust among consumers and stakeholders.

For example, in the food and fashion industries, blockchain can be used to trace the origin of products, presenting consumers with relevant information regarding the production processes, sourcing of materials, and adherence to sustainability standards (Agrawal et al., 2021). Through the utilization of blockchain, organizations can enhance the credibility of the sustainability assertions linked to their products and outsourcing practices.

6.3.6   Focus on Social Impact Outsourcing

The concept of social impact outsourcing goes beyond traditional corporate social responsibility initiatives. It involves integrating social impact goals directly into outsourcing strategies, thereby aligning business operations with broader societal and environmental objectives. Social impact outsourcing encompasses initiatives such as creating employment opportunities for marginalized communities, supporting fair labor practices, and contributing to community development (Nicholson et al., 2016).

Companies are increasingly recognizing the potential of social impact outsourcing not only to fulfill ethical responsibilities but also as a source of competitive advantage. Integrating social impact goals into outsourcing decisions allows organizations to have a positive influence on the communities in which they operate. This not only enhances their brand reputation but also helps to foster stronger relationships with socially conscious consumers.

6.3.7   Green Finance for Sustainable Outsourcing

Green finance is becoming instrumental in steering organizations toward sustainable outsourcing practices. Through instruments like sustainable bonds and loans, companies can secure funding expressly for environmentally and socially responsible initiatives within their outsourcing strategies (Li & Umair, 2023). The concept operates on the principle of incentivizing eco-friendly practices, with organizations showcasing sustainability commitments and gaining access to favorable financial terms (Li & Umair, 2023). Investors, emphasizing ESG metrics, are influencing the adoption of green finance, aligning their portfolios with socially responsible companies engaged in sustainable outsourcing. Collaborative efforts with sustainable financial institutions are also on the rise, tailoring financial solutions that specifically support outsourcing sustainability goals. Strategically allocating green funds to enhance energy efficiency, sustainable sourcing, and other eco-conscious initiatives, organizations are leveraging green finance to reinforce their commitment to responsible, sustainable, and socially conscious business practices.

6.4   Emergent Concerns and Future Directions

As sustainable outsourcing evolves in response to global dynamics, emerging concerns and future directions come to the forefront, shaping the trajectory of responsible business practices. Addressing these concerns and navigating future trends are critical for organizations committed to embedding sustainability into their outsourcing strategies.

6.4.1   Climate Change and Environmental Impact

An emergent concern in sustainable outsourcing is the escalating impact of climate change and the associated environmental risks (Jorgenson et al., 2022). Companies are grappling with the need to align outsourcing decisions with climate action goals. From the carbon footprint of supply chains to the sustainable sourcing of materials, organizations are increasingly under pressure to mitigate environmental impacts (Kannan et al., 2022). Future directions entail a more robust integration of environmental considerations into outsourcing strategies, leveraging innovations such as blockchain for transparent and traceable supply chains and embracing circular economy principles to minimize waste.

6.4.2   Ethical Labor Practices and Social Responsibility

As awareness of ethical labor practices grows, concerns regarding fair wages, working conditions, and workers' rights within the outsourcing ecosystem are coming to the forefront (Ang, 2015). Future directions involve a heightened focus on social responsibility, not just in terms of compliance but as an integral part of outsourcing decisions. Companies are expected to conduct thorough due diligence on the ethical practices of their outsourcing partners, fostering a culture of fair labor and human rights (Babin & Nicholson, 2012). Technology, including AI, can play a role in monitoring and ensuring ethical labor practices throughout the supply chain.

6.4.3   Resilience to Global Disruptions and Regionalization

The COVID-19 pandemic has underscored the vulnerability of global supply chains to unforeseen disruptions (Akbari, 2023). Future directions in sustainable outsourcing involve a strategic shift toward enhancing resilience. This includes diversifying sourcing strategies, adopting technologies for real-time monitoring and adaptability, and exploring regionalization or nearshoring to reduce dependence on distant suppliers (Akbari, 2022). Resilience becomes a key consideration, not only for risk management but also for ensuring continuous operations with minimal environmental impact during crises.

6.4.4   Biodiversity Preservation and Ecosystem Impact

The depletion of biodiversity and the impact on ecosystems are emerging concerns within sustainable outsourcing. Organizations are recognizing the need to assess and address the biodiversity implications of their outsourcing decisions, especially in industries with significant environmental footprints. Future directions involve incorporating biodiversity impact assessments into sourcing strategies, promoting sustainable practices that safeguard ecosystems, and engaging in conservation initiatives (Hughes et al., 2023). Companies are expected to take a proactive stance on preserving biodiversity, not only as a regulatory requirement but as a fundamental aspect of responsible outsourcing.

6.4.5   Data Privacy, Cybersecurity, and Transparency

As outsourcing involves the exchange of vast amounts of sensitive data, data privacy and cybersecurity are becoming critical concerns. Future directions involve stringent measures to ensure the protection of customer data, intellectual property, and sensitive business information (Benaroch, 2020). Organizations will need to incorporate robust cybersecurity protocols into their outsourcing agreements, conduct regular audits, and stay abreast of evolving data protection regulations globally. Ensuring data privacy and cybersecurity will be paramount to building trust with customers and stakeholders (Nguyen et al., 2023).

6.4.6   Global Environmental Policies and Carbon Tax Impact

The incorporation of environmental measures, such as carbon taxes and similar regulatory policies, contributes to the intricacy of the global supply chain (Babagolzadeh et al., 2020). Governments imposing carbon taxes to compensate for greenhouse gas emissions incentivize manufacturers to reduce local production and outsource functions. This results in a reduction of home country emissions. Additionally, customer awareness of sustainable practices positively impacts emission reduction. Governments should strategically introduce measures like low-carbon awareness campaigns to raise customer awareness and contribute to overall sustainability goals (Yang et al., 2021).

In summary, sustainable outsourcing stands at a critical juncture, necessitating the proactive resolution of emerging challenges and the adoption of forward-looking strategies. The infusion of environmental, social, and ethical factors into outsourcing approaches serves not only to mitigate risks but also positions organizations for success in a future where sustainability is an indispensable facet of achievement. As enterprises traverse this terrain, their capacity to adapt, innovate, and systematically address emerging concerns emerges as pivotal in sculpting a sustainable and responsible outsourcing ecosystem.

6.5   MANAGERIAL IMPLICATIONS

As organizations increasingly recognize the imperative of integrating sustainability into their outsourcing strategies, there are profound managerial implications that guide decision-making and operations. These implications extend beyond mere compliance, urging managers to adopt a proactive stance on environmental, social, and ethical considerations. Here are key managerial implications that pave the way for responsible and sustainable outsourcing.

- Strategic Alignment with Corporate Values: Managers play a pivotal role in aligning outsourcing decisions with the core values and mission of the corporation (Duhamel et al., 2021). Beyond the pursuit of cost savings, sustainability should be embedded as a fundamental criterion in the outsourcing decision-making process. This requires a strategic re-evaluation of suppliers, taking into account their environmental practices, labor standards, and overall commitment to responsible business conduct (Duhamel et al., 2021). By ensuring that outsourcing partners align with the organization's values, managers contribute to building a supply chain that reflects and reinforces the company's commitment to sustainability.
- Risk Management and Resilience Planning: In the face of global disruptions, effective risk management becomes a crucial aspect of sustainable outsourcing (Shoushtari & Ghafourian, 2023). Managers

should proactively assess the vulnerabilities in the supply chain, considering environmental, geopolitical, and social factors. This involves diversifying suppliers, adopting a regionalized approach, and incorporating flexibility into contractual agreements to enhance resilience (König & Spinler, 2016). By incorporating risk management strategies, managers not only mitigate the impact of disruptions but also contribute to the overall sustainability and longevity of the outsourcing relationships.

- Integration of Technology for Transparency: Technology, particularly blockchain and data analytics, plays a pivotal role in ensuring transparency and traceability within the supply chain. Managers should prioritize the integration of such technologies to monitor and verify sustainability claims made by outsourcing partners. Blockchain, for instance, can provide an immutable record of every transaction, offering a transparent view of the supply chain (Agrawal et al., 2021). By leveraging technology for transparency, managers enhance the credibility of sustainability efforts, build trust with stakeholders, and actively contribute to responsible business practices (Agrawal et al., 2021).

- Talent Management and Skill Development: Sustainable outsourcing demands a workforce equipped with the skills and knowledge to navigate complex environmental and ethical considerations (Shikweni et al., 2019). Managers need to invest in talent management and skill development programs that empower employees to understand and implement sustainability practices in outsourcing (Kok & Akbari, 2023). This may involve training programs on ethical sourcing, environmental impact assessments, and social responsibility within the supply chain. By fostering a culture of continuous learning, managers ensure that the workforce is well prepared to contribute to and execute sustainable outsourcing strategies.

- Collaboration and Stakeholder Engagement: Sustainable outsourcing transcends organizational boundaries, necessitating collaboration with various stakeholders (Velter et al., 2020). Managers should actively engage with suppliers, local communities, and non-government organizations to foster a collaborative approach to sustainability (Akbari, 2022). This involves regular communication, partnerships, and joint initiatives that contribute to shared environmental and social goals. Through effective collaboration, managers not only enhance the impact of sustainability efforts but also foster a positive reputation and stronger relationships with stakeholders.

- Compliance with Global Standards: Managers must stay abreast of evolving global standards and regulations related to sustainable outsourcing. Compliance with these standards is not only a legal requirement but also a key element in building trust with consumers and investors (Babin & Nicholson, 2012). Regular audits and assessments should be conducted to ensure that outsourcing practices align with international frameworks on environmental stewardship, ethical labor practices, and overall sustainability. By embracing global standards, managers position their organizations as responsible global citizens committed to meeting and exceeding ethical and environmental expectations (Mirvis & Googins, 2006).

- Measuring and Reporting Sustainability Metrics: Managers need to establish robust systems for measuring and reporting sustainability metrics within the outsourcing ecosystem. This involves defining KPIs related to environmental impact, social responsibility, and ethical considerations (Kacani et al., 2022). Regular reporting on these metrics, both internally and externally, showcases a commitment to transparency and accountability. Additionally, it allows organizations to track progress, identify areas for improvement, and communicate their sustainability achievements to stakeholders effectively (Sahoo et al., 2023).

- Ethical AI Deployment in Outsourcing: As AI becomes integral to outsourcing processes, managers bear the responsibility of ensuring ethical deployment. This entails taking into account the social and environmental implications of AI applications (Lo Piano, 2020). Managers should advocate for the ethical treatment of workers, transparency in algorithmic decision-making, and mitigating biases. By incorporating ethical considerations into AI deployment, managers not only uphold responsible practices but also contribute to developing a sustainable and equitable outsourcing landscape.

Ultimately, the managerial implications of sustainable outsourcing underscore the need for a holistic and proactive approach to responsible business practices. Managers serve as the architects of sustainable strategies, shaping outsourcing decisions that not only optimize efficiency but also contribute positively to the environment, society, and the long-term success of the organization. By embracing these implications, managers position their organizations as pioneers in the evolving landscape of sustainable outsourcing, driving positive change and creating lasting value for all stakeholders.

6.6   SUMMARY AND CONCLUSION

In this comprehensive exploration of sustainable outsourcing, the chapter delved into the multifaceted dimensions and evolving dynamics shaping the contemporary business landscape. The discourse began by elucidating the concept of sustainable outsourcing, elucidating its foundations in ethical, environmental, and social considerations. The narrative unfolded with an insightful analysis of the global trends driving organizations toward embedding sustainability into their outsourcing strategies.

The chapter extensively covered the pivotal role of managers as the architects of sustainable strategies, emphasizing their responsibility in shaping outsourcing decisions that transcend mere cost considerations. From strategic alignment with corporate values to the integration of technology for transparency, managers are pivotal players in steering organizations toward responsible and sustainable business practices.

Environmental impact, ethical labor practices, and resilience to global disruptions emerge as critical themes, reflecting the increasing importance of organizations in mitigating risks and contributing positively to the global ecosystem. The incorporation of technology, talent management, and adherence to global standards further underscore the nuanced approach required for successful sustainable outsourcing.

Moreover, the chapter highlighted the emerging concerns and future directions in sustainable outsourcing, encapsulating the urgency of addressing climate change, fostering ethical AI deployment, and navigating the complexities of green finance. The narrative was enriched with real-world examples, providing a tangible understanding of how organizations are currently navigating and contributing to sustainable outsourcing practices.

In closing, the managerial implications elucidated throughout the chapter underscore the imperative of a holistic and proactive approach to responsible business practices. Managers, as the linchpins of sustainable strategies, are urged to embrace these implications to position their organizations as pioneers in the evolving landscape of sustainable outsourcing. By doing so, they not only drive positive change but also create lasting value for all stakeholders, embodying the ethos of responsible and resilient business in the modern era. This chapter serves as a guiding compass for organizations seeking to navigate the intricate intersection of sustainability and outsourcing in the pursuit of enduring success.

References

Adams, R., Jeanrenaud, S., Bessant, J., Denyer, D., & Overy, P. (2016). Sustainability-oriented innovation: A systematic review. *International Journal of Management Reviews, 18*(2), 180–205. https://doi.org/10.1111/ijmr.12068

Agrawal, T. K., Kumar, V., Pal, R., Wang, L., & Chen, Y. (2021). Blockchain-based framework for supply chain traceability: A case example of textile and clothing industry. *Computers & Industrial Engineering, 154*, 107130. https://doi.org/10.1016/j.cie.2021.107130

Akbari, M. (2022). Outsourcing in supply chain management. In J. Sarkis (Ed.), *Handbook of supply chain management—A major reference work* (Chapter 47). Palgrave. https://doi.org/10.1007/978-3-030-89822-9_47-1

Akbari, M. (2023, in press). Revolutionizing supply chain and circular economy with edge computing: Systematic review, research themes and future directions. *Management Decision*. https://doi.org/10.1108/MD-03-2023-0412

Akbari, M., & Do, T. N. A. (2021). A systematic review of machine learning in logistics and supply chain management: Current trends and future directions. *Benchmarking: An International Journal, 28*(10), 2977–3005. https://doi.org/10.1108/BIJ-10-2020-0514

Akbari, M., & Hopkins, J. (2022). Digital technologies as enablers of supply chain sustainability in an emerging economy. *Operations Management Research, 15*, 689–710. https://doi.org/10.1007/s12063-021-00226-8

Akbari, M., & McClelland, R. (2020). Corporate social responsibility and corporate citizenship in sustainable supply chain: A structured literature review. *Benchmarking: An International Journal, 27*(6), 1799–1841. https://doi.org/10.1108/BIJ-11-2019-0509

Aldrighetti, R., Battini, D., Ivanov, D., & Zennaro, I. (2021). Costs of resilience and disruptions in supply chain network design models: A review and future research directions. *International Journal of Production Economics, 235*, 108103. https://doi.org/10.1016/j.ijpe.2021.108103

Ang, Y. S. (2015). Ethical outsourcing and the act of acting together. In *Empowering organizations through corporate social responsibility* (pp. 113–130). IGI Global.

Aslam, J., Saleem, A., Khan, N. T., & Kim, Y. B. (2021). Factors influencing blockchain adoption in supply chain management practices: A study based on the oil industry. *Journal of Innovation & Knowledge, 6*(2), 124–134. https:// doi.org/10.1016/j.jik.2021.01.002

Attaran, M. (2020). Digital technology enablers and their implications for supply chain management. *Supply Chain Forum: An International Journal, 21*(3), 158–172. https://doi.org/10.1080/16258312.2020.1751568

Awan, U., Sroufe, R., & Shahbaz, M. (2021). Industry 4.0 and the circular economy: A literature review and recommendations for future research. *Business Strategy and the Environment, 30*(4), 2038–2060. https://doi.org/10. 1002/bse.2731

Babagolzadeh, M., Shrestha, A., Abbasi, B., Zhang, Y., Woodhead, A., & Zhang, A. (2020). Sustainable cold supply chain management under demand uncertainty and carbon tax regulation. *Transportation Research Part D: Transport and Environment, 80*, 102245. https://doi.org/10.1016/j.trd.2020.102245

Babin, R., & Nicholson, B. (2012). *Sustainable global outsourcing: Achieving social and environmental responsibility in global IT and business process outsourcing.* Springer.

Benaroch, M. (2020). Cybersecurity risk in IT outsourcing—Challenges and emerging realities. In *Information systems outsourcing: The era of digital transformation* (pp. 313–334). Springer. https://doi.org/10.1007/978-3-030-45819-5_13

Carl, J., & Fedor, D. (2016). Tracking global carbon revenues: A survey of carbon taxes versus cap-and-trade in the real world. *Energy Policy, 96*, 50–77. https://doi.org/10.1016/j.enpol.2016.05.023

Choudhary, N. A., Ramkumar, M., Schoenherr, T., Rana, N. P., & Dwivedi, Y. K. (2023). Does reshoring affect the resilience and sustainability of supply chain networks? The cases of Apple and Jaguar Land Rover. *British Journal of Management, 34*(3), 1138–1156. https://doi.org/10.1111/1467-8551. 12614

Dhillon, G., Syed, R., & de Sá-Soares, F. (2017). Information security concerns in IT outsourcing: Identifying (in) congruence between clients and vendors. *Information & Management, 54*(4), 452–464. https://doi.org/10.1016/j. im.2016.10.002

Di Vaio, A., Palladino, R., Hassan, R., & Escobar, O. (2020). Artificial intelligence and business models in the sustainable development goals perspective: A systematic literature review. *Journal of Business Research, 121*, 283–314. https://doi.org/10.3390/su12124851

Dubey, R., Gunasekaran, A., & Papadopoulos, T. (2017). Green supply chain management: Theoretical framework and further research directions. *Benchmarking: An International Journal, 24*(1), 184–218. https://doi.org/10. 1108/BIJ-01-2016-0011

Duhamel, F., Gutiérrez-Martínez, I., Picazo-Vela, S., & Luna-Reyes, L. F. (2021). Strategic alignment, process improvements and public value in public-private IT outsourcing in Mexico. *International Journal of Public Sector Management, 34*(5), 489–507. https://doi.org/10.1108/IJPSM-07-2020-0183

Fiorini, P. C., & Jabbour, C. J. C. (2017). Information systems and sustainable supply chain management towards a more sustainable society: Where we are and where we are going. *International Journal of Information Management, 37*(4), 241–249. https://doi.org/10.1016/j.ijinfomgt.2016.12.004

Fisher, D. R., Campbell, L. K., & Svendsen, E. S. (2012). The organisational structure of urban environmental stewardship. *Environmental Politics, 21*(1), 26–48. https://doi.org/10.1080/09644016.2011.643367

Garg, C. P., & Sharma, A. (2020). Sustainable outsourcing partner selection and evaluation using an integrated BWM–VIKOR framework. *Environment, Development and Sustainability, 22,* 1529–1557. https://doi.org/10.1007/s10668-018-0261-5

Herold, D. M., Nowicka, K., Pluta-Zaremba, A., & Kummer, S. (2021). COVID-19 and the pursuit of supply chain resilience: Reactions and "lessons learned" from logistics service providers (LSPs). *Supply Chain Management: An International Journal, 26*(6), 702–714. https://doi.org/10.1108/SCM-09-2020-0439

Hughes, A. C., Tougeron, K., Martin, D. A., Menga, F., Rosado, B. H., Villasante, S., Madgulkar, S., Gonçalves, F., Geneletti, D., Diele-Viegas, L. M., & Berger, S. (2023). Smaller human populations are neither a necessary nor sufficient condition for biodiversity conservation. *Biological Conservation, 277,* 109841. https://doi.org/10.1016/j.biocon.2022.109841

Jorgenson, A., Clark, R., Kentor, J., & Rieger, A. (2022). Networks, stocks, and climate change: A new approach to the study of foreign investment and the environment. *Energy Research & Social Science, 87,* 102461. https://doi.org/10.1016/j.erss.2021.102461

Kacani, J., Mukli, L., & Hysa, E. (2022). A framework for short-vs. long-term risk indicators for outsourcing potential for enterprises participating in global value chains: Evidence from Western Balkan countries. *Journal of Risk and Financial Management, 15*(9), 401. https://doi.org/10.3390/jrfm15090401

Kane, V., Akbari, M., Nguyen, L., & Nguyen, T. (2021). Corporate social responsibility in Vietnam: Views from corporate and NGO executives. *Social Responsibility Journal, 18*(2), 316–347. https://doi.org/10.1108/SRJ-10-2020-0434

Kannan, D., Solanki, R., Kaul, A., & Jha, P. C. (2022). Barrier analysis for carbon regulatory environmental policies implementation in manufacturing supply chains to achieve zero carbon. *Journal of Cleaner Production, 358,* 131910. https://doi.org/10.1016/j.jclepro.2022.131910

Kantaros, A., Diegel, O., Piromalis, D., Tsaramirsis, G., Khadidos, A. O., Khadidos, A. O., Khan, F. Q., & Jan, S. (2022). 3D printing: Making an innovative technology widely accessible through makerspaces and outsourced services. *Materials Today: Proceedings, 49,* 2712–2723. https://doi.org/10.1016/j.matpr.2021.09.074

Khan, S. A. R., Yu, Z., & Farooq, K. (2023). Green capabilities, green purchasing, and triple bottom line performance: Leading toward environmental sustainability. *Business Strategy and the Environment, 32*(4), 2022–2034. https://doi.org/10.1002/bse.3234

Kiørboe, N. (2015). *Moving towards a circular economy: Successful Nordic business models: Policy brief.* Nordic Council of Ministers.

Kok, S. K., & Akbari, M. (2023). Human resource management in supply chains. In J. Sarkis (Ed.), *The Palgrave handbook of supply chain management.* Palgrave Macmillan. https://doi.org/10.1007/978-3-030-89822-9_38-1

König, A., & Spinler, S. (2016). The effect of logistics outsourcing on the supply chain vulnerability of shippers: Development of a conceptual risk management framework. *The International Journal of Logistics Management, 27*(1), 122–141. https://doi.org/10.1108/IJLM-03-2014-0043

Li, C., & Umair, M. (2023). Does green finance development goals affects renewable energy in China. *Renewable Energy, 203,* 898–905. https://doi.org/10.1016/j.renene.2022.12.066

Lo Piano, S. (2020). Ethical principles in machine learning and artificial intelligence: Cases from the field and possible ways forward. *Humanities and Social Sciences Communications, 7*(1), 1–7. https://doi.org/10.1057/s41599-020-0501-9

Ma, L., Zhang, X., & Dong, L. (2023). Enhancing sustainable performance: The innovative strategy of digital transformation leading green collaborative management. *Sustainability, 15*(17), 13085. https://doi.org/10.3390/su151713085

Mendoza, A. J., & Clemen, R. T. (2013). Outsourcing sustainability: A game-theoretic modeling approach. *Environment System Decision, 33,* 224–236. https://doi.org/10.1007/s10669-013-9443-8

Millar, M. (2015). *Global supply chain ecosystems: Strategies for competitive advantage in a complex, connected world.* Kogan Page Publishers.

Mirvis, P., & Googins, B. (2006). Stages of corporate citizenship. *California Management Review, 48*(2), 104–126.

Montiel, I., & Delgado-Ceballos, J. (2014). Defining and measuring corporate sustainability: Are we there yet? *Organization & Environment, 27*(2), 113–139. https://doi.org/10.1177/1086026614526413

Nguyen, T. V., Pham, H. C., Nguyen, M. N., Zhou, L., & Akbari, M. (2023). Data-driven review of blockchain applications in supply chain management: Key research themes and future directions. *International Journal of Production Research*, 1–23. https://doi.org/10.1080/00207543.2023.216 5190

Nicholson, B., Babin, R., & Lacity, M. C. (Eds.). (2016). *Socially responsible outsourcing: Global sourcing with social impact*. Palgrave Macmillan.

Plambeck, E. L., Lee, H. L., & Yatsko, P. (2012). Improving environmental performance in your Chinese supply chain. *MIT Sloan Management Review*, 53(2), 42–51.

Rissman, J., Bataille, C., Masanet, E., Aden, N., Morrow, W. R., III., Zhou, N., Elliott, N., Dell, R., Heeren, N., Huckestein, B., & Cresko, J. (2020). Technologies and policies to decarbonize global industry: Review and assessment of mitigation drivers through 2070. *Applied Energy, 266*, 114848. https://doi.org/10.1016/j.apenergy.2020.114848

Ryan, M., & Stahl, B. C. (2020). Artificial intelligence ethics guidelines for developers and users: Clarifying their content and normative implications. *Journal of Information, Communication and Ethics in Society, 19*(1), 61–86. https://doi.org/10.1108/JICES-12-2019-0138

Sahoo, S., Kumar, A., & Upadhyay, A. (2023). How do green knowledge management and green technology innovation impact corporate environmental performance? Understanding the role of green knowledge acquisition. *Business Strategy and the Environment, 32*(1), 551–569. https://doi.org/10.1002/bse.3160

Sardá, R., & Pogutz, S. (2018). *Corporate sustainability in the 21st century: Increasing the resilience of social-ecological systems*. Routledge.

Settembre-Blundo, D., González-Sánchez, R., Medina-Salgado, S., & García-Muiña, F. E. (2021). Flexibility and resilience in corporate decision making: A new sustainability-based risk management system in uncertain times. *Global Journal of Flexible Systems Management, 22*(Suppl. 2), 107–132. https://doi.org/10.1007/s40171-021-00277-7

Shikweni, S., Schurink, W., & Van Wyk, R. (2019). Talent management in the South African construction industry. *SA Journal of Human Resource Management, 17*(1), 1–12. https://hdl.handle.net/10520/EJC-178607b345

Shoushtari, F., & Ghafourian, E. (2023). Antifragile, sustainable, and agile supply chain network design with a risk approach. *International Journal of Industrial Engineering and Operational Research, 5*(1), 19–28. http://bgsiran.ir/journal/ojs-3.1.1-4/index.php/IJIEOR/article/view/33

Stahl, G. K., Brewster, C. J., Collings, D. G., & Hajro, A. (2020). Enhancing the role of human resource management in corporate sustainability and social responsibility: A multi-stakeholder, multidimensional approach to HRM.

Human Resource Management Review, 30(3), 100708. https://doi.org/10.1016/j.hrmr.2019.100708

Stevens, G. C., & Johnson, M. (2016). Integrating the supply chain… 25 years on. *International Journal of Physical Distribution & Logistics Management, 46*(1), 19–42. https://doi.org/10.1108/IJPDLM-07-2015-0175

Tafti, M. H. (2005). Risks factors associated with offshore IT outsourcing. *Industrial Management & Data Systems, 105*(5), 549–560. https://doi.org/10.1108/02635570510599940

Taghipour, A., Khazaei, M., Azar, A., Rajabzadeh Ghatari, A., Hajiaghaei-Keshteli, M., & Ramezani, M. (2022). Creating shared value and strategic corporate social responsibility through outsourcing within supply chain management. *Sustainability, 14*(4), 1940. https://doi.org/10.3390/su14041940

Tetrick, M. (2023). *Rise of AI In business process outsourcing*. Rely Services. https://www.relyservices.com/blog/ai-business-process-outsourcing. Accessed 1 October 2023.

Velter, M. G. E., Bitzer, V., Bocken, N. M. P., & Kemp, R. (2020). Sustainable business model innovation: The role of boundary work for multi-stakeholder alignment. *Journal of Cleaner Production, 247*, 119497. https://doi.org/10.1016/j.jclepro.2019.119497

Voegtlin, C., & Scherer, A. G. (2017). Responsible innovation and the innovation of responsibility: Governing sustainable development in a globalized world. *Journal of Business Ethics, 143*, 227–243. https://doi.org/10.1007/s10551-015-2769-z

World Commission on Environment and Development. (1987). *Our common future*. Oxford University Press. https://digitallibrary.un.org/record/139811?ln=en. Accessed 4 October 2023.

Yang, Y., Goodarzi, S., Jabbarzadeh, A., & Fahimnia, B. (2021). In-house production and outsourcing under different emissions reduction regulations: An equilibrium decision model for global supply chains. *Transportation Research Part E: Logistics and Transportation Review, 157*, 102446. https://doi.org/10.1016/j.tre.2021.102446

Zhao, J., & Gómez Fariñas, B. (2023). Artificial intelligence and sustainable decisions. *European Business Organization Law Review, 24*(1), 1–39. https://doi.org/10.1007/s40804-022-00262-2

CHAPTER 7

Navigating the Spectrum from 1 to 6PL in the Age of Technology and Innovation

7.1 INTRODUCTION

In today's globalized and competitive business environment, it is increasingly vital for enterprises to concentrate on their core competencies and seek external support to enhance their competitiveness. Third-party providers such as suppliers, logistics companies, and technology partners can help firms to access new markets, lower costs, and increase efficiency (Niu & Mu, 2020).

Logistics outsourcing, also known as third-party logistics (3PL/TPL), has become an increasingly critical topic in today's global business setting (Akbari, 2022). As companies face growing competition and complexity in their supply chains, they are recognizing the need to leverage external expertise and resources to enhance their competitiveness (Anderson et al., 2010). Outsourcing logistics functions to third-party providers is one such strategy that many firms have adopted in recent years (De & Singh, 2022; Dong et al., 2023).

Logistics outsourcing is the practice of delegating all or some of an organization's logistics functions to an external service provider (Lynch, 2000). This can include functions such as transportation, warehousing, inventory management, and distribution (Akbari & Hopkins, 2016). The third-party provider may be a specialist logistics company or a supplier that offers logistics services as part of a broader product or service offering (Anderson et al., 2010).

M. Akbari, *The Road to Outsourcing 4.0*, https://doi.org/10.1007/978-981-97-2708-7_7

Logistics outsourcing has gained popularity for several reasons. First, it allows firms to concentrate on their core competencies and free up internal resources. By outsourcing logistics functions, companies can shift their attention to areas such as research and development, marketing, or customer service, which are often critical for maintaining a competitive edge (Auramo et al., 2002). Second, outsourcing may provide cost savings by allowing companies to access economies of scale and expertise that may not be available internally. Third, it also helps companies to reduce risk by diversifying their supplier base and building redundancy into their supply chain (El Mokrini & Aouam, 2022; Voss et al., 2006). By working with multiple logistics providers, companies can avoid disruptions caused by supply chain failures or other issues, which could lead to costly delays and loss of business.

Despite its benefits, logistics outsourcing is not without its challenges. Companies must carefully evaluate potential providers and ensure that they have the expertise and capacity to meet their needs (Rahman et al., 2011). They must also establish clear performance metrics and communication channels to ensure that the outsourced functions are being performed to the desired level of quality (Solakivi et al., 2022). Finally, companies must ensure that they maintain appropriate levels of control and visibility over their outsourced logistics functions to avoid potential disruptions or quality issues (Brown & Wilson, 2007; Kalubanga & Namagembe, 2022). This requires establishing strong contractual agreements, implementing effective monitoring mechanisms, and building collaborative relationships with logistics providers (Akbari, 2018).

This chapter will explore the history of logistics outsourcing from 1 to 6PL, the key drivers, and benefits of logistics outsourcing, as well as the challenges that companies may encounter when implementing this strategy. The chapter will also examine best practices for selecting and managing third-party logistics providers and provide practical guidance for companies looking to leverage outsourcing as a strategic tool for enhancing their competitiveness. By the end of this chapter, readers will have a solid understanding of the role of logistics outsourcing in SCM and be equipped with the tools and knowledge to successfully implement this strategy in their organizations.

7.2   OVERVIEW

Over the past 25 years, outsourcing has become a prominent global supply chain strategy (Akbari & Hopkins, 2016; Miah et al., 2014; Pettersson & Segerstedt, 2013). Since the mid-1990s, there has been a significant increase in the importance of SCM, leading to a surge in the study of supply chain and outsourcing by practitioners and scholars alike (König & Spinler, 2016).

The practice of outsourcing logistics activities has empowered companies to enhance their overall SCM efficiency by concentrating on their core competencies. As supply chains continue to evolve in complexity, the importance of logistics has increased, and third-party logistics providers (3PLs or TPLs) have become key players in managing supply chain operations (König & Spinler, 2016).

Efficient management of logistics is a critical instrument for a global supply chain, as most markets have been globalized (Cohen & Russel, 2013). Logistics management involves overseeing the procurement, transportation, and storage of goods, materials, parts, and inventories (Christopher, 2016). The goal is to optimize profitability through the efficient fulfillment of orders (Christopher, 2016). It is crucial to recognize the impact of logistics on profits. Efficient logistics management can have a substantial impact on the Return on Investment (ROI), representing the ratio of net profit to the capital employed (investment) to generate a profit (Wisner et al., 2012).

$$ROI = [\text{Net profit/Sales}] \times [\text{Sales/Capital Employed(Investment)}].$$

Logistics, being a non-core business function, is often outsourced, enabling companies to allocate resources more efficiently and focus on their primary strengths (König & Spinler, 2016). The term "logistics outsourcing" refers to a process where external or third-party logistics firms provide services within agreed-upon budgets and time frames (Hsiao et al., 2010; Skjoett-Larsen, 2000).

Logistics outsourcing is a strategic practice whereby companies contract out some or all their logistics functions to third-party service providers (Tian et al., 2008). The outsourcing of logistics functions has become an ever more popular practice in today's global business environment, as companies face growing competition and complexity in their supply chains (Akbari et al., 2020).

In pursuit of heightened competitiveness, many companies have adopted specialization strategies, foregoing self-sufficiency (Baeza et al., 2019). This often includes outsourcing the transportation function to harness the expertise of specialists and cut down on operational costs (Baeza et al., 2019).

While logistics outsourcing offers potential benefits, it also carries risks (Akbari et al., 2020). While numerous papers emphasize the advantages of logistics outsourcing, there is a dearth of literature that addresses the associated risks (Govindan & Chaudhuri, 2016; Stojanović & Aas, 2015). To address this, Stojanović and Aas (2015) compiled a list of logistics outsourcing risks, categorized into external and internal dimensions. External risks stem from uncertainties in transport demand, whereas internal risks are associated with uncertainties related to service providers (Stojanović & Aas, 2015). Table 7.1 below summarizes the risks of logistics outsourcing.

To successfully implement logistics outsourcing, companies must follow a number of best practices. Implementation can be a complex process and success requires careful planning, effective execution, and ongoing management (Akbari, 2022). Here are some key steps that supply chain firms can take to become successful in implementing logistics outsourcing (de Grahl, 2011):

- *Identify objectives and goals:* Before beginning the outsourcing of logistics functions, it's important to identify what you hope to achieve through outsourcing. This might include reducing costs, improving service levels, or gaining access to specialized expertise. Clear objectives and goals will help guide outsourcing decisions and ensure that the right choices are made for the business.
- *Choose the right outsourcing partner:* Once you have a clear idea of objectives and goals, companies need to find the right outsourcing partner. They should look for a logistics provider that has experience in their industry, a strong track record of success, and a reputation for reliability and customer service. It's also important to choose a provider that has the right technology and infrastructure to support their needs.
- *Develop a detailed implementation plan:* After selecting the outsourcing partner, companies need to work together to develop a detailed implementation plan. This plan should outline all of the steps that will be taken to transition logistics functions to the

Table 7.1 Logistics outsourcing risks

Internal Risks	External risks
There are risks associated with the intricacies of supply chains, including strategic, operational, supply, customer, asset impairment, and reputational risks (Harland et al., 2003)	The absence of flexibility could result in the failure to adapt and configure resources to meet the evolving demands of the market (Harland et al., 2003)
Inadequate management of outsourcing relationships with selected vendors can result in failure (Harland et al., 2005)	Rigidity of businesses to adapt to changing business environments and varying demands for products, services, and technologies is a significant issue (Greaver & Greaver II, 1999)
Inadequate communication and poorly designed service level agreements with the outsourcing partner can lead to failure (Harland et al., 2005)	Demand is unpredictable and the associated risks are magnified (Potter & Lalwani, 2008)
The absence of in-house expertise in making outsourcing decisions can be a challenge (Solakivi et al., 2013)	Business can be impacted by both currency exchange rate fluctuations and the implementation of nontariff barriers (Chang et al., 2015)
Risks related to the relationship between parties include power asymmetry, vendor opportunism, and the absence of shared goals (Tsai et al., 2012)	Variation in social, cultural, and legal frameworks between various countries, as well as the stability of governments and legal systems, can have an impact (Schniederjans & Zuckweiler, 2004)
There are risks associated with logistics outsourcing, including ineffective management, reduced control over 3PL providers, diminished logistics innovation capability, and heightened reliance on service providers (Blom & Niemann, 2022)	
The 3PL provider may provide inadequate and/or inferior performance (Best Practice Group, 2019)	

Source adapted fromAkbari (2022)

outsourcing provider, as well as timelines, responsibilities, and key milestones. Involving all stakeholders in the planning process ensures that everyone is on the same page.

- *Communicate effectively:* Effective communication is essential throughout the outsourcing process. Companies should regularly communicate with their outsourcing partner to ensure smooth operations and address any issues that arise. It's also important to communicate with internal stakeholders to keep them informed about the outsourcing process and to address any concerns they may have.

- *Monitor performance and make adjustments:* Once logistics functions have been outsourced, it's important to monitor performance to ensure that objectives and goals are being met. This may involve tracking KPIs such as delivery times, inventory levels, and order accuracy. If performance is not meeting expectations, companies should work with their outsourcing partner to make adjustments and improvements.

By following these steps, supply chain firms could increase their chances of success in implementing logistics outsourcing. However, it's important to remember that outsourcing is an ongoing process that requires ongoing management and attention. Firms must regularly review outsourcing arrangements and make adjustments as needed to ensure the best possible results from the outsourcing partnership.

In brief, logistics outsourcing is an important strategic tool for companies looking to enhance their competitiveness in today's global business environment. By leveraging the expertise and resources of third-party logistics providers, firms can concentrate on their core competencies, reduce costs, and increase flexibility. However, to successfully implement logistics outsourcing, companies must carefully evaluate potential providers, establish clear performance metrics, and maintain adequate oversight and control over outsourced functions. By following best practices and building collaborative relationships with their logistics providers, companies could effectively leverage outsourcing as a tool for enhancing their SCM capabilities and driving long-term success.

7.3   Emerging Trends and Practices

In the current business landscape, with competition escalating, organizations are increasingly prioritizing their core competencies as the key focus of their strategic efforts (Akbari, 2023). This has led to significant global growth in logistics outsourcing (de Grahl, 2011). Outsourcing logistics-related tasks to logistics service providers (LSPs) has become a prevalent strategy in SCM (Akbari et al., 2017). Typically, outsourcing in the supply chain pertains to the delegation of warehousing and transportation functions (Akbari, 2018, 2022). LSPs can be classified into five levels (1PL, 2PL, 3PL, 4PL, and 5PL) (see Fig. 7.1).

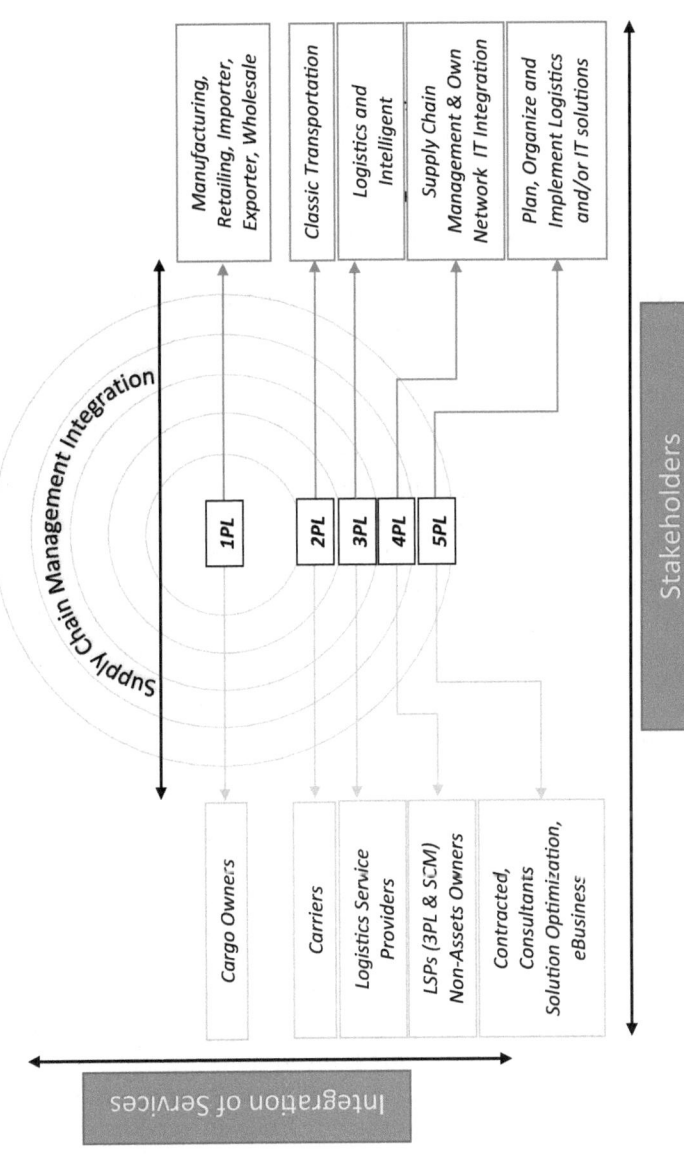

Fig. 7.1 Classification of logistics service providers 20222020 (*Source* Author's own work—Adapted from Akbari [2022] and Akbari et al. [2020])

The logistics industry is classified into different categories of service providers, depending on the level of service offered, as follows.

1PL: This term refers to in-house logistics, where companies use their vehicles, warehouses, and facilities without relying on external firms (Odnokonnaya, 2017). A real-life example of 1PL would be a company like Walmart, which manages its own logistics operations in-house. Walmart has a fleet of trucks, warehouses, and distribution centers to manage the movement of goods from its suppliers to its stores. They have their own transportation management system which schedules and manages product deliveries to stores. This means that Walmart does not rely on external firms to manage its logistics functions and has complete control over its supply chain operations.

2PL: 2PLs are carriers that specialize in a particular segment of the supply chain like transportation or warehousing (Rodrigue et al., 2016). An example of a 2PL provider is FedEx Freight. They specialize in transportation and logistics services, including freight forwarding, SCM, and warehousing. They have a fleet of trucks and offer transportation services for businesses that need to move their goods from one location to another. They may also offer some warehousing services to customers, but their main focus is on transportation.

3PL: 3PLs provide services that extend beyond those offered by 2PLs, including value-added services such as packaging, labeling, bundling/unbundling, reverse logistics, and repair services (Beamberlin, 2018). A real example of a 3PL is DHL Supply Chain. DHL Supply Chain is a global logistics provider that provides a variety of services such as transportation, warehousing, and distribution. They have a vast network of warehouses and transportation hubs, which allows them to provide customized logistics solutions for their clients. DHL Supply Chain works with companies in a variety of industries such as automotive, consumer, and healthcare, to manage their logistics needs and improve their supply chain efficiency. They use advanced technologies such as real-time tracking and data analytics to optimize their operations and provide visibility to their clients.

4PL: These independent companies do not own any assets but subcontract to other LSPs (Saglietto, 2013). A real-life example of a 4PL provider is Accenture. Accenture is a global management consulting and professional services firm that provides a range of services, including 4PL solutions. They work with businesses to design and manage their supply chain operations, often through the use of technology and data analytics. For example, Accenture worked with a global pharmaceutical company to optimize its supply chain operations. The 4PL provider used advanced analytics to provide visibility and insights into the company's supply chain, enabling them to identify inefficiencies and areas for improvement. Accenture then designed and implemented new supply chain processes and technologies to improve the company's overall efficiency and reduce costs. In another example, Accenture worked with a leading automotive company to streamline its supply chain operations. The 4PL provider implemented a centralized platform that provided real-time visibility into the company's supply chain, enabling them to optimize inventory management, reduce lead times, and improve delivery times.

5PL: Logistics aggregators are also known as 5PLs, and they organize and implement logistics solutions for numerous customers (Matlack Leasing, 2019). This novel model leverages technologies in collaboration with 3PLs and 4PLs to manage the complete supply chain (Matlack Leasing, 2019). A real-world example of a logistics aggregator is Flexport. Flexport is a San Francisco-based technology company that offers a platform for freight forwarding and customs brokerage services. The company uses technology to connect with carriers, warehouses, and customs agencies worldwide and offers end-to-end supply chain solutions to its customers. Flexport acts as a single point of contact for its customers and manages the entire supply chain on their behalf, from sourcing and shipping to customs clearance and delivery.

7.4   EMERGENT CONCERNS AND FUTURE DIRECTIONS

The rapid pace of technological advancement in today's world, including the digital revolution of Industry 4.0, is transforming global business models (Arlbjørn et al., 2011; Hoyer et al., 2021). The emergence of I4.0 is a significant catalyst for this transformation in supply chains (Akbari et al., 2022) including logistics outsourcing as a primary activity. In recent years, researchers have conducted numerous studies on logistics and delivery issues in various production systems. These studies, including those by Pournader et al. (2020), Koh et al. (2020), Liu et al. (2022), and Zhou et al. (2022), have shed light on the significance of I4.0 technologies in enhancing logistics efficiency. These studies acknowledge that the implementation of I4.0 technologies can significantly improve the efficiency of logistics operations. The focus is now on developing a new generation of LSPs that are fully integrated and automated, utilizing ML,

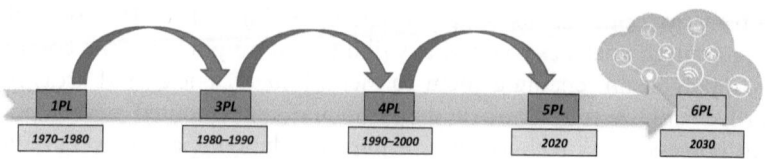

Fig. 7.2 Emergence of 6PL 20222018 (*Source* Author's own work—Adapted from Akbari [2022] and Gruchmann et al. [2018])

AI, and IoT to optimize the entire supply chain process (Akbari & Do, 2021; Niu et al., 2022).

The term "6PL" has been coined to describe this fully integrated and automated supply chain managed and controlled by AI (see Fig. 7.2).

The potential impact of I4.0 emerging technologies on the entire supply chain process is significant (Ha et al., 2022), as it can enable the automation of many routine tasks, reduce lead times, optimize inventory levels, and improve the overall efficiency of the supply chain process (Yang et al., 2021). This can result in cost savings and improved customer satisfaction. While still in the theoretical stage, the potential impact of AI, ML, and IoT on the entire SCM is significant, and the development of 6PL could greatly influence the future of logistics outsourcing. Despite the challenges that need to be addressed, such as data security, integration of logistics providers, and the need for skilled professionals, the development of 6PL has the potential to significantly impact the future of logistics outsourcing and SCM.

6PL is a model of logistics outsourcing that offers a fully integrated and automated supply chain managed and controlled by AI. This model leverages the I4.0 emerging technologies to optimize the entire supply chain process, which can lead to several benefits for businesses.

One of the main benefits of 6PL is improved supply chain efficiency. The automated system can optimize logistics processes, reduce manual errors, and speed up delivery times, resulting in a more efficient supply chain process. This can ultimately lead to cost savings for businesses by reducing waste, improving productivity, and increasing customer satisfaction.

Another benefit of 6PL is cost reduction. By optimizing the entire supply chain process, including transportation, warehousing, and inventory management, businesses can reduce the costs associated with these activities. The automated system can also help to identify cost-saving opportunities and optimize routes and delivery times, further reducing costs.

6PL also offers increased flexibility in meeting changing customer demands. The 6PL provider designs and implements a customized supply chain solution that meets the specific needs of its customers, allowing for more flexibility in adapting to changing market conditions or customer requirements.

Moreover, 6PL provides better visibility and control over the supply chain process. The AI-controlled system provides real-time data and insights into the supply chain process, allowing businesses to track and monitor inventory levels, manage orders and shipments, and make informed decisions based on the latest information. This can help to reduce supply chain disruptions and improve overall SCM.

Additionally, a Sustainability Service Provider (SSP) is a type of 6PL that focuses on integrating sustainability principles into the supply chain (Gruchmann et al., 2018). SSPs work with companies to assess their environmental impact and develop strategies to reduce waste, conserve resources, and minimize greenhouse gas emissions. They also help companies meet regulatory requirements and adopt best practices for sustainability. SSPs leverage technology, data analytics, and ML to optimize sustainable supply chain practices (Gruchmann et al., 2018). For example, they may use sensors to track energy consumption and carbon emissions in real time or use predictive analytics to identify areas where sustainability improvements can be made. By partnering with an SSP, companies could improve their sustainability performance while also reducing costs and improving efficiency.

However, 6PL also presents several challenges that need to be addressed before it can be implemented on a large scale. These challenges include data security, integration of different logistics providers and systems, and the need for skilled professionals to manage and operate the system.

Example 1: Electronic product

Let's consider an example of a company that produces electronic products and is looking to improve its supply chain process through the implementation of 6PL.

The company partners with a 6PL provider who designs and implements a customized supply chain solution for their business. The solution is fully integrated and automated, utilizing ML and AI to optimize the entire supply chain process.

The first step in implementing 6PL is to identify the specific needs of the company. The 6PL provider conducts a thorough analysis of the company's supply chain process, including transportation, warehousing, and inventory management, to identify areas for improvement.

Based on this analysis, the 6PL provider designs a customized solution that meets the specific needs of the company. The solution includes the utilization of advanced technology, such as AI-powered demand forecasting, to optimize inventory levels and ensure that the company has the right products in the right quantities at the right time.

The solution also includes the use of advanced routing and scheduling software, which optimizes delivery routes and reduces lead times. The system is fully automated, reducing the risk of manual errors and improving overall supply chain efficiency.

One of the key benefits of 6PL is the increased visibility and control over the supply chain process. The 6PL provider provides real-time data and insights into the supply chain process, allowing the company to track and monitor inventory levels, manage orders and shipments, and make informed decisions based on the latest information.

Another benefit is the increased flexibility in meeting changing customer demands. The 6PL provider designs the supply chain solution to be flexible and adaptable, allowing the company to quickly respond to changing market conditions or customer requirements.

Example 2: Fashion retailer

Let's say a fashion retailer wants to improve their supply chain process and ensure they have the right products in stock at all times. They partner with a 6PL provider to design and implement a customized solution.

The first step is for the 6PL provider to conduct an analysis of the retailer's current supply chain process. This includes analyzing their inventory management system, transportation process, and warehousing operations.

Based on this analysis, the 6PL provider designs a solution that incorporates AI-powered demand forecasting to ensure the retailer has the right products in stock at all times. This is achieved by analyzing data such as historical sales trends, seasonal demand, and customer preferences.

The solution also includes advanced transportation management software that optimizes delivery routes and reduces lead times. This software can even be integrated with GPS technology to provide real-time updates on the status of shipments.

In addition to these technological solutions, the 6PL provider also ensures that the retailer has access to a team of skilled professionals who can manage and operate the system effectively. This includes supply chain experts who can analyze data and make informed decisions, as well as IT professionals who can ensure the system is running smoothly.

One of the key benefits of 6PL in this example is the increased accuracy of demand forecasting. By utilizing AI-powered forecasting, the retailer can ensure they have the right products in stock at all times, reducing the risk of overstocking or understocking.

Another benefit is the increased efficiency of the transportation process. By optimizing delivery routes and reducing lead times, the retailer can improve customer satisfaction and reduce costs associated with transportation.

Example 3: DHL's "Green Solutions"

DHL's "Green Solutions" program is a comprehensive sustainability service that helps businesses reduce their carbon footprint and environmental impact. The program offers a range of services, including sustainable packaging, carbon reporting, and green transport solutions. DHL's sustainability experts work with businesses to recognize areas where they can progress their sustainability performance, such as optimizing transport routes to reduce emissions, using renewable energy sources, and implementing energy-efficient technologies.

One key feature of the program is DHL's Carbon Dashboard, which provides businesses with detailed information about their carbon footprint and emissions, including data on transport, energy consumption, and waste generation. The dashboard allows businesses to monitor and analyze their sustainability performance, track progress toward emissions reduction targets, and identify opportunities for further improvement.

Another aspect of the program is DHL's sustainable packaging solutions, which include recyclable and biodegradable packaging materials, as well as innovative packaging designs that reduce waste and improve transport efficiency. DHL also offers a range of green transport options, such as electric and hybrid vehicles, and encourages customers to use these low-emission vehicles wherever possible. Overall, DHL's Green Solutions program is an example of a 6PL service that leverages technology, expertise, and partnerships with other logistics providers to help businesses achieve their sustainability goals and reduce their environmental impact.

In conclusion, these examples illustrate how 6PL can be used to transform traditional SCM processes. By leveraging AI-powered technologies and skilled professionals, companies can improve inventory management, optimize transportation processes, and reduce costs. However, it's important to note that there are challenges that need to be addressed before 6PL can be implemented on a large scale. Nevertheless, the potential benefits of 6PL are significant, and it could greatly influence the future of logistics outsourcing and SCM. As companies continue to adopt Industry 4.0 technologies, it's likely that we will see more examples of 6PL being implemented to streamline supply chain processes and improve overall efficiency.

7.5   Managerial Implications

Logistics outsourcing has become an increasingly popular practice among businesses looking to outsource their logistics and SCM functions as this approach has numerous benefits which are discussed throughout the chapter. However, managers must carefully evaluate the service providers to ensure that they can provide customized solutions that meet their specific needs. In this section, I will present the key managerial implications of using service providers and provide insights into how managers can effectively navigate this complex area of logistics management.

The most significant advantage of using a 3PL provider is the potential for cost savings (de Grahl, 2011). By outsourcing transportation, warehousing, and other logistics-related functions to a 3PL provider, companies can save money on infrastructure, labor, and overhead costs (El Mokrini & Aouam, 2022). However, managers should be careful when evaluating 3PL providers' pricing structures to ensure that they are cost-effective and aligned with their budgets. Another benefit of 3PL providers is access to a vast network of carriers and warehouses that can improve service levels (Hsiao et al., 2010). Managers should prioritize choosing 3PL providers with a reliable and efficient transportation and warehousing network to ensure optimal service levels. Additionally, 3PL providers offer greater flexibility in managing logistics and supply chain operations (Harland et al., 2003). Managers should choose providers who can provide customized solutions tailored to their company's specific needs. 3PL providers also assist in risk management by having robust risk management procedures in place (Voss et al., 2006). Managers should choose providers with robust tracking and reporting capabilities to ensure optimal visibility. Lastly, 3PL providers have the capability to improve customer service by providing faster and more accurate order fulfillment (Auramo et al., 2002). It is essential to choose a provider with a customer-centric approach to service delivery to maximize this benefit.

Further, the development and implementation of 6PL have significant managerial implications for companies. Here are some of the most important implications.

- *Need for skilled professionals:* 6PL requires highly skilled professionals to effectively manage and operate the system. Companies need to invest in training and hiring employees with the necessary skills to handle this new technology. In addition, they need to create a culture of innovation and continuous learning to keep up with the rapidly evolving technology.
- *Data management:* With 6PL, companies have access to substantial amounts of data that can be used to make informed decisions. However, this also means that there is a need for effective data management to ensure data security and accuracy. Companies need to develop effective data governance policies and procedures to protect sensitive data and ensure data quality.
- *Collaboration:* 6PL involves integrating different logistics providers and systems. To ensure the success of 6PL, companies need to develop effective collaboration strategies that involve open communication and sharing information between all parties involved.
- *Change management:* The implementation of 6PL involves a significant change in the way companies manage their supply chain processes. To ensure the success of this new technology, companies need to invest in effective change management strategies to ensure that employees understand and support the new system.
- *Cost implications:* The implementation of 6PL involves significant investment in technology and skilled professionals. Companies need to carefully consider the cost implications of implementing 6PL and ensure that the benefits outweigh the costs.

Overall, the development and implementation of 6PL have significant managerial implications that require careful consideration and planning. Companies that are able to effectively manage these implications can leverage 6PL to enhance their supply chain activities and gain a competitive advantage in the marketplace.

7.6   SUMMARY AND CONCLUSION

In conclusion, the book chapter provides an insightful analysis of the concept of 6PL and its potential impact on the future of logistics outsourcing and SCM. The chapter began by discussing the history and background of logistics outsourcing and the emergence of service providers from 1Pl to 5PL. It then explained how logistics outsourcing is one of the primary outsourcing activities in supply chains and how emerging technologies like ML and AI can be leveraged to develop a new generation of logistics providers, framed through the concept of 6PL.

The chapter also highlighted the benefits and challenges of 6PL. On the one hand, 6PL offers significant potential benefits, such as improved inventory management, optimization of transportation processes, and reduced costs. On the other hand, there are challenges that need to be addressed before 6PL can be implemented on a large scale, such as data security, integration of different logistics providers and systems, and the need for skilled professionals to manage and operate the system.

One of the key takeaways from the chapter is that the development and implementation of 6PL require a significant investment in technology and skilled professionals. Companies need to carefully consider the cost implications of implementing 6PL and ensure that the benefits outweigh the costs. They also need to invest in effective change management strategies to ensure that employees understand and support the new system. The chapter also underscored the importance of effective collaboration, data management, and change management in implementing 6PL.

In summary, the chapter provided an insightful analysis of the challenges and benefits associated with 6PL, which is a new generation of logistics providers that leverages ML and AI to streamline supply chain processes. The chapter offers valuable insights for business leaders and logistics professionals looking to stay ahead of the curve and leverage the latest technological advances to improve their supply chain processes.

References

Akbari, M. (2018). Logistics outsourcing: A structured literature review. *Benchmarking: An International Journal, 25*(5), 1548–1580. https://doi.org/10.1108/BIJ-04-2017-0066

Akbari, M. (2022). Chapter 47—Outsourcing in supply chain management. In J. Sarkis (Ed.), *Handbook of supply chain management—A major reference work,* Palgrave. https://doi.org/10.1007/978-3-030-89822-9_47-1

Akbari, M. (2023). Data-driven review of additive manufacturing on supply chains: Regionalization, key research themes and future directions. *Computers & Industrial Engineering, 184,* 109600. https://doi.org/10.1016/j.cie.2023.109600

Akbari, M., & Do, T. N. A. (2021). A systematic review of machine learning in logistics and supply chain management: current trends and future directions. *Benchmarking: An International Journal, 28*(10), 2977–3005. https://doi.org/10.1108/BIJ-10-2020-0514

Akbari, M., & Hopkins, J. (2016). The changing business landscape in Iran: Establishing outsourcing best practices. *Operations and Supply Chain Management: An International Journal, 9*(3), 184–197. https://doi.org/10.31387/oscm0250172

Akbari, M., Clarke, S. J., & Maleki Far, S. (2017). Outsourcing best practice— The case of large construction firms in Iran. In *Proceedings of the informing science and information technology education conference.* (pp. 39–50). From: InSITE 2017: Informing Science and Information Technology Education Conference, July 31–August 5, 2017. https://doi.org/10.28945/3737

Akbari, M., Ha, N., & Kok, S. (2022). A systematic review of AR/VR in operations and supply chain management: Maturity, current trends and future directions. *Journal of Global Operations and Strategic Sourcing, 15*(4), 534–565. https://doi.org/10.1108/JGOSS-09-2021-0078

Akbari, M., Ha, N., & Majo, G. (2020). Chapter 5: Role of logistics service providers in the supply chain. In R. Nayak (Ed.), *Supply chain management and logistics in the global fashion sector: The sustainability challenge.* https://doi.org/10.4324/9781003089063-6

Anderson, E., Coltman, T., Devinney, T. M., & Keating, B. (2010). What drives the choice of a third party logistics provider? *Journal of Supply Chain Management: a global review of purchasing and supply, 47*(2), 97–115. https://ro.uow.edu.au/commpapers/767/

Arlbjørn, J. S., de Haas, H., & Munksgaard, K. B. (2011). Exploring supply chain innovation. *Logistics Research, 3*(1), 3–18. https://doi.org/10.1007/s12159-010-0044-3

Auramo, J., Aminoff, A., & Punakivi, M. (2002). Research agenda for e-business logistics based on professional opinions. *International Journal of Physical*

Distribution & Logistics Management, 32(7), 513–531. https://doi.org/10. 1108/09600030210442568

Baeza, E., Montt, C., & Quezada, L. (2019). Methodological proposal to evaluate the alternative of outsourcing the transportation fleet of a company. *Procedia Manufacturing, 39*, 1545–1551. https://doi.org/10.1016/j.pro mfg.2020.01.292

Beamberlin. (2018). Our guide to 1PL, 2PL, 3PL, 4PL, 5PL. https://beambe rlin.com/logistics-101-1pl-2pl-3pl-4pl-5pl/. Accessed 1 April 2023.

Best Practice Group. (2019). Problematic outsourcing relationship?—8 steps to improve performance, rebuild trust and maximise value. https://www. ops.gov.ie/app/uploads/2019/12/Problematic-Outsourcing-Relationship-8-Steps.pdf. Accessed 2 April 2023.

Blom, T., & Niemann, W. (2022). Managing reputational risk during supply chain disruption recovery: A triadic logistics outsourcing perspective. *Journal of Transport and Supply Chain Management, 16*, a623. https://doi.org/10. 4102/jtscm.v16i0.623

Brown, D., & Wilson, S. (2007). *The black books of outsourcing: How to manage the changes, challenges, and opportunities*. John Wiley & Sons.

Chang, C. H., Xu, J., & Song, D. P. (2015). Risk analysis for container shipping: From a logistics perspective. *The International Journal of Logistics Management, 26*(1), 147–171. https://doi.org/10.1108/IJLM-07-2012-0068

Christopher, M. (2016). *Logistics and supply chain management* (5th ed.). Pearson.

Cohen, S., & Roussel, J. (2013). *Strategic supply chain management: The five core disciplines for top performance* (2nd ed.). McGraw-Hill.

de Grahl, A. (2011). Success factors in logistics outsourcing. *Gabler Verlag, Springer*. https://doi.org/10.1007/978-3-8349-7084-8

De, A., & Singh, S. P. (2022). Analysis of competitiveness in Agri-supply chain logistics outsourcing: A B2B contractual framework. *Sustainability, 14*(11), 6866. https://doi.org/10.3390/su14116866

Dong, C., Huang, Q., Pan, Y., Ng, C. T., & Liu, R. (2023). Logistics outsourcing: Effects of greenwashing and blockchain technology. *Transportation Research Part e: Logistics and Transportation Review, 170*, 103015. https://doi.org/10.1016/j.tre.2023.103015

El Mokrini, A., & Aouam, T. (2022). A decision-support tool for policy makers in healthcare supply chains to balance between perceived risk in logistics outsourcing and cost-efficiency. *Expert Systems with Applications, 201*, 116999. https://doi.org/10.1016/j.eswa.2022.116999

Govindan, K., & Chaudhuri, A. (2016). Interrelationships of risks faced by third party logistics service providers: A DEMATEL based approach. *Transportation Research Part e: Logistics and Transportation Review, 90*, 177–195. https:// doi.org/10.1016/j.tre.2015.11.010

Greaver, M. F., & Greaver, M. F. (1999). *II*. A structured approach to outsourcing decisions and initiatives. Amacom Books.

Gruchmann, T., Melkonyan, A., & Krumme, K. (2018). Logistics business transformation for sustainability: Assessing the role of the lead sustainability service provider (6PL). *Logistics, 2*(4), 25. https://doi.org/10.3390/logistics2040025

Ha, N. T., Akbari, M., & Au, B. (2022). Last mile delivery in logistics and supply chain management: A bibliometric analysis and future directions. *Benchmarking: An International Journal, 30*(4), 1137–1170. https://doi.org/10.1108/BIJ-07-2021-0409

Harland, C., Brenchley, R., & Walker, H. (2003). Risk in supply networks. *Journal of Purchasing and Supply Management, 9*(2), 51–62. https://doi.org/10.1016/S1478-4092(03)00004-9

Harland, C., Knight, L., Lamming, R., & Walker, H. (2005). Outsourcing: Assessing the risks and benefits for organisations, sectors and nations. *International Journal of Operations & Production Management, 25*(9), 831–850. https://doi.org/10.1108/01443570510613929

Hoyer, C., Gunawan, I., & Reaiche, C. H. (2021). Implementing industry 4.0—The need for a holistic approach. In A. Dingli, F. Haddod & C. Klüver (Eds.), *Artificial intelligence in industry 4.0*. Studies in Computational Intelligence, vol 928. Springer. https://doi.org/10.1007/978-3-030-61045-6_1

Hsiao, H. I., Van Der Vorst, J. G. A. J., Kemp, R. G. M., & Omta, S. W. F. (2010). Developing a decision-making framework for levels of logistics outsourcing in food supply chain networks. *International Journal of Physical Distribution & Logistics Management, 40*(5), 395–414. https://doi.org/10.1108/09600031011052840

Kalubanga, M., & Namagembe, S. (2022). Trust, commitment, logistics outsourcing relationship quality, relationship satisfaction, strategy alignment and logistics performance—a case of selected manufacturing firms in Uganda. *The International Journal of Logistics Management, 33*(1), 102–140. https://doi.org/10.1108/IJLM-05-2020-0215

Koh, L., Dolgui, A., & Sarkis, J. (2020). Blockchain in transport and logistics—Paradigms and transitions. *International Journal of Production Research, 58*(7), 2054–2062. https://doi.org/10.1080/00207543.2020.1736428

König, A., & Spinler, S. (2016). The effect of logistics outsourcing on the supply chain vulnerability of shippers. *The International Journal of Logistics Management, 27*(1), 122–141. https://doi.org/10.1108/IJLM-03-2014-0043

Liu, W., Long, S., Wei, S., Xie, D., Wang, J., & Liu, X. (2022). Smart logistics ecological cooperation with data sharing and platform empowerment: An examination with evolutionary game model. *International Journal of Production Research, 60*(13), 4295–4315. https://doi.org/10.1080/002 07543.2021.1925173

Lynch, C. F. (2000). Logistics outsourcing: A management guide. Council of Logistics Management, Oak Brook.

Matlack Leasing (2019). 3PL, 4PL or 5PL logistic services, what's the difference? www.matlackleasing.com/article/3pl-4pl-5pl-logistic-services-whats-dif ference/. Accessed 1 April 2023.

Miah, S. J., Ahsan, K., & Msimangira, K. A. B. (2014). An approach of purchasing decision support in healthcare supply chain management. *Operations and Supply Chain Management: An International Journal, 6*(2), 43–53. https://doi.org/10.31387/oscm0140087

Niu, B., & Mu, Z. (2020). Sustainable efforts, procurement outsourcing, and channel co-opetition in emerging markets. *Transportation Research Part e: Logistics and Transportation Review, 138*, 101960. https://doi.org/10. 1016/j.tre.2020.101960

Niu, B., Zhang, J., & Mu, Z. (2022). IoT-enabled delivery time guarantee in logistics outsourcing and efficiency improvement. *International Journal of Production Research, 1–22.* https://doi.org/10.1080/00207543.2022.211 7868

Odnokonnaya, M. (2017). Logistics outsourcing. Current state of the market of outsourcing logistics services. Bachelor thesis, South-Eastern Finland University of Applied Sciences.

Pettersson, A. I., & Segerstedt, A. (2013). To evaluate cost saving in a supply chain: Two examples from Ericsson in the telecom industry. *Operations and Supply Chain Management: An International Journal, 6*(3), 94–102. https:// doi.org/10.31387/oscm0150094

Potter, A., & Lalwani, C. (2008). Investigating the impact of demand amplification on freight transport. *Transportation Research Part e: Logistics and Transportation Review, 44*(5), 835–846. https://doi.org/10.1016/j.tre. 2007.06.001

Pournader, M., Shi, Y., Seuring, S., & Koh, S. L. (2020). Blockchain applications in supply chains, Transport and logistics: A systematic review of the literature. *International Journal of Production Research, 58*(7), 2063–2081. https:// doi.org/10.1080/00207543.2019.1650976

Rahman, S., & Jim Wu, Y. C. (2011). Logistics outsourcing in China: The manufacturer-cum-supplier perspective. *Supply Chain Management, 16*(6), 462–473. https://doi.org/10.1108/13598541111171156

Rodrigue, J. P., Comtois, C., & Slack, B. (2016). *The geography of transport systems* (4th ed.). Routledge.

Saglietto, L. (2013). Towards a classification of fourth party logistics (4PL). *Universal Journal of Industrial and Business Management, 1*(3), 104–116. https://doi.org/10.13189/ujibm.2013.010305

Schniederjans, M. J., & Zuckweiler, K. M. (2004). A quantitative approach to the outsourcing-insourcing decision in an international context. *Management Decision, 42*(8), 974–986. https://doi.org/10.1108/00251740410555461

Skjoett-Larsen, T. (2000). Third party logistics—from an interorganizational point of view. *International Journal of Physical Distribution & Logistics Management, 30*(2), 112–127. https://doi.org/10.1108/096000300 10318838

Solakivi, T., Kiisler, A., & Hilmola, O. P. (2022). A comparative study of market potential for logistics outsourcing in Estonia and Finland. *Journal of Global Operations and Strategic Sourcing, 15*(1), 79–95. https://doi.org/10.1108/ JGOSS-01-2021-0004

Solakivi, T., Töyli, J., & Ojala, L. (2013). Logistics outsourcing, its motives and the level of logistics costs in manufacturing and trading companies operating in Finland. *Production Planning & Control, 24*(4–5), 388–398. https://doi. org/10.1080/09537287.2011.648490

Stojanović, Đ. M., & Aas, B. (2015). Transport outsourcing and transport collaboration relationship-the risk hedging perspective. *Serbian Journal of Management, 10*(1), 33–49.

Tian, Y., Lai, F., & Daniel, F. (2008). An examination of the nature of trust in logistics outsourcing relationship: Empirical evidence from China. *Industrial Management & Data Systems, 108*(3), 346–367. https://doi.org/10.1108/ 02635570810858769

Tsai, M. C., Lai, K. H., Lloyd, A. E., & Lin, H. J. (2012). The dark side of logistics outsourcing—Unraveling the potential risks leading to failed relationships. *Transportation Research Part e: Logistics and Transportation Review, 48*(1), 178–189. https://doi.org/10.1016/j.tre.2011.07.003

Voss, D. M., Page, T. J., Keller, S., & Ozment, J. (2006). Determining important carrier attributes: A fresh perspective using the theory of reasoned action. *Transportation Journal, 45*(3), 7–19. http://www.jstor.org/stable/ 20713641

Wisner, J. D., Tan, K. C., & Leong, G. K. (2012). *Principles of supply chain management: A balanced approach* (3rd Edn.). South-Western Cengage.

Yang, C., Lan, S., Lin, T., Wang, L., Zhuang, Z., & Huang, G. O. (2021). Transforming Hong Kong's Warehousing Industry with a novel business model: A game-theory analysis. *Robotics and Computer-Integrated Manufacturing, 68*, 102073. https://doi.org/10.1016/j.rcim.2020.102073

Zhou, L., Jiang, Z., Geng, N., Niu, Y., Cui, F., Liu, K., & Qi, N. (2022). Production and operations management for intelligent manufacturing: A systematic literature review. *International Journal of Production Research, 60*(2), 808–846. https://doi.org/10.1080/00207543.2021.2017055

CHAPTER 8

The Evolution of Outsourcing: Embracing the Era of Outsourcing 4.0

8.1 Introduction

The rapid and extensive impact of the pandemic caught many firms off guard, necessitating swift adaptation to volatile conditions (Akbari et al., 2023; Raj et al., 2022). This unforeseen challenge has resulted in bottlenecks, delays, and shortages within supply chains, consequently influencing economic growth and consumer confidence (Alblowi et al., 2022).

Concurrently, a notable change in consumer spending patterns has unfolded (Ha et al., 2022; Zwanka & Buff, 2021). With a substantial reduction in spending on services, consumers have redirected their expenditure toward products, particularly those associated with home and health (Roll et al., 2022). This change in demand has imposed additional strains on supply chains already grappling with increased demand due to the pandemic (Pujawan & Bah, 2022). The compounding effects of these factors underscore the intricate challenges that businesses and supply chains face in navigating the repercussions of the ongoing global health crisis.

Prior to the COVID-19 pandemic, the 2018 global survey by Deloitte underscored the crucial role of Industry 4.0 (I4.0) technologies in transforming supply chains, with a specific emphasis on the digitalization of supply chain processes (Deloitte, 2018). The survey focused on automation and robotics, revealing a shift away from hazardous tasks. This aligns

© The Author(s), under exclusive license to Springer Nature Singapore Pte Ltd. 2024
M. Akbari, *The Road to Outsourcing 4.0*,
https://doi.org/10.1007/978-981-97-2708-7_8

169

with Lyall et al.'s (2018) findings, highlighting a transformative impact on supply chain work environments through self-regulating utilities.

> Without data, you're just another person with an opinion.—Edwards Deming (1900–1993)

The integration of emerging I4.0 technologies plays a pivotal role in shaping digital transformation in supply chains. It facilitates the generation, accumulation, and interpretation of extensive datasets, thereby improving operational efficiency across various industries (Hoyer et al., 2023; Kache & Seuring, 2017; LaValle et al., 2011). Notably, ongoing research with AI, exemplified by the ChatGPT solution, explores its potential to engage with customers and address queries autonomously, eliminating the basic need for human intervention (Nunez, 2023). In the context of a Supply Chain 4.0 strategy, the success of the digital transformation hinges not only on technological advancements but also on the necessary managerial and resource capabilities for a seamless implementation (Frederico et al., 2021). The convergence of virtual and physical technologies is critical in fortifying resilience in supply chains (Frederico et al., 2021). Strategic deployment of digital technologies during the uncertainties of the pandemic can significantly enhance the agility, resilience, and long-term performance of global supply chain companies (Papadopoulos et al., 2020).

I4.0 underscores intelligent manufacturing and automated ecosystems, harnessing state-of-the-art technologies to facilitate streamlined and adaptable production activities that result in high-quality products (Raja Santhi & Muthuswamy, 2023). This method emphasizes efficiency and flexibility in operations (Hofmann & Rüsch, 2017; Machado et al., 2020). A McKinsey survey conducted in China in 2016 revealed that only 57% of manufacturers had adequately prepared for the implementation of I4.0 technologies at that time, attributed to a lack of understanding regarding the benefits and economic impacts of these technologies (McKinsey, 2016). Therefore, an emphasis on effective knowledge management becomes increasingly important for the seamless incorporation of I4.0 technologies into global supply chains (Sartori et al., 2022). There is a chance to enhance this comprehension and assist manufacturers to integrate and implement I4.0 technologies, unlocking their complete economic potential (Bai et al., 2020).

The landscape of outsourcing has undergone a remarkable evolution over the years, adapting and transforming in response to the dynamic interplay of business and technology. In its early days, outsourcing primarily involved the delegation of non-core tasks to external vendors, offering cost savings and operational efficiency (Akbari, 2022). However, as technological advancements and global connectivity accelerated, outsourcing evolved into more sophisticated forms, culminating in what is now termed "Outsourcing 4.0". This represents a paradigm shift that transcends mere cost considerations, delving into the realms of digital innovation, strategic partnerships, and enhanced collaboration.

In the forthcoming segments of this chapter, I will thoroughly examine each phase of the outsourcing evolution, dissecting the trends, challenges, and opportunities that have been instrumental in shaping the landscape of outsourcing 4.0. As organizations traverse this transformative era, a nuanced comprehension of the historical context, covered in preceding chapters, coupled with an adept embrace of the diverse facets of outsourcing 4.0, is imperative for success in an ever more interconnected and digitally-driven business environment.

8.2   INDUSTRY 4.0

Over the past three decades, IT systems have undergone a transformative revolution (Dal Mas et al., 2023). This evolution has given rise to what is now termed "Industry 4.0", denoting the implementation of interconnected networks operating autonomously within the realms of production and operations, eliminating the need for direct human intervention (Oesterreich & Teuteberg, 2016).

I4.0 encapsulates the essence of the Fourth Industrial Revolution, marking the advent of digital transformation that facilitates automation and the development of smart factories and manufacturing processes (Akbari et al., 2023; Hoye et al., 2021). This paradigm shift is poised to have a profound impact on the supply chain, influencing future investments, employment dynamics, and trade practices (Piccarozzi et al., 2018). The Fourth Industrial Revolution is anticipated to usher in significant changes, bringing about a new era characterized by advanced technologies, increased efficiency, and innovative approaches to various facets of industry and commerce (see Fig. 8.1).

Within the vast spectrum of I4.0 technologies, a myriad of transformative innovations is reshaping industries and catalyzing unparalleled

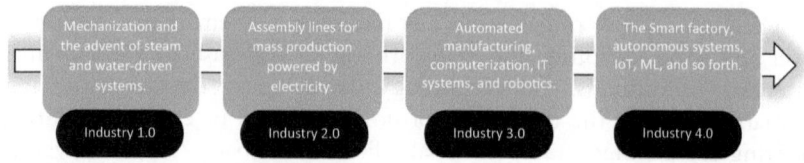

Fig. 8.1 Evolution of industry: from 1.0 to 4.0—the Fourth Industrial Revolution journey (*Source* Author's own work)

efficiency and innovation (Bai et al., 2020). Among these, automation, robotics, AI, IoT, and ML stand out as the cornerstones of this technological revolution (Akbari, 2023). These dynamic technologies are not merely tools; they are catalysts propelling a paradigm shift in the way supply chains operate, optimizing processes and fostering a new era of industrial prowess (Vahdat, 2022). From streamlined manufacturing processes to intelligent decision-making systems, these technologies collectively usher in an age of heightened productivity and groundbreaking advancements (Hansen & Bøgh, 2021; Queiroz & Wamba, 2022) (see Table 8.1).

The integration of automation, robotics, AI, IoT, and ML is not only transforming industrial landscapes but also influencing global business strategies (Vu et al., 2022). This convergence of technologies, often referred to as I4.0, is reshaping traditional manufacturing and operational processes, introducing unprecedented levels of efficiency and innovation (Akbari & Do, 2021). As industries embrace this technological revolution, the concept of outsourcing 4.0 emerges as a pivotal component in navigating the changing business landscape.

In the subsequent section, an in-depth analysis will delve into the nuances of outsourcing 4.0, exploring how these advanced technologies are shaping the outsourcing landscape and fostering a new era of collaborative and tech-driven business partnerships. The synergies between I4.0 technologies and outsourcing strategies hold the promise of unlocking unprecedented value, efficiency, and innovation in the supply chain ecosystem.

Table 8.1 Technological landscape for industrial advancements

Technology	Description	Applications in industries
Automation	This is the use of technology to perform tasks without human intervention, ranging from simple processes to sophisticated systems. It is implemented to streamline operations, reduce errors, and increase productivity (Cugno et al., 2021; Deloitte, 2018; Lyall et al., 2018)	Process automation in business and industrial automation in manufacturing
Robotics	Robotics involves the design, construction, operation, and use of robots. Industrial robots are programmed for precision and speed in repetitive tasks, improving manufacturing processes. Collaborative robots (cobots) work alongside humans, enhancing efficiency and safety (Eckert et al., 2016)	Industrial tasks requiring precision, speed, and safety, such as manufacturing
AI	This represents the simulation of human intelligence in machines. It is used in industries for data analysis, predictive maintenance, and decision-making. AI-driven systems adapt and learn from data, optimizing processes over time (Bashir & Harky, 2019; Schinkel et al., 2019)	Data analysis, predictive maintenance, and decision-making in various industries
IoT	IoT involves connecting everyday objects to the internet, enabling data exchange. In an industrial context, it allows for remote monitoring and control of devices and systems, enhancing real-time decision-making and operational efficiency (Benyezza et al., 2023; Li et al., 2015)	Remote monitoring, control of devices and systems, real-time decision-making in industrial settings
ML	ML concentrates on developing algorithms for systems to learn from data and make predictions. It is applied in industries to analyze datasets, identify patterns, and optimize processes (Ahmad et al., 2022; Akbari & Do, 2021)	Quality control, demand forecasting, energy optimization, and process optimization in industrial applications

8.3   OUTSOURCING 4.0: CONVERGENCE, INNOVATION, AND STRATEGIC EVOLUTION

Outsourcing 4.0 signifies the convergence of digital technologies, strategic partnerships, and a comprehensive approach to outsourcing. In this era, outsourcing is not only a cost-cutting measure but a strategic decision to drive innovation, agility, and competitiveness. The focus has shifted from transactions to transformations, with outsourcing becoming an integral part of companies' digital strategies.

The historical trajectory from the rudimentary models of outsourcing 1.0 to the interconnected and technologically sophisticated landscape of outsourcing 4.0 embodies a compelling narrative of organizational adaptation, propelled by the unstoppable march of digital progress and the seamless connectivity afforded by a globalized world. This narrative unfolds as a dynamic story, weaving through the various stages that characterize the evolution of outsourcing.

Outsourcing 1.0 marked the inception—a phase where businesses embraced cost-centric delegation, endeavoring to streamline processes and curtail operational expenses. This period was foundational, laying the bedrock for subsequent developments. As technology progressed and the business terrain became more intricate, outsourcing 2.0 emerged, characterized by a significant shift toward a sophisticated approach to relationship management. In outsourcing 2.0, the emphasis was on increased collaboration, collective stability, and efficient communication, with relationships taking center stage in the creation of business value. Suppliers and companies were mutually invested in each other's successes, fostering a collaborative environment that led to enhanced access to supply chain information. Organizations sought external expertise not solely for cost reduction but with a strategic focus on gaining a competitive edge through access to niche skills and knowledge.

The narrative progresses further into the era of outsourcing 3.0, where the complexities of a globalized economy demanded more intricate outsourcing strategies. The integration of cloud services with on-premises virtual private clouds further propelled the evolution, leading to the emergence of "Outsourcing 3.0" or "Web 3.0" (Gedda, 2011), where businesses began outsourcing not just tasks but entire processes, often on a global scale. The focus shifted from local optimization to the orchestration of a global network of interconnected activities.

Now, in the contemporary epoch of outsourcing 4.0, the story reaches its zenith. Outsourcing is no longer confined to a transactional exchange of services; it has evolved into a transformative endeavor intricately interwoven with the digital fabric of modern supply chain strategy. The synergy of cutting-edge technologies, strategic partnerships, and a holistic approach defines a new paradigm, outsourcing 4.0, where outsourcing becomes a dynamic force propelling innovation, agility, and competitiveness (see Fig. 8.2). This model is tailored to accelerate marketplace dynamics by leveraging strategic relationships, enabling future-forward organizations to swiftly collaborate, develop new capabilities, integrate them for value creation, and drive that value seamlessly into the supply chain (Deloitte, 2022a).

This narrative illuminates the adaptive resilience of supply chains amid technological advancements, highlighting the necessity to remain pertinent in a globally connected world. It unfolds as a tale of unwavering

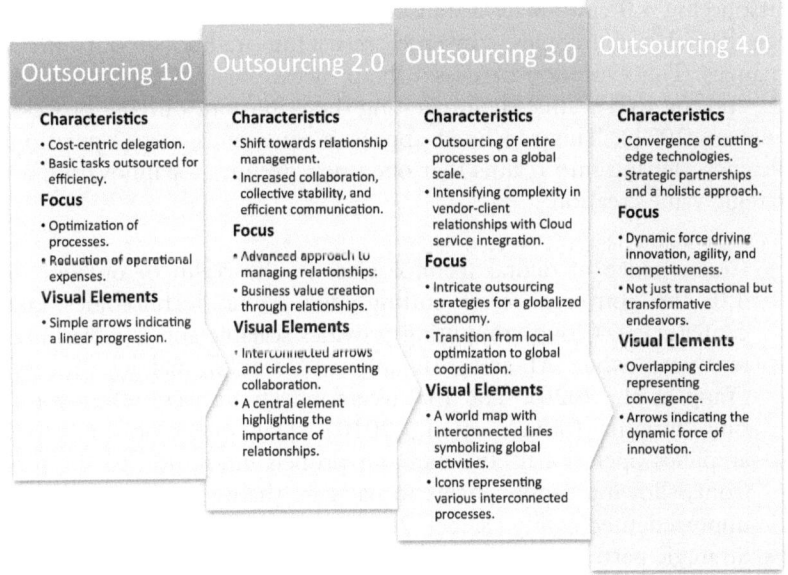

Fig. 8.2 Outsourcing's evolution—journey from 1.0 to 4.0 (*Source* Author's own work)

resilience, foresight, and strategic evolution, where each developmental stage assimilates the wisdom of its precursors. This journey culminates in the era of outsourcing 4.0—a period wherein the fundamental nature of outsourcing undergoes a profound redefinition within the swiftly advancing digital age.

The dawn of the digital era coupled with heightened global connectivity has acted as catalyst propelling the evolution of outsourcing (Deloitte, 2022b). In this progression, technology's sophistication and the seamlessness of communication channels have prompted supply chains to aspire for more from their outsourcing relationships than mere operational efficiency and cost savings. The narrative captures a transformative trajectory where supply chains, spurred by technological innovation and global interconnection, are seeking to extract strategic value and innovation from their outsourcing engagements.

8.3.1   Defining Outsourcing 4.0

Outsourcing 4.0 epitomizes a transformative paradigm in which cutting-edge digital technologies converge, reshaping traditional outsourcing dynamics. This evolution harnesses the prowess of cloud computing, AI, ML, and the IoT, seamlessly integrating them into outsourcing processes (Sullivan, 2021). This redefined approach transcends mere operational efficiency, delving into realms that open new avenues for innovation and strategic value creation.

- Convergence of digital technologies: In the realm of outsourcing 4.0, the convergence of cutting-edge digital technologies takes center stage. Cloud computing provides scalable and flexible infrastructures, while AI and ML augment decision-making processes (Yang et al., 2020). The IoT interconnects devices, offering real-time insights (Sisinni et al., 2018). This integration not only amplifies operational efficiency but propels innovation to the forefront, allowing supply chains to navigate the digital landscape with unprecedented agility (Siebel, 2019).
- Strategic partnerships: Diverging from its predecessors, outsourcing 4.0 underscores the pivotal role of strategic partnerships. This evolution transcends traditional vendor relationships, fostering collaborations that extend beyond transactional exchanges (Chukwu et al., 2023). Strategic partners are now perceived as integral extensions

of the supply chains, sharing goals and objectives (Altekar, 2023). Together, they embark on a journey of mutual growth and innovation, leveraging each other's strengths to navigate the complexities of the modern business landscape.

- Holistic approach to outsourcing: Within the paradigm of outsourcing 4.0, outsourcing ceases to be a standalone strategy; rather, it transforms into an integral component of the overarching business strategy. This marks a shift toward a holistic approach where outsourcing is intricately aligned with the broader digital strategy of the company. The synergy between these elements contributes not only to operational efficiency but becomes a catalyst for innovation, agility, and competitiveness, ensuring that the organization is not merely keeping pace but leading in the digital age.

Therefore, outsourcing 4.0 is defined as:

> a paradigm shift in business strategy, involving the convergence of advanced digital technologies, strategic partnerships, and a holistic approach to outsourcing for enhanced innovation and competitiveness.

After comprehensively defining outsourcing 4.0, the following graph visually elucidates the interconnected components and relationships that characterize this paradigm shift in business strategy (see Fig. 8.3).

This transformative evolution is characterized by a departure from transactional engagements toward collaborative relationships that extend beyond mere operational efficiency. In this era, outsourcing is not isolated but intricately aligned with the broader digital strategy, contributing synergistically to innovation, agility, and a heightened competitive edge. Outsourcing 4.0 transcends conventional boundaries, propelling organizations into a realm where the fusion of technology, collaboration, and strategic alignment becomes the cornerstone of sustainable success in the ever evolving digital landscape (Deloitte, 2022a).

8.3.2 Real-World Examples of Outsourcing 4.0

The emergence of outsourcing 4.0 is not just a theoretical concept; it manifests in tangible and transformative ways across industries globally.

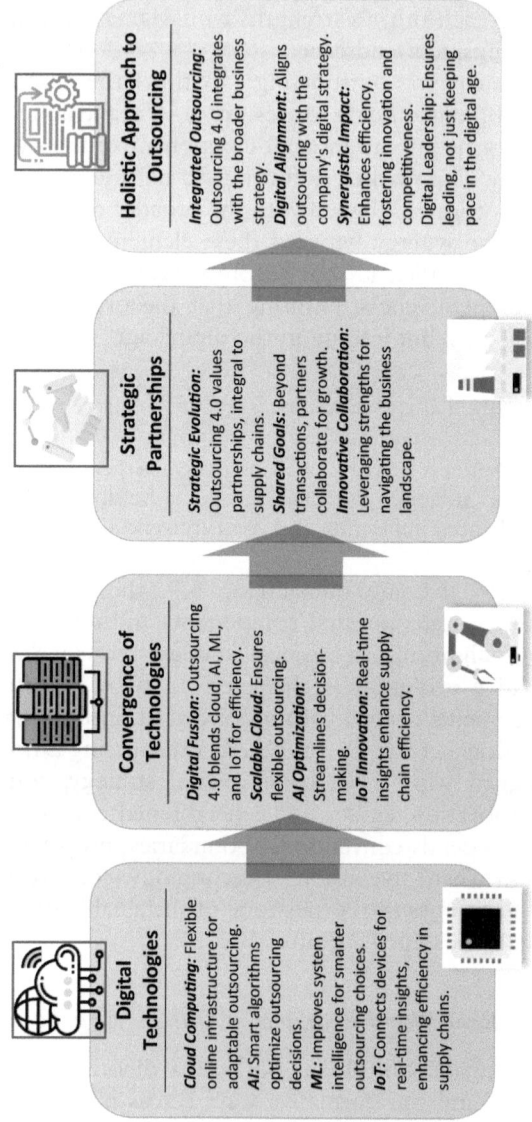

Digital Technologies

Cloud Computing: Flexible online infrastructure for adaptable outsourcing.
AI: Smart algorithms optimize outsourcing decisions.
ML: Improves system intelligence for smarter outsourcing choices.
IoT: Connects devices for real-time insights, enhancing efficiency in supply chains.

Convergence of Technologies

Digital Fusion: Outsourcing 4.0 blends cloud, AI, ML, and IoT for efficiency.
Scalable Cloud: Ensures flexible outsourcing.
AI Optimization: Streamlines decision-making.
IoT Innovation: Real-time insights enhance supply chain efficiency.

Strategic Partnerships

Strategic Evolution: Outsourcing 4.0 values partnerships, integral to supply chains.
Shared Goals: Beyond transactions, partners collaborate for growth.
Innovative Collaboration: Leveraging strengths for navigating the business landscape.

Holistic Approach to Outsourcing

Integrated Outsourcing: Outsourcing 4.0 integrates with the broader business strategy.
Digital Alignment: Aligns outsourcing with the company's digital strategy.
Synergistic Impact: Enhances efficiency, fostering innovation and competitiveness.
Digital Leadership: Ensures leading, not just keeping pace in the digital age.

Fig. 8.3 Outsourcing 4.0 paradigm (*Source* Author's own work)

A glimpse into possible scenarios illustrates how supply chains are leveraging advanced digital technologies, forging strategic partnerships, and embracing a holistic approach to outsourcing.

- *Data analytics for decision support*: In the realm of outsourcing 4.0, supply chains are navigating the data-rich landscape with advanced analytics capabilities attained through strategic collaborations. Consider a multinational corporation entering into a partnership with a specialized analytics firm to extract actionable insights from vast datasets. This collaborative effort not only refines decision-making processes but also sparks innovation in areas such as product development and market strategies. The integration of data analytics becomes a driving force, propelling supply chains toward informed, agile, and competitive decision-making.
- *AI-powered customer support*: Outsourcing 4.0 is reshaping customer support through the infusion of AI. Companies are forging alliances with AI-driven service providers to deploy chatbots and virtual assistants. These intelligent systems provide instantaneous responses to customer queries, elevating the overall quality of service while concurrently reducing operational costs. The incorporation of AI in customer support exemplifies how outsourcing 4.0 redefines conventional service paradigms, ushering in an era of efficient and technology-driven customer interactions.
- *Blockchain for supply chain management*: In the dynamic landscape of outsourcing 4.0, businesses are revolutionizing SCM through strategic engagements with blockchain experts. Collaborations aim to establish transparent and secure supply chains, mitigating risks and enhancing traceability in today's intricate and globalized supply networks. Blockchain not only acts as a technological disruptor but also serves as a foundational element in the quest for resilient and reliable supply chain solutions.
- *Robotic Process Automation (RPA) in finance*: Outsourcing 4.0 finds concrete expression in the finance sector through the adoption of RPA. Financial institutions, recognizing the potential, collaborate with RPA specialists to automate routine, rule-based tasks such as data entry and reconciliation. This strategic partnership not only reduces errors and enhances accuracy but also liberates human resources to focus on tasks demanding strategic analysis and

decision-making, ushering in a new era of efficiency and precision in financial operations.

- *Collaborative innovation labs*: Outsourcing 4.0 transcends traditional outsourcing paradigms with the establishment of collaborative innovation labs. Supply chains engage with external innovation hubs, often situated in technology-rich ecosystems, to co-create and innovate. This approach fosters the cross-pollination of ideas, leading to breakthrough innovations that extend beyond the capabilities of a single organization. The collaborative innovation lab model showcases how outsourcing 4.0 is not confined to transactional exchanges but is a catalyst for transformative and boundary-pushing innovations. It exemplifies a strategic shift toward collaborative ideation, driving industry-wide progress in an era where innovation is paramount.

To sum up, outsourcing 4.0 marks a pivotal shift in the outsourcing paradigm. It is no longer just about cost savings; rather, it is a strategic imperative for driving innovation, agility, and competitiveness. The progression from historical outsourcing models to outsourcing 4.0 reflects the dynamic interplay of technology, globalization, and strategic thinking. The scenarios provided illustrate how businesses are embracing this paradigm shift to stay ahead in an increasingly digital and interconnected business environment. In navigating this transformative era, a nuanced understanding of the historical context and proactive engagement with the diverse facets of outsourcing 4.0 are crucial for sustained success.

8.4   Navigating Outsourcing 4.0: Unveiling Benefits, Challenges, and Opportunities

8.4.1   Benefits of Outsourcing 4.0

Outsourcing 4.0 heralds a new era of innovation acceleration, where the integration of cutting-edge technologies becomes a driving force for transformation. Supply chains strategically leverage advanced tools such as AI, ML, and the IoT to not only improve operational efficiency but also foster unparalleled creativity and problem-solving (Allioui & Mourdi, 2023). The collaborative innovation labs established in this paradigm exemplify how external expertise converges with internal capabilities, leading to breakthrough innovations that transcend organizational boundaries.

- *Innovation acceleration:*

Advanced technologies: Outsourcing 4.0 brings forth the integration of cutting-edge technologies like AI, ML, and the IoT. This infusion of innovation into outsourcing processes not only enhances operational efficiency but also opens up new frontiers for creativity and problem-solving.

Collaborative innovation labs: The collaborative nature of outsourcing 4.0, exemplified by the establishment of collaborative innovation labs, fosters an environment where external expertise converges with internal capabilities. This collaboration sparks innovation that transcends the confines of a single organization, leading to breakthroughs that might not have been possible in isolation (Wang et al., 2023).

- *Strategic partnerships:*

Mutual growth: Outsourcing 4.0 moves beyond the transactional nature of previous outsourcing models, emphasizing strategic partnerships. In this paradigm, outsourcing relationships become collaborations that extend beyond the traditional vendor–client dynamic. Strategic partners are viewed as integral extensions of the supply chain, working together toward shared goals, thereby fostering mutual growth and success (Pereira et al., 2023).

Extended expertise: Organizations leverage strategic partnerships to access specialized expertise. For example, a manufacturing company might collaborate with a robotics specialist to integrate automation into its production processes. This access to external knowledge enhances the overall capabilities of the supply chain, contributing to its competitive edge (Kok & Akbari, 2023).

- *Operational efficiency and cost savings:*

RPA: Outsourcing 4.0 facilitates the adoption of RPA in various industries, particularly in finance. RPA enables the automation of routine, rule-based tasks, leading to significant improvements in operational efficiency (Nayak et al., 2024). This not only reduces errors but also allows human resources to focus on tasks that require critical thinking and strategic decision-making.

Cloud computing: The utilization of cloud computing in outsourcing 4.0 provides supply chains with scalable and flexible infrastructures. This flexibility enables organizations to swiftly respond to shifting demands, optimizing resource utilization and leading to cost savings (Akbari, 2023).

- *Global talent access:*

Niche skills and knowledge: Outsourcing 4.0 enables organizations to tap into a global pool of talent with specialized skills and knowledge (Kok & Akbari, 2023). For instance, a technology company based in the US might collaborate with a data analytics firm in India to harness the expertise required for complex data projects.

24/7 operations: Global outsourcing allows businesses to operate around the clock. Teams in different time zones can collaborate to ensure continuous progress and support, enhancing productivity and responsiveness (Akbari, 2022).

8.4.2   Challenges of Outsourcing 4.0

While outsourcing 4.0 presents numerous benefits, it is not without its challenges. Data security and privacy concerns loom large as organizations navigate the integration of advanced technologies (Mekdad et al., 2023). Sharing sensitive information across borders exposes supply chains to cyber threats, necessitating vigilant management and mitigation of cybersecurity risks. Additionally, adherence to data protection regulations such as the GDPR becomes imperative, adding complexity to the outsourcing landscape.

- *Data security and privacy concerns:*

Cybersecurity risks: The integration of advanced technologies, particularly in data analytics and AI, brings forth concerns regarding data security (Salah et al., 2023). The growing reliance on cloud computing and the cross-border exchange of sensitive information makes supply chains vulnerable to cybersecurity risks. Managing and mitigating these risks become paramount in outsourcing 4.0.

Regulatory compliance: As data protection regulations become more stringent globally, organizations engaging in outsourcing must navigate complex regulatory landscapes. Ensuring compliance with regulations such as the GDPR poses a challenge, especially when outsourcing involves processing personal and sensitive data (Brandy, 2023).

- *Dependency on technology:*

Technological disruptions: While advanced technologies contribute to the benefits of outsourcing 4.0, they also pose challenges. Rapid technological advancements can lead to disruptions, and supply chains need to adapt quickly to stay competitive (Steffen et al., 2018). This creates a constant demand for upskilling and reskilling the workforce to keep pace with evolving technologies (Kok & Akbari, 2023).

Initial investment: The integration of new technologies often requires significant initial investment. Supply chains must carefully assess the costs and benefits of adopting these technologies, particularly when considering the potential for rapid technological obsolescence (Akbari et al., 2023).

- *Cultural and communication challenges:*

Diversity and communication: Global outsourcing involves collaboration across diverse cultures and languages. Effective communication becomes crucial in overcoming language barriers and ensuring that all team members are aligned with project goals (Nguyen et al., 2022). Cultural differences can also impact working styles and expectations, requiring organizations to implement strategies for effective cross-cultural collaboration (Gasteiger et al., 2023).

Management of remote teams: The shift toward collaborative relationships in outsourcing 4.0 means that teams may be geographically dispersed. Managing remote teams poses challenges in terms of communication, team cohesion, and ensuring that everyone is working toward shared objectives (Hopkins & Bardoel, 2023).

8.4.3   Opportunities of Outsourcing 4.0

Outsourcing 4.0 unveils a multitude of possibilities for supply chains. Market expansion becomes achievable through strategic partnerships that facilitate access to new and diverse markets (Tjemkes et al., 2023).

Collaborative innovation labs, often situated in technology-rich ecosystems, provide a platform for companies to establish a global presence, capitalizing on external expertise and resources.

- *Market expansion:*

  Access to global markets: Outsourcing 4.0 allows supply chains to access new and diverse markets. Strategic partnerships can facilitate market expansion by utilizing the expertise and knowledge of local partners (Tjemkes et al., 2023). This is especially pertinent in industries where localization is essential for success.

  Global presence: Collaborative innovation labs, where companies engage with external innovation hubs, provide an opportunity to establish a global presence. These innovation hubs are often located in technology-rich ecosystems, offering access to a network of expertise and resources.

- *Flexibility and scalability:*

  Adaptive business models: The integration of cloud computing in outsourcing 4.0 enables supply chains to adopt more flexible and scalable business models. This adaptability allows organizations to respond quickly to changing market dynamics, scaling operations up or down as needed (He et al., 2023).

  Agile operations: Outsourcing 4.0 promotes agile operations, allowing supply chains to pivot and adapt rapidly to market changes. This agility is crucial in industries with fast-paced technological advancements and evolving consumer preferences (Alghamdi & Agag, 2024).

- *Continuous learning and skill development:*

  Upskilling opportunities: The adoption of advanced technologies in outsourcing 4.0 creates opportunities for continuous learning and skill development. Organizations can make investments in upskilling their workforce to ensure they possess the capabilities to leverage new technologies effectively (Akbari, 2022).

  Knowledge transfer: Collaborative partnerships, especially those involving strategic alliances with external experts, provide opportunities for knowledge transfer. This knowledge transfer not only enhances the capabilities of the workforce but also contributes to the overall innovation and competitiveness of the organization (Kok & Akbari, 2023).

In navigating the complex terrain of outsourcing 4.0, organizations must recognize that success is not merely about overcoming challenges or seizing opportunities in isolation. It's about orchestrating a harmonious symphony, where the benefits are maximized, the challenges are mitigated, and the opportunities are strategically embraced (Vu et al., 2022). As outsourcing 4.0 unfolds its transformative potential, supply chains are called upon not just to react but to proactively shape their destiny in the digital age (Akbari et al., 2023). The road to sustained success in this dynamic landscape demands continuous innovation, a keen awareness of market shifts, and an unwavering commitment to staying at the forefront of technological advancements (Frederico et al., 2021). In doing so, organizations can not only weather the storms of change but also ride the waves of opportunity, positioning themselves as industry leaders in the ever-evolving tapestry of outsourcing 4.0.

8.5   Emergent Concerns and Future Directions

The landscape of outsourcing 4.0, while promising unprecedented benefits and opportunities, is not devoid of emergent concerns that warrant careful consideration. As supply chains navigate this transformative era, certain considerations come to the forefront, and, simultaneously, a set of intriguing future directions beckon as the next phase of evolution in outsourcing unfolds.

8.5.1   Emergent Concerns

Ethical implications of advanced technologies: Incorporating advanced technologies like AI raises the importance of ethical considerations (Kumar et al., 2020). The utilization of AI and ML in decision-making processes, particularly in areas such as talent acquisition and customer interactions, raises concerns about bias, transparency, and accountability (Busuioc, 2021). Organizations must grapple with the ethical implications of these technologies, ensuring that their deployment aligns with principles of fairness, equity, and responsible use.

Cybersecurity and data privacy: As outsourcing 4.0 relies heavily on data analytics, cloud computing, and global collaborations, the specter of cybersecurity threats looms large (Nguyen et al., 2020). The interconnected nature of outsourcing operations increases vulnerability to cyberattacks, and businesses must fortify their defenses. Additionally, the evolving landscape of data protection regulations requires organizations to maintain a vigilant stance to protect sensitive information and uphold privacy standards.

Resilience in the face of technological disruptions: While technological advancements are a cornerstone of outsourcing 4.0, they also introduce an element of vulnerability (Lewallen, 2021). Rapid changes in technology can lead to disruptions, and organizations must cultivate resilience to adapt swiftly (Frederico et al., 2021). This involves not only staying abreast of technological trends but also building flexible systems that can withstand and recover from unforeseen disruptions, ensuring business continuity in the face of technological shifts.

Dependency on global supply chains: The globalization inherent in outsourcing operations exposes businesses to risks associated with global supply chains (Akbari, 2022). Events such as geopolitical tensions or wars, natural disasters, or pandemics can disrupt the seamless flow of goods and services. Organizations need robust contingency plans to navigate these challenges and potentially reconsider aspects of their supply chain strategies to enhance resilience.

8.5.2   Future Directions

Sustainability in outsourcing: The future of outsourcing lies in a heightened focus on sustainability. Organizations will increasingly consider ESG factors in their outsourcing decisions (Moreira & Rodrigues, 2023). This involves assessing the carbon footprint of outsourcing operations, promoting ethical labor practices, and incorporating sustainable practices into the supply chain (Alvarez & Rubio, 2015). Sustainable outsourcing will not only align with global initiatives but also resonate with environmentally conscious consumers.

Integration of augmented reality (AR) and virtual reality (VR): The next wave of technological integration in outsourcing 4.0 may involve the use of AR and VR. These emerging technologies have the potential to revolutionize training, collaboration, and customer interactions (Numfu et al., 2019). For example, in manufacturing, AR can assist remote workers in troubleshooting machinery, and VR can simulate realistic training environments. The integration of AR and VR can enhance not only operational efficiency but also the overall user experience.

Emphasis on circular economy practices: A shift toward circular economy practices is anticipated in future outsourcing models (Lahti et al., 2018). This involves minimizing waste, recycling materials, and designing products for longevity and reusability. Supply chains will increasingly look for outsourcing partners that align with circular economy principles, contributing to a more sustainable and environmentally-friendly approach to production and consumption (Akbari, 2022).

Enhanced AI ethics and governance: As AI continues to play a pivotal role in outsourcing, there will be a growing emphasis on AI ethics and governance. Organizations will develop robust frameworks to ensure the responsible and ethical use of AI, addressing concerns related to bias, accountability, and transparency (Kumar et al., 2020). AI governance will become an integral part of outsourcing strategies, reflecting a commitment to ethical AI practices.

Reskilling initiatives for the workforce: The evolution of outsourcing models will necessitate reskilling initiatives to align the workforce with the demands of emerging technologies (Kok & Akbari, 2023). As automation and AI reshape job roles, organizations will invest in reskilling programs to equip employees with the necessary skills for the digital age (Adepoju, 2022). This proactive approach to workforce development will be crucial in fostering a workforce that is adaptable, innovative, and capable of navigating the complexities of outsourcing 4.0.

8.6 Managerial Implications

The advent of outsourcing 4.0 brings about a paradigm shift in how supply chains approach and manage their outsourcing strategies. This transformative era, marked by the integration of advanced digital technologies and a holistic approach to outsourcing, necessitates a re-evaluation of managerial practices. Here, I dig into the key managerial implications of outsourcing 4.0, exploring how organizations and leaders can navigate the challenges and leverage the opportunities presented by this dynamic landscape.

- Strategic alignment with digital initiatives: Managers must align outsourcing strategies with broader digital initiatives (Yeow et al., 2018). Outsourcing is no longer a transactional exchange; it is an integral part of the overall digital strategy. This requires a nuanced understanding of how outsourcing can contribute to innovation, agility, and competitiveness in the digital age. Managers need to actively collaborate with IT leaders and other relevant stakeholders to ensure that outsourcing decisions align with the organization's overarching digital goals.

- Enhanced risk management: As outsourcing operations become more global and interconnected, the complexity of risks also increases. Managers must prioritize enhanced risk management strategies (Majumdar et al., 2021). This involves identifying and mitigating risks associated with cybersecurity, data privacy, geopolitical factors, and technological disruptions. The development of robust contingency plans and proactive risk mitigation measures is crucial to ensuring the resilience of outsourcing operations in the face of unforeseen challenges.
- Cultural competence and communication: The globalized nature of outsourcing 4.0 demands heightened cultural competence among managers. Effective communication becomes paramount in managing diverse teams across borders. Managers need to foster an inclusive and collaborative culture that transcends geographical boundaries (Stone et al., 2020). This involves understanding and appreciating cultural nuances, leveraging technology for seamless communication, and ensuring that teams are aligned with organizational goals, regardless of their physical location.
- Strategic partner selection: Outsourcing 4.0 emphasizes strategic partnerships over transactional vendor relationships. Managers play a pivotal role in selecting strategic partners that align with the organization's values, goals, and digital roadmap (Akbari, 2022). This involves comprehensive due diligence, assessing the partner's technological capabilities, ethical standards, and ability to collaborate effectively. Strategic partner selection is not merely a procurement decision; it is a strategic choice that can significantly impact the organization's long-term success.
- Data governance and security: Given the central role of data analytics and advanced technologies in outsourcing 4.0, managers must prioritize robust data governance and security measures. This includes defining clear data ownership, implementing encryption protocols, and ensuring compliance with data protection regulations (Salah et al., 2023). Managers need to stay informed about evolving cybersecurity threats and proactively implement measures to safeguard sensitive information, fostering trust among stakeholders and customers.

- Continuous learning and workforce development: The integration of advanced technologies requires a skilled workforce. Managers must invest in continuous learning and workforce development initiatives to ensure that employees possess the necessary skills for the digital age (Kok & Akbari, 2023). This involves identifying skill gaps, providing training programs, and fostering a culture of continuous learning (Akbari et al., 2022). Additionally, managers can explore strategic partnerships with educational institutions and external training providers to enhance the capabilities of their workforce.

- Agile project management: Outsourcing 4.0 is characterized by agility and adaptability. Traditional project management approaches may not suffice in this dynamic landscape. Managers need to adopt agile project management methodologies that prioritize flexibility, collaboration, and iterative development (Wu, 2022). This approach enables teams to respond swiftly to changing requirements and market dynamics, ensuring that outsourcing projects align with evolving business needs.

- Performance measurement and KPIs: Managers must redefine performance measurement metrics and KPIs in the context of outsourcing 4.0. Traditional metrics focused on cost savings may not capture the full spectrum of value that strategic outsourcing partnerships can bring. KPIs should align with broader business objectives, emphasizing innovation, customer satisfaction, and overall supply chain agility (Govindan et al., 2021). Managers need to regularly reassess and adjust performance metrics to ensure they reflect the evolving priorities of the organization.

- Legal and compliance considerations: The globalized nature of outsourcing brings forth legal and compliance complexities. Managers need to stay abreast of international regulations, particularly in areas such as data protection, intellectual property, and contractual agreements (Kurpjuweit et al., 2021). Legal considerations should be integrated into the strategic decision-making process, and organizations should work closely with legal experts to navigate the intricacies of international business laws.

- Strategic exit planning: In the dynamic landscape of outsourcing 4.0, managers must consider strategic exit planning. The flexibility to exit or transition out from outsourcing arrangements is as important as the decision to enter into them. This involves clearly defined exit strategies, contingency plans, and a thorough understanding of contractual obligations (Pereira et al., 2019). Managers need to anticipate potential scenarios that might necessitate a change in outsourcing arrangements and plan accordingly to minimize disruptions.

In the era of outsourcing 4.0, managerial success hinges on a strategic, adaptive approach. Managers, pivotal in shaping outsourcing triumphs, align decisions with digital strategies, prioritize risk management, foster cultural competence, and invest in continuous learning. The dynamic nature of outsourcing 4.0 demands agile and responsive management, viewing change as an avenue for innovation. As technology evolves, effective managerial practices become vital for navigating challenges and unlocking the potential of strategic outsourcing partnerships, positioning organizations for success in this era of digital disruption.

8.7   Summary and Conclusion

The journey through the landscape of outsourcing 4.0 has been one marked by transformative evolution, bringing forth a paradigm shift in how supply chains conceptualize and implement outsourcing strategies. This dynamic era, characterized by the convergence of cutting-edge digital technologies, strategic partnerships, and a holistic approach to outsourcing, presents a tapestry of opportunities and challenges that demand strategic vision and adaptability.

The evolution from outsourcing 1.0's rudimentary models to the technologically sophisticated realm of outsourcing 4.0 narrates a story of adaptation in the digital age. Outsourcing 1.0 was initiated with cost-centric delegation, evolving into outsourcing 2.0's focus on relationship management. Outsourcing 3.0 extended to global process outsourcing via cloud. In outsourcing 4.0, strategic partnerships, advanced technologies, and a holistic approach redefine outsourcing as a transformative element in digital supply chain strategy.

The managerial implications of outsourcing 4.0 underscore the need for a strategic, adaptive, and forward-thinking approach. Managers, as central architects of outsourcing success, must align decisions with broader digital initiatives, prioritize risk management, foster cultural competence, select strategic partners, and invest in continuous learning. The dynamic nature of outsourcing 4.0 demands agile and responsive management, viewing change as an opportunity for innovation. Effective managerial practices become instrumental in navigating challenges and unlocking the potential of strategic outsourcing partnerships.

As outsourcing 4.0 continues to unfold, organizations stand at the crossroads of challenges and opportunities. The convergence of digital technologies, strategic partnerships, and a holistic approach reshapes the outsourcing landscape. Ethical considerations, cybersecurity, resilience, and the dependency on global supply chains emerge as concerns that necessitate proactive management. Simultaneously, future directions point toward sustainability, integration of AR and VR, circular economy practices, enhanced AI ethics, and workforce reskilling.

The success of outsourcing 4.0 lies in adeptly managing these challenges while leveraging the myriad opportunities it offers. Organizations that balance benefits, address challenges, and capitalize on opportunities gain a significant competitive advantage. As supply chains traverse this transformative era, remaining agile, adaptive, and forward-thinking is imperative to harnessing the full potential of outsourcing 4.0.

In this era of digital disruption, organizations led by proactive and visionary managers are poised not only to thrive but also to lead in the ever-evolving landscape of outsourcing 4.0. The journey forward involves not just reacting to change but actively shaping the future trajectory of outsourcing to align with broader digital strategies. As technology evolves and outsourcing models continue to evolve, the strategic vision of leaders will be the compass guiding organizations toward sustainable success in the digital age.

Outsourcing 4.0 is not merely a phase in the evolution of business practices; it is a transformative epoch that requires organizations to embrace change, innovate relentlessly, and forge strategic partnerships that transcend traditional boundaries. It is a call to action for leaders to navigate uncharted territories, where the fusion of technology, collaboration, and strategic alignment becomes the cornerstone of sustainable success. As the story of outsourcing 4.0 unfolds, it is clear that the organizations that dare to embrace the challenges and opportunities of this dynamic era will be the trailblazers shaping the future of global supply chains.

REFERENCES

Adepoju, O. (2022). Reskilling for construction 4.0. In *Re-skilling human resources for construction 4.0*. Springer Tracts in Civil Engineering. Springer. https://doi.org/10.1007/978-3-030-85973-2_9

Ahmad, T., Madonski, R., Zhang, D., Huang, C., & Mujeeb, A. (2022). Data-driven probabilistic machine learning in sustainable smart energy/smart energy systems: Key developments, challenges, and future research opportunities in the context of smart grid paradigm. *Renewable and Sustainable Energy Reviews, 160*, 112128. https://doi.org/10.1016/j.rser.2022.112128

Akbari, M. (2022). Outsourcing and insourcing in global supply chain. In J. Sarkis (Ed.), *Handbook of supply chain management—A major reference work* (Chapter 47). Palgrave. https://doi.org/10.1007/978-3-030-89822-9_47-1

Akbari, M. (2023, in press). Revolutionizing supply chain and circular economy with edge computing: Systematic review, research themes and future directions. *Management Decision*. https://doi.org/10.1108/MD-03-2023-0412

Akbari, M., & Do, T. N. A. (2021). A systematic review of machine learning in logistics and supply chain management: Current trends and future directions. *Benchmarking: An International Journal, 28*(10), 2977–3005. https://doi.org/10.1108/BIJ-10-2020-0514

Akbari, M., Kok, S. K., Hopkins, J., Frederico, G. F., Nguyen, H., & Alonso, A. D. (2023, in press). The changing landscape of digital transformation in supply chains: Impacts of Industry 4.0 in Vietnam. *The International Journal of Logistics Management*. https://doi.org/10.1108/IJLM-11-2022-0442

Akbari, M., Nguyen, H. M., McClelland, R., & Van Houdt, K. (2022). Design, implementation and academic perspectives on authentic assessment for applied business higher education in a top performing Asian economy. *Education + Training, 64*(1), 69–88. https://doi.org/10.1108/ET-04-2021-0121

Alblowi, R., Brydges, T., Henninger, C. E., Heinze, L., Retamal, M., Parker-Strak, R., & Blazquez, M. (2022). Exploring supply chain sustainability drivers during COVID-19- Tale of 2 cities. *Journal of Cleaner Production, 373*, 133956. https://doi.org/10.1016/j.jclepro.2022.133956

Alghamdi, O., & Agag, G. (2024). Competitive advantage: A longitudinal analysis of the roles of data-driven innovation capabilities, marketing agility, and market turbulence. *Journal of Retailing and Consumer Services, 76*, 103547. https://doi.org/10.1016/j.jretconser.2023.103547

Allioui, H., & Mourdi, Y. (2023). Unleashing the potential of AI: Investigating cutting-edge technologies that are transforming businesses. *International Journal of Computer Engineering and Data Science (IJCEDS), 3*(2), 1–12. https://ijceds.com/ijceds/article/view/59

Altekar, R. V. (2023). *Supply chain management: Concepts and cases*. PHI Learning Pvt. Ltd.

Alvarez, S., & Rubio, A. (2015). Carbon footprint in Green Public Procurement: A case study in the services sector. *Journal of Cleaner Production, 93*, 159–166. https://doi.org/10.1016/j.jclepro.2015.01.048

Bai, C., Dallasega, P., Orzes, G., & Sarkis, J. (2020). Industry 4.0 technologies assessment: A sustainability perspective. *International Journal of Production Economics, 229*, 107776. https://doi.org/10.1016/j.ijpe.2020.107776

Bashir, M., & Harky, A. (2019). Artificial intelligence in aortic surgery: The rise of the machine. *Seminars in Thoracic and Cardiovascular Surgery, 31*(4), 635–637. https://doi.org/10.1053/j.semtcvs.2019.05.040

Benyezza, H., Bouhedda, M., Kara, R., & Rebouh, S. (2023). Smart platform based on IoT and WSN for monitoring and control of a greenhouse in the context of precision agriculture. *Internet of Things, 23*, 100830. https://doi.org/10.1016/j.iot.2023.100830

Brandy, S. (2023). Overcoming challenges and unlocking the potential: Empowering Small and Medium Enterprises (SMEs) with data analytics solutions. *International Journal of Information Technology and Computer Science Applications, 1*(3), 150–160. https://doi.org/10.58776/ijitcsa.v1i3.47

Busuioc, M. (2021). Accountable artificial intelligence: Holding algorithms to account. *Public Administration Review, 81*(5), 825–836. https://doi.org/10.1111/puar.13293

Chukwu, E., Adu-Baah, A., Niaz, M., Nwagwu, U., & Chukwu, M. U. (2023). Navigating ethical supply chains: The intersection of diplomatic management and theological ethics. *International Journal of Multidisciplinary Sciences and Arts, 2*(1), 127–139. https://doi.org/10.47709/ijmdsa.vxix.xxxx

Cugno, M., Castegnoli, R., Buchi, G., & Pini, M. (2021). Industry 4.0 and production recovery in the covid era. *Technovation, 114*, 102443. https://doi.org/10.1016/j.technovation.2021.102443

Dal Mas, F., Massaro, M., Rippa, P., & Secundo, G. (2023). The challenges of digital transformation in healthcare: An interdisciplinary literature review, framework, and future research agenda. *Technovation, 123*, 102716. https://doi.org/10.1016/j.technovation.2023.102716

Deloitte. (2018). *Overcoming barriers to NextGen supply chain innovation*. The MHI Annual Industry Report. https://www2.deloitte.com/fr/fr/pages/strategie-et-innovation/articles/mhi-annual-industry-report.html. Accessed 25 May 2023.

Deloitte. (2022a). *Outsourcing 4.0—Adding value through trusted relationships*. Deloitte. https://www2.deloitte.com/content/dam/Deloitte/us/Documents/technology/us-cons-nextgen-sourcing-cloud.pdf. Accessed 10 October 2023.

Deloitte. (2022b). *Outsourcing 4.0: Cloud-based IT outsourcing services—The future of IT outsourcing strategy*. Deloitte. https://www2.deloitte.com/us/en/pages/consulting/solutions/us-outsourcing-4-cloud-based-it-outsourcing-services.html. Accessed 10 October 2023.

Eckert, V., Curran, C., & Bhardwaj, S. C. (2016). *Tech breakthroughs megatrend: How to prepare for its impact*. PwC India. www.pwc.es/es/digital/assets/tech-breakthroughsmegatrend-how-to-prepare-for-its-impact.pdf. Accessed 4 March 2023.

Frederico, G. F., Kumar, V., Garza-Reyes, J. A., Kumar, A., & Agrawal, R. (2021). Impact of I4.0 technologies and their interoperability on performance: Future pathways for supply chain resilience post-COVID-19. *The International Journal of Logistics Management, 34*, 1020–1049. https://doi.org/10.1108/IJLM-03-2021-0181

Gasteiger, N., Hellou, M., & Ahn, H. S. (2023). Factors for personalization and localization to optimize human–robot interaction: A literature review. *International Journal of Social Robotics, 15*(4), 689–701. https://doi.org/10.1007/s12369-021-00811-8

Gedda, R. (2011, July/August). Beyond today's cloud to outsourcing 3.0. *CIO, 26*. https://search.informit.org/doi/pdf/10.3316/informit.488905828267796

Govindan, K., Aditi, Dhingra Darbari, J., Kaul, A., & Jha, P. C. (2021). Structural model for analysis of key performance indicators for sustainable manufacturer–supplier collaboration: A grey-decision-making trial and evaluation laboratory-based approach. *Business Strategy and the Environment, 30*(4), 1702–1722. https://doi.org/10.1002/bse.2703

Ha, N. T., Akbari, M., & Au, B. (2022). Last mile delivery in logistics and supply chain management: A bibliometric analysis and future directions. *Benchmarking: An International Journal, 30*, 1137–1170. https://doi.org/10.1108/BIJ-07-2021-0409

Hansen, E. B., & Bøgh, S. (2021). Artificial intelligence and internet of things in small and medium-sized enterprises: A survey. *Journal of Manufacturing Systems, 58*(Part-B), 362–372. https://doi.org/10.1016/j.jmsy.2020.08.009

He, Z., Huang, H., Choi, H., & Bilgihan, A. (2023). Building organizational resilience with digital transformation. *Journal of Service Management, 34*(1), 147–171. https://doi.org/10.1108/JOSM-06-2021-0216

Hofmann, E., & Rüsch, M. (2017). Industry 4.0 and the current status as well as future prospects on logistics. *Computer Industry, 89*, 23–34. https://doi.org/10.1016/j.compind.2017.04.002

Hopkins, J., & Bardoel, A. (2023). The future is hybrid: How organisations are designing and supporting sustainable hybrid work models in post-pandemic Australia. *Sustainability, 15*(4), 3086. https://doi.org/10.3390/su15043086

Hoyer, C., Gunawan, I., & Reaiche, C. H. (2021). Implementing Industry 4.0—The need for a holistic approach. In A. Dingli, F. Haddod, & C. Klüver

(Eds.), *Artificial intelligence in Industry 4.0*. Studies in Computational Intelligence, Vol. 928. Springer. https://doi.org/10.1007/978-3-030-61045-6_1

Hoyer, C., Gunawan, I., & Reaiche, C. H. (2023). Exploring the relationships between Industry 4.0 implementation factors through systems thinking and network analysis. *Systems Research and Behavioral Science, 40*(4), 723–739. https://doi.org/10.1002/sres.2947

Kache, F., & Seuring, S. (2017). Challenges and opportunities of digital information at the intersection of big data analytics and supply chain management. *International Journal of Operations and Production Management, 37*(1), 10–36. https://doi.org/10.1108/IJOPM-02-2015-0078

Kok, S. K., & Akbari, M. (2023). Human resource management in supply chains. In J. Sarkis (Ed.), *The Palgrave handbook of supply chain management*. Palgrave Macmillan. https://doi.org/10.1007/978-3-030-89822-9_38-1

Kumar, R., Singh, R. K., & Dwivedi, Y. K. (2020). Application of Industry 4.0 technologies in SMEs for ethical and sustainable operations: Analysis of challenges. *Journal of Cleaner Production, 275*, 124063. https://doi.org/10.1016/j.jclepro.2020.124063

Kurpjuweit, S., Schmidt, C. G., Klöckner, M., & Wagner, S. M. (2021). Blockchain in additive manufacturing and its impact on supply chains. *Journal of Business Logistics, 42*(1), 46–70. https://doi.org/10.1111/jbl.12231

Lahti, T., Wincent, J., & Parida, V. (2018). A definition and theoretical review of the circular economy, value creation, and sustainable business models: Where are we now and where should research move in the future? *Sustainability, 10*(8), 2799. https://doi.org/10.3390/su10082799

LaValle, S., Lesser, E., Shockley, R., Hopkins, M. S., & Kruschwitz, N. (2011). Big data, analytics and the path from insights to value. *MIT Sloan Management Review, 2*(2), 21.

Lewallen, J. (2021). Emerging technologies and problem definition uncertainty: The case of cybersecurity. *Regulation & Governance, 15*(4), 1035–1052. https://doi.org/10.1111/rego.12341

Li, S., Xu, L. D., & Zhao, S. (2015). The internet of things: A survey. *Information Systems Frontiers, 17*, 243–259. https://doi.org/10.1007/s10796-014-9492-7

Lyall, A., Mercier, P., & Gstettner, S. (2018). The death of supply chain management. *Harvard Business Review, 1*.

Machado, C. G., Winroth, M. P., & Ribeiro da Silva E. H. D. (2020). Sustainable manufacturing in Industry 4.0: An emerging research agenda. *International Journal of Production Research, 58*(50), 1462–1484. https://doi.org/10.1080/00207543.2019.1652777

Majumdar, A., Sinha, S. K., & Govindan, K. (2021). Prioritising risk mitigation strategies for environmentally sustainable clothing supply chains: Insights from selected organisational theories. *Sustainable Production and Consumption, 28*, 543–555. https://doi.org/10.1016/j.spc.2021.06.021

Mekdad, Y., Aris, A., Babun, L., El Fergougui, A., Conti, M., Lazzeretti, R., & Uluagac, A. S. (2023). A survey on security and privacy issues of UAVs. *Computer Networks, 224*, 109626. https://doi.org/10.1016/j.comnet.2023.109626

McKinsey. (2016). *China's Industry 4.0 road*. McKinsey. https://www.mckinsey.com.cn/%e4%b8%ad%e5%9b%bd%e5%b7%a5%e4%b8%9a4-0%e4%b9%8b%e8%b7%af/. Accessed 20 October 2023.

Moreira, O. J., & Rodrigues, M. C. M. (2023). Sourcing third party logistics service providers based on environmental, social and corporate governance: A case study. *Discover Sustainability, 4*(1), 36. https://doi.org/10.1007/s43621-023-00149-3

Nayak, A., Satpathy, I., Patnaik, B. C. M., Gujrati, R., & Uygun, H. (2024). Simplified hospital management system: Robotic Process Automation (RPA) to rescue. In *Data-centric AI solutions and emerging technologies in the healthcare ecosystem* (pp. 281–302). CRC Press.

Nguyen, T., Gosine, R. G., & Warrian, P. (2020). A systematic review of big data analytics for oil and gas industry 4.0. *IEEE Access, 8*, 61183–61201. https://doi.org/10.1109/ACCESS.2020.2979678

Nguyen, H., Onofrei, G., Akbari, M., & McClelland, R. (2022). Enhancing quality and innovation performance: The role of supplier communication and knowledge development. *Total Quality Management & Business Excellence, 33*(3–4), 410–433. https://doi.org/10.1080/14783363.2020.1858711

Nunez, V. (2023). *How Chat GPT thinks it can revolutionize the logistics industry?* https://www.shiplilly.com/blog/how-chat-gpt-thinks-it-can-revolutionize-the-logistics-industry/. Accessed 16 September 2023.

Numfu, M., Riel, A., & Noël, F. (2019). Virtual reality based digital chain for maintenance training. *Procedia CIRP, 84*, 1069–1074. https://doi.org/10.1016/j.procir.2019.04.268

Oesterreich, T. D., & Teuteberg, F. (2016). Understanding the implications of digitisation and automation in the context of Industry 4.0: A triangulation approach and elements of a research agenda for the construction industry. *Computers in Industry, 83*, 121–139. https://doi.org/10.1016/j.compind.2016.09.006

Papadopoulos, T., Baltas, K. N., & Balta, M. E. (2020). The use of digital technologies by small and medium enterprises during COVID-19: Implications for theory and practice. *International Journal of Information Management, 55*, 102192. https://doi.org/10.1016/j.ijinfomgt.2020.102192

Pereira, D., Leitão, J., Oliveira, T., & Peirone, D. (2023). Proposing a holistic research framework for university strategic alliances in sustainable entrepreneurship. *Heliyon*. https://doi.org/10.1016/j.heliyon.2023.e16087

Pereira, V., Munjal, S., & Ishizaka, A. (2019). Outsourcing and offshoring decision making and its implications for businesses—A synthesis of research pursuing five pertinent questions. *Journal of Business Research, 103*, 348–355. https://doi.org/10.1016/j.jbusres.2019.07.009

Piccarozzi, M., Aquilani, B., & Gatti, C. (2018). Industry 4.0 in management studies: A systematic literature review. *Sustainability, 10*(10), 3821. https://doi.org/10.3390/su10103821

Pujawan, N., & Bah, A. U. (2022). Supply chains under COVID-19 disruptions: Literature review and research agenda. *Supply Chain Forum: An International Journal, 23*(1), 81–95. https://doi.org/10.1080/16258312.2021.1932568

Queiroz, M. M., & Wamba, S. F. (2022). *Managing the digital transformation.* CRC Press. https://doi.org/10.1201/9781003226468

Raj, A., Mukherjee, A. A., de Sousa Jabbour, A. B. L., & Srivastava, S. K. (2022). Supply chain management during and post-COVID-19 pandemic: Mitigation strategies and practical lessons learned. *Journal of Business Research, 142*, 1125–1139. https://doi.org/10.1016/j.jbusres.2022.01.037

Raja Santhi, A., & Muthuswamy, P. (2023). Industry 5.0 or industry 4.0S? Introduction to Industry 4.0 and a peek into the prospective Industry 5.0 technologies. *International Journal on Interactive Design and Manufacturing, 17*, 947–979. https://doi.org/10.1007/s12008-023-01217-8

Roll, S., Chun, Y., Kondratjeva, O., Despard, M., Schwartz-Tayri, T. M., & Grinstein-Weiss, M. (2022). Household spending patterns and hardships during COVID-19: A comparative study of the U.S. and Israel. *Journal of Family and Economic Issues, 43*, 261–281. https://doi.org/10.1007/s10834-021-09814-z

Salah, M., Al Halbusi, H., & Abdelfattah, F. (2023). May the force of text data analysis be with you: Unleashing the power of generative AI for social psychology research. *Computers in Human Behavior: Artificial Humans*, 100006. https://doi.org/10.1016/j.chbah.2023.100006

Sartori, J. T. D., Frederico, G. F., & Silva, H. F. N. (2022). Organizational knowledge management in the context of supply chain 4.0: A systematic literature review and conceptual model proposal. *Knowledge & Process Management, 29*(2), 147–161. https://doi.org/10.1002/kpm.1682

Schinkel, M., Paranjape, K., Nannan Panday, R. S., Skyttberg, N., & Nanayakkara, P. W. B. (2019). Clinical applications of artificial intelligence in sepsis: A narrative review. *Computers in Biology and Medicine, 115*. https://doi.org/10.1016/j.compbiomed.2019.103488

Siebel, T. M. (2019). *Digital transformation: Survive and thrive in an era of mass extinction.* RosettaBooks.

Sisinni, E., Saifullah, A., Han, S., Jennehag, U., & Gidlund, M. (2018). Industrial internet of things: Challenges, opportunities, and directions. *IEEE*

Transactions on Industrial Informatics, 14(11), 4724–4734. https://doi.org/10.1109/TII.2018.2852491

Steffen, W., Rockström, J., Richardson, K., Lenton, T. M., Folke, C., Liverman, D., Summerhayes, C. P., Barnosky, A. D., Cornell, S. E., Crucifix, M., & Schellnhuber, H. J. (2018). Trajectories of the earth system in the Anthropocene. *Proceedings of the National Academy of Sciences, 115*(33), 8252–8259. https://doi.org/10.1073/pnas.1810141115

Stone, R. J., Cox, A., & Gavin, M. (2020). *Human resource management.* Wiley.

Sullivan, M. (2021). Demystifying the impacts of the Fourth Industrial Revolution on logistics: An introduction. In *The digital transformation of logistics: Demystifying impacts of the Fourth Industrial Revolution* (pp. 1–19). Wiley. https://doi.org/10.1002/9781119646495.ch1

Tjemkes, B., Vos, P., & Burgers, K. (2023). *Strategic alliance management.* Taylor & Francis.

Vahdat, S. (2022). The role of IT-based technologies on the management of human resources in the COVID-19 era. *Kybernetes, 51*(6), 2065–2088. https://doi.org/10.1108/K-04-2021-0333

Vu, O. T. K., Duarte Alonso, A., Bressan, A., Kok, S. K., Quang Nguyen, T., Akbari, M., & Nguyen, H. T. T. (2022). Enabling environmentally sustainable practices in Vietnam through knowledge management: The case of TONTOTON. *Knowledge Management Research & Practice*, 1–15. https://doi.org/10.1080/14778238.2022.2159556

Wang, Y., Wen, H., Hu, Z., & Zhang, Y. (2023). Collaborative innovation strategy of supply chain in the context of MCU domestic substitution: A differential game analysis. *Computational Economics, 61*(3), 1039–1074. https://doi.org/10.1016/j.ocecoaman.2022.106387

Wu, T. (2022). Digital project management: Rapid changes define new working environments. *Journal of Business Strategy, 43*(5), 323–331. https://doi.org/10.1108/JBS-03-2021-0047

Yang, H., Alphones, A., Xiong, Z., Niyato, D., Zhao, J., & Wu, K. (2020). Artificial-intelligence-enabled intelligent 6G networks. *IEEE Network, 34*(6), 272–280. https://doi.org/10.1109/MNET.011.2000195

Yeow, A., Soh, C., & Hansen, R. (2018). Aligning with new digital strategy: A dynamic capabilities approach. *The Journal of Strategic Information Systems, 27*(1), 43–58. https://doi.org/10.1016/j.jsis.2017.09.001

Zwanka, R. J., & Buff, C. (2021). COVID-19 generation: A conceptual framework of the consumer behavioral shifts to be caused by the COVID-19 pandemic. *Journal of International Consumer Marketing, 33*(1), 58–67. https://doi.org/10.1080/08961530.2020.1771646

Index